Everest the Hard Way

Chris Bonington is one of Britain's most distinguished climbers. He started climbing at the age of sixteen and, among his many achievements as a mountaineer, he has made a first ascent of the Old Man of Hoy, a first ascent of the Central Pillar of Freney, Mont Blanc, and the first British ascent of the North Wall of the Eiger. In 1960, Bonington reached the summit of Annapurna II and, ten years later, led an expedition on the South Face of Annapurna, the first major Himalayan Wall to be attempted. In autumn 1972, he led the first expedition to the South West Face but was defeated by the winter wind and cold. Two years later he was among the team that made the first ascent of Changabang.

Well known as a freelance writer, Chris Bonington's autobiographical books, *I Chose To Climb* and *The Next Horizon* are published by Arrow.

Arrow Books Limited
3 Fitzroy Square, London W1P 6JD

An imprint of the Hutchinson Publishing Group

London Melbourne Sydney Auckland
Wellington Johannesburg and agencies
throughout the world

First published by Hodder & Stoughton 1976
Arrow Books edition 1977
© British Everest Expedition 1975/
Barclays Bank International 1976

Set in Monotype Times

Made and printed in Great Britain by
The Anchor Press Ltd, Tiptree, Essex

ISBN 0 09 915940 6

Parts of Pete Boardman's account of events
in chapter 15 have already appeared in a different
form in *Mountain Life*, No. 23, December–January 1976

Cover photographs

Front Haston climbing the Hillary step (*Photo Doug Scott*)

Back Haston finds a route through a crevasse in the
Western Cwm (*Photo Doug Scott*)

Everest the Hard Way

Chris Bonington

Arrow Books

Contents

To Mick Burke and Mingma Nuru

List of black and white illustrations

between pages 160 and 161

List of colour illustrations

Foreword
by Lord Hunt of Llanvair Waterdine

In December 1972 I greeted Chris Bonington and his team at a reception on their return from his previous attempt on the South West Face, from which they had been turned back at 27 300 feet, and at the very limits of human endurance, by the combined effects of low temperatures and high wind at very high altitude. 'Never again,' was his verdict.

I knew how he felt. Many years before, in the winter of 1937, with my wife and Reggie Cook, I had taken part in a light expedition during the months of October to December to the eastern surroundings of Kangchenjunga, third highest mountain in the world. One of our purposes was to try out climbing conditions during the long clear spell at the beginning of winter, so as to prove whether that period might offer a better chance to climb Everest than the usually favoured, but brief opportunity before the monsoon brings heavy snowfalls to the South East Himalaya. We had some successes, including a 23 500-foot peak; and we pushed a reconnaissance on Kangchenjunga to within a few hundred feet of its North Col, from which a ridge leads to the summit. But an indelible memory had been the bitter cold and a terrifying wind – especially that wind. Yet looking through my diaries, I find that I wrote later: 'Taken all round, I feel that it is unwise to generalize as a result of this experience, and that it is most desirable to visit Everest in the post-monsoon period.'

So it came as no surprise when Chris phoned me in September 1973, to tell me that a Canadian expedition had cancelled their permit to attempt Everest in the autumn of 1975, and said he was keen to have another go. What did I think? Of course I agreed, and I meant it. Maybe the chances of success would not be much greater than before – I gave the odds at evens – but we both knew that some day that face would be climbed by someone. The urge to be that somebody was irresistible and with all the experience he had gained, Chris just had to try again.

There were certain lessons from the last attempt by which he was determined to profit. One of these was to start earlier and be off the mountain before life was made intolerable. But this meant beginning the climb before the monsoon ended; there would still be masses of snow on the mountain and fresh snow would be falling from time to time. I agreed with that proposition, too, despite its snags. On our way up the Zemu Glacier in 1937 we had met a German party on their way down, flushed with triumph after climbing Siniolchu, a beautiful and very difficult peak, during September, in spite of the difficult snow conditions. Even more impressive had been the astonishing skill and endurance of an earlier German party led by Paul Bauer which, during more than two months of continuous hard climbing between July and September 1931, had forced their way up the North East Spur of Kangchenjunga, living in ice caves, to reach a height of 25 260 feet. They were finally defeated by an avalanche-prone snow slope just below the crest of the main North Ridge, whence the route to the summit appeared to be relatively straightforward.

So one of the problems attaching to Bonington's choice of that earlier period was the danger of avalanches. This point was tragically brought home to us again a year after our telephone conversation when, while we were attending the centenary celebrations of the French Alpine Club at Chamonix the leader of a French expedition on Everest and five Sherpas were swept to their deaths down a couloir leading to the West Ridge.

Reading this book, that word 'avalanche' looms large. An avalanche badly damaged Camp 4; a much bigger one wrought havoc in the Advance Base Camp at the foot of the Face; smaller snow slides, some of them serious enough to carry climbers out of their steps, were an almost daily occurrence on the great steep slopes between the high camps. That the climbers pressed on, taking calculated risks, without loss of life from this danger, speaks worlds for the new equipment they used, for their mastery of modern techniques, sheer determination – and a large slice of luck; there were some very narrow escapes.

As for equipment, there is no doubt that it played an important role. I will mention only the matter of the expedition tents. Watching members of the team, armed with improbable climbing weapons – spanners – laboriously piecing together the steel framework of a MacInnes box tent on a gentle grassy slope above the waters of Windermere on a sunny morning last summer, I found it hard to imagine the same operation being performed on a slope on ice tilted at 50 degrees, at 25 000 feet on Everest, with the temperature well below zero centigrade. Yet it was done, not once but at every one of the four camps on the Face. Those boxes, products of the inventive genius of Hamish MacInnes, were further proof of the foresight of the team; credit is also due to the inventor of their prototype, Don Whillans, whose own performance on earlier attempts by this route had made such a great contribution to the final result. The robustness of these tents, with the relative comfort and protection they provided, was an important factor in success.

On techniques, the extensive use of fixed ropes, up and down which all the climbers, attached by jumar clamps, can slide with security and relative ease once the leading climber has forced a passage, is the most revolutionary change in climbing big mountain faces during the past twenty years. It played an important part in all the onslaughts on the South West Face of Everest, and but for its skilful use last September several climbers would have been carried away by avalanches. But I think that all members of the party would concede (with the exception of the person I allude to) that the supreme example of climbing technique, applied with exceptional determination, was Nick Estcourt's superb lead, without the normal safeguards or oxygen at 27 000 feet, up the rickety, outward-leaning ramp of snow-covered rubble which led from the gully in the Rock Band up to the Upper Snow Field. This must be one of the greatest leads in climbing history, comparable, at least in its psychological effect, with the original lead across the Hinterstösser Traverse or the exit gully above the Spide, on the North Face of the Eiger.

I would like to say more about determination, for the urge to press on pervades the whole of this story. The will to get up Everest must be there in large measure in every Everest climber before he sets out, if he is to reach the top. It is a necessary reserve of inner strength which, if – and only if – it is in abundant supply at the foot of the mountain, may just about see him through – perhaps ebbing slightly all the time. It is a peculiarly personal thing, for which the word 'ambition' in its conventional sense is quite inadequate to explain the motive power needed for this kind of high endeavour. But no one reading those graphic passages from the diaries of the summit climbers, floundering and flaying their agonizing way in deep, incoherent snow up the couloir below the South Summit, can question that it was this matter of will, reinforced by confidence, that carried Dougal Haston and Doug Scott to the crest. It was this same will alone, flickering through a bitter night, which made it possible for them to return and tell their story to the world.

Everest imposes enormous emotional strains on the climber, which are an inescapable consequence of his determination and will; and those tensions are movingly conveyed to the reader of this book. Upon no one was the stress so great and so prolonged as on the leader of the expedition. His was the original decision to make the bid; his the choice of companions, the general strategy, the supervision of the whole complex plan and its unfolding on Everest. His was the responsibility for the lives of more than seventy men, exposed to risks of many kinds and for a considerable time: from crevasses and séracs in the Ice Fall; from the labyrinth of monstrous hidden chasms on the Western Cwm; from avalanches on the Face and the sudden onset of bad weather on the summit ridge. On the leader would be heaped the chorus of criticism – even obloquy – from some climbers and many members of the public if this expensive venture were to prove to be yet another failure.

Chris Bonington is such an effective writer partly because he writes himself, his doubts and fears, his irritations and rejoicings, into the story. We can feel his edginess as the effects of mental stress, physical exhaustion and oxygen lack during eight days and nights spent at and above Camp 5. Through his perceptive understanding of his fellow climbers, and by the inclusion of excerpts from their own accounts, we experience their moods, too. Nothing moved me more than Bonington's tears when Dougal's radio message from Camp 6 on the morning of 25 September announced success – and their safe return; and the unashamed weeping of Pete Boardman, youngest member of the team, when he staggered into that same camp after his own triumph and ordeal, with its accompanying tragedy of the loss of Mick Burke.

But when all has been said about equipment, climbing techniques and the individual qualities of the climbers, my final word must be about the team as a whole and their inter-action one with another during this epic enterprise. For me, this is the most fascinating aspect of the story. Much has been written in praise of small, light expeditions, in condemnation of large ones. I share with most other climbers a strong preference for going to the mountains with a few close friends: some of my happiest memories derive from expeditions of this nature. But where the objectives are diverse, or when the scale of the undertaking demand larger numbers, there is also much reward to be enjoyed from its complexity, with many members playing different roles to produce a combined result. The satisfaction may come from the fact that unison in these circumstances is that much harder to achieve and, if it can be made to work, the experience can be exhilarating. I can say about this team that the quality of their achievement lies not only in the fact that they reached their objective; not only in some brilliant climbing, nor the perfect timing of the plan, which avoided the worst onslaught of the elements. It is to be found in the manner of the doing by the very individualistic members working as a team, in accepting their various parts, tempering their disappointments and being such a happy united band.

The British triumph on the South West Face is the culmina-tion of a succession of attempts to solve this problem during the past five years: an international expedition in 1971; a European expedition in the spring of 1972, followed by Bonington's first attempt that autumn. And before and after these three efforts came climbers from Japan: in the autumn of 1969, the spring of 1970 and finally the autumn of 1973. To all of these, but especially to the Japanese, much credit should be given for their contribution to the eventual British success.

This book is entitled *Everest the Hard Way*. Undoubtedly, the South West Face is a very difficult and arduous climb. Some day, no doubt, climbers will have so far improved their performances that this climb will be classified in a lower order of difficulty; such is the way of progress. Meanwhile, let nobody suppose that Everest by any other way, including our route in 1953, is an easy mountain; it is not. And at all times it is dangerous, as the sad toll of life in the Ice Fall, the West Cwm and on the Lhotse Face bears witness. Whenever the wind is blowing strongly it is impossible to move along the summit ridges, and that means on most days in the year.

And it is well that this should be the case, for man should be humble before the greatest works of nature.

JOHN HUNT
Henley on Thames

Author's note

So many people have helped make this book possible, for a start the huge number of individuals and organizations who helped get the expedition under way. Without these, of course, there would be no book. I hope we have mentioned everyone, expressing our appreciation, either in the text or the appendices. I should like to express our very special gratitude, however, to Barclays Bank International for underwriting the expedition, for without this support it is unlikely that it would ever have taken place. We are particularly grateful to the chairman, Anthony Tuke, whose ultimate decision it was, and to Alan Tritton, who sat on our Committee of Management and looked after our interests throughout the expedition.

I should like to give my special thanks to all the members of the climbing team, who not only gave me their utmost support and friendship throughout the climb, but also made available to me their diaries, letters home and, in several instances, original writing of their experience on the expedition. They gave me a wealth of superb material from which to select what I hope represents a balanced, living account of an expedition, not just from my point of view, but also from the viewpoint of many other members of the team, re-creating the day-to-day emotions, fears, enjoyment and stress of a group of climbers on Everest.

I should also like to thank the many helpers who remain in the background but without whom I should never have managed to write this book within my deadline: Margaret Body, my editor at Hodder and Stoughton, who has constantly helped me with encouragement, balanced advice and judicious editing; Ronnie Richards and an old friend of mine, David Hellings, for their painstaking proof-reading and helpful suggestions; Betty Prentice, who not only typed most of the manuscript but also did some very useful initial editing; my secretary, Louise Wilson, who helped close the expedition down, completed one of the appendices and protected me from the outside world whilst I struggled with the book; my wife, Wendy, who looked after all the expedition transparencies and made the basic picture selection for the book; George Greenfield, the expedition literary agent, for his support and sound advice.

Finally I should like to thank John Hunt, both for writing the foreword to this book, and for providing me with inspiration and an example to follow from studying his leadership of the 1953 Everest Expedition which provides a blueprint for organizing any major venture, and for the kind support and advice he has given me at every stage.

Tragically Dougal Haston died in a powder snow avalanche on 17 January 1977, whilst ski-ing near his home in Leysin, Switzerland. We all grieve the loss of a close friend, climbing companion and superb mountaineer whose friendship, support and ability contributed so much to our success on Everest and many other expeditions. We shall miss him in the climbs we plan for the future.

CHRISTIAN BONINGTON

1   A second chance

After we gave up our attempt on the South West Face of Everest in November 1972, I remember saying to Chris Brasher who had come out to Base Camp to report our story for *The Observer*: 'Climbing is all about gambling. It's not about sure things. It's about challenging the impossible. I think we have found that the South West Face of Everest in the post-monsoon period is impossible!' Rash words for, of course, the story of mountaineering has proven time and again that there is no such thing as impossible – although, I think, we could be allowed this self-indulgence immediately after our beating.

Only two days before, on 14 November, I had been lying in my hoar-frost-encrusted sleeping bag in the battered box tent at Camp 4, at about 24 600 feet on the South West Face. The wind was hammering at the walls, driving small spurts of spindrift through the many rents caused by stones dislodged from the Face above. Outside there was a brilliant blue sky and a sun that blazed without warmth. From out of this void had come the wind tearing and probing at tent and climber.

Somewhere above, Dougal Haston, Hamish MacInnes, Doug Scott and Mick Burke were pulling across the line of fixed ropes towards Camp 6. The wind was so strong that it had liften Doug, a big thirteen-stoner, bodily from his steps and hurled him down; only the fixed rope saved him. I had had some inkling what it was like, for the previous day I had made a solitary carry up to the site of Camp 6 – even then the wind had been buffeting hard and I had wondered just how they were going to be able to erect the box tent in those conditions.

But there had been nothing I could do but wait. Jimmy Roberts, my deputy leader, was far below, camped on Kala Pattar, the rocky hummock of just over 18 000 feet that rises above the Khumbu Glacier forming a perfect dress-circle from which to view climbers on the upper part of the South West Face of Everest. He had a walkie-talkie with him and throughout the day reported on the tiny black dots which were making their slow progress across the snow slopes below the Rock Band. One had turned back early but then, having reached the site of Camp 6, the remaining three turned back. For some reason Dougal Haston and Hamish MacInnes had decided not to stay at the camp as originally planned and I could only guess that, because of the strength of the wind, they had been unable to erect their box tent. There was no way of knowing for certain until they got back to their tents at Camp 5 and made the seven o'clock call that night. Night fell quickly but then the time crept by slowly until, at last, I could switch on the radio.

I got Dougal. They had pressed on to the site of Camp 6, but as I had suspected, they had been unable to get the tent up and even if they had, there is little they could have done. The gully ahead had been swept clear of snow, and the rock could not be climbed in that intense wind and cold. They were coming down the next day. And so I started to arrange our retreat from the mountain; all the Sherpas at Camp 2 to come up to Camp 4 the next day to pick up loads; the Nepalese foreign office to be informed.

It was all so terse and matter of fact but after switching off the radio I could not stop myself crying in the solitude of that small dark tent. We had tried so hard but in those last few days I suspect that all of us had realized that there was no chance of success, although none of us was prepared to admit openly to defeat. It was too late in the season; the winds of Everest were reaching over a hundred miles per hour; the temperature was dropping as low as $-40°C$. We were all much too tired and our equipment was in tatters.

We returned to Britain with a mixture of emotions. There was sadness at the loss of Tony Tighe, a young Australian who had helped us at Base Camp during the expedition and who had been killed by the collapse of a sérac wall on the last day of the evacuation of the mountain. This was mingled with satisfaction at having taken ourselves beyond limits that we had previously thought possible and feelings of heightened friendship and respect for each other cemented by the experience. There were memories of fearsome nights in Camp 4 with the wind hammering at the box tent, bringing stones from the Rock Band above thundering over the roof as one huddled against the inner side of the tent and wondered when it would be crushed. But there had been moments as well which made all the struggle and suffering worthwhile. I shall never forget my solitary trip to Camp 6 on the penultimate day of the expedition as I plodded laboriously up the line of fixed rope. My oxygen system was only working for part of the time but as I slowly gained height, creeping above the confines of the Western Cwm – higher at that moment than any other person on the surface of the earth – the very effort I had made and the loneliness of my position made the ever-expanding vista of mountains seem even more beautiful.

Before leaving Kathmandu at the end of November 1972, I had already filed an application for another attempt on the South West Face in the next available spring slot. This was a slightly hopeless gesture since the mountain was now fully booked, autumn and spring, until 1979. The Nepalese only allowed one expedition on the mountain at a time, and such is the popularity of Everest that it becomes booked up years in advance. There are two periods in which the mountain is considered climbable – spring and autumn. The former season, undoubtedly, has much to recommend it; there is less wind particularly at altitude but, most important of all, squeezed as it is between the end of winter and the arrival of the monsoon (sometime at the end of May or the beginning of June) an expedition starts at Base Camp at the coldest period of the season and then enjoys relatively warmer weather as it progresses up the mountain, having the warmest possible period just before making a summit bid. On the other hand, in the autumn the climbing period is slotted between the end of the monsoon, around the middle of September, and the arrival of the winter winds and cold which we had found, to our cost, come in mid-October giving an uncomfortably short period of tolerable weather in which to climb the mountain.

It seemed highly probable that the South West Face would be climbed before we could have another chance at it, even though a fair proportion of the expeditions that had booked Everest were not planning to attempt the South West Face. There did seem to be one hope, however, for the Army Mountaineering Association had the booking for the spring 1976 slot; by themselves they were not strong enough to tackle the South West Face and had no plans for doing so. During the previous few years the Army had organized a number of successful expeditions to the Himalayas, climbing both Tirich Mir and Annapurna from the North side. I had been a regular soldier and was a founder member of the Army Mountaineering Association; this seemed an excellent opportunity to persuade the Army to incorporate three or four strong civilian climbers, such as Haston or Scott, and try the South West Face at what appeared to be the best time of year for such an attempt. I was prepared to take on the role of climbing leader under the overall leadership of an active soldier, feeling that in this way the expedition could have been fully cohesive and that the civilian members could have fitted in.

I went down to Warminster to see Major-General Brockbank, who was Chairman of the Army Mountaineering Association, and put my plan across. He did not like the idea and turned it down. I can sympathize with his thinking for there were obviously several problems. The Army Mountaineering Association naturally wanted to maintain its own identity and, although I was an ex-member, there was the possibility that my own reputation as a mountaineer could have engulfed them. Success could have been portrayed by the press as that of myself and the talented civilian climbers who had been brought in, rather than of the team as a whole. There could also have been personality problems inevitably created by bringing two groups of climbers together for reasons of convenience rather than selecting a team from scratch. I would, nevertheless, have been prepared to take this risk and make it work, since this seemed the only chance we had of reaching Everest.

In the spring of 1973, Guido Monzino – the Italian millionaire who had relinquished the autumn 1972 booking, thus allowing us our chance – organized a massive expedition to

repeat the South Col route. This expedition used two helicopters, hoping to ferry gear up the Ice Fall and even into the
Western Cwm. This was a controversial step since the Ice
Fall and lower part of the mountain are an integral part of the
climb and the use of aircraft to solve logistic problems
seemed an unpleasant erosion of the climbing ethic. Monzino
could have argued that it is preferable to use an aircraft rather
than risk the lives of Sherpas who carry the brunt of the risk
ferrying loads in the Ice Fall and Western Cwm but, in the
event, this argument was proved specious. The helicopters, at
altitude, could not manage a sufficiently effective pay-load to
eliminate the use of the Sherpas and were used instead for
ferrying members of the climbing team up and down the
mountain for their rest periods. In the end, fate took a hand –
one of the helicopters crashed, fortunately without any
injury to the occupants, and this ended a very expensive
experiment. Our objection to the use of helicopters on Everest
is on aesthetic grounds, for one of the beauties of the Western
Cwm is its majestic silence; both the sound and sight of a
helicopter chattering up the Cwm would be an unpleasant, if
not unbearable, intrusion. In spite of these problems, the
Italians were successful, placing eight men on the summit of
Everest by the original South East Ridge route.

In the autumn of 1973 came the next serious onslaught onto
the South West Face, with the biggest expedition so far;
thirty-six Japanese climbers, sixty-two Sherpas and a twelve-
man Base Camp group. The expedition was organized by the
Japanese Rock Climbers' Club. They started earlier than we
had done, with an eight-man advance party going out to
Kathmandu in early April, sending part of their gear by light
plane to Luglha, the airstrip in the Dudh Kosi valley just
below Namche Bazar. They brought the rest of their gear out
with them in mid-July which meant that they had to carry it
through the worst of the monsoon rains to Sola Khumbu.

They established their Base Camp on 25 August and at first
made excellent progress, following the same route as
ourselves in 1972. They were hit by a savage seven-day storm
at the beginning of October, just after they had reached the
site of Camp 5 at 26000 feet. Sadly they lost Jangbo, one of

their best Sherpas, who had been with us in 1972, in an
avalanche on the lower part of the Face. Influenced by this
tragedy and the deterioration of the weather, they resolved to
turn their main effort to an attempt on the South Col route.
Two of the party, Ishiguro and Kato, reached the summit of
Everest in a single push from the South Col on 26 October.
They had to bivouac on the way down and suffered from
frostbite. This was the first post-monsoon ascent of Everest
and a magnificent achievement, but the South West Face
remained unclimbed. The Japanese had not abandoned the
attempt on the Face when they turned to the South Col, but
on 28 October, after two other members of the expedition had
reached the site of Camp 6 on the Face, they decided to call
off the expedition.

Back in England I followed the Japanese progress as closely
as sparse newspaper reports and intermittent letters from
friends in Kathmandu would allow. In some ways I should
have been quite relieved had the Japanese succeeded, since
this would have removed the nagging problem, enabling
myself and other British climbers to get on with our more
modest but nonetheless satisfying schemes. It did seem fairly
unlikely, anyway, that the South West Face would still be
unclimbed in 1979 – the next date there was a free booking –
and so, that autumn, I was already immersed in other plans.
In the spring of 1974, Doug Scott, Dougal Haston, Martin
Boysen and I were going to Changabang, a shapely rock peak
of 22 700 feet in the Garhwal Himalaya. I had also applied
for permission to attempt the Trango Tower, a magnificent
rock spire off the Baltoro Glacier in the Karakorum for the
summer of 1975.

And then, one morning in early December 1973, a cable
arrived from Kathmandu. It was from Mike Cheney, who
helps to run a trekking business called Mountain Travel. It
was founded by Jimmy Roberts, who had been the leader of
the first Himalayan expedition to Annapurna II in 1960, had
given me advice and help in the intervening years, and had
been deputy leader in our 1972 attempt. Mike had always been
the back-room boy, doing all the donkey work of arranging
documentation, booking porters, helping our gear through

Customs, but had never actually been a full member of an expedition. He had also always kept me very well informed of happenings in Nepal.

The cable read: 'Canadians cancelled for Autumn 1975 stop Do you want to apply Reply urgent Cheney.'

Suddenly all my nicely laid plans were upset: I had another chance of going for the South West Face but at the wrong time of year. We had already found that it was too cold and windy to climb the South West Face in the autumn. The Japanese had also failed but at least that had shown that a man could reach the summit of Everest in late October by the South Col route and that he could even survive a bivouac within a thousand feet of the summit, admittedly at the price of severe frostbite.

It took me several days to decide. If I were to attempt the South West Face again I felt strongly that it should be in the spring rather than in the autumn. The memories of the bitter wind and cold of the autumn, the problems of leadership and organization, the worries of finding the money to pay for it were all too fresh. Could I go through all this again for what might be little more than a forlorn hope of success? Every consideration of reason and common sense said 'Don't go!'

But the fact that Everest is the highest mountain the world, the variety of mountaineering challenges it presents, the richness of its history, combine to make it difficult for any mountaineer to resist. And for me it had a special magnetism. I had been there before and failed, and in the end I knew that I could not let pass the opportunity to go to Everest again, even if an attempt on the South West Face seemed impractical.

One challenge that intrigued me was the possibility of organizing a lightweight expedition to climb Everest by the original South Col route, employing no Sherpas and moving up the mountain as a self-contained unit of twelve climbers. I had pursued the same line of thought before committing myself to the South West Face in 1972, from similar motives of worry about the practical feasibility of a full-scale attempt on the South West Face. I talked to Doug Scott, Dougal Haston and Graham Tiso about my plans. All three had been with me in 1972. Doug and Dougal were non-committal but

Graham, who had organized all the equipment for my first Everest expedition was positively enthusiastic about the scheme. All too well he knew the problems of assembling the equipment necessary for a major expedition. He had put in a brilliant performance as a support climber on our 1972 trip, reaching 26000 feet without using oxygen and staying at altitude as long as anyone on the expedition; the thought of taking part in a small, compact expedition, where he could even have the opportunity of reaching the summit of Everest, obviously appealed to him.

Through the winter of 1973–4, Mike Cheney pushed our cause in Kathmandu and I did what I could from this country, enlisting the help of the Foreign Office and any other contacts I could think of. But Everest filled only a small part of my mind for I was busy planning our expedition to Changabang which we hoped to climb with a group of Indian mountaineers. Even more important, we were in the throes of moving from suburban Manchester to a small cottage on the northern side of the Lake District.

I had lived in the Lake District from 1962–8 but then found myself getting more involved in photo-jouralism than in climbing, with all my work coming from London. The move to Manchester was rather an unsatisfactory compromise between staying in the Lakes and moving all the way down to London. I very much doubt, however, if I could have organized my first two expeditions – to the South Face of Annapurna in 1970 and Everest in 1972 – from the Lake District. At that stage I needed the amenities provided by a large city, near the centre of the country. We bought a small cottage in the Lake District for weekends and holidays and, in the spring of 1973, whilst lying in the garden one day, relaxing from the stress of closing down the 1972 expedition and writing its book, I suddenly realized how important was this quiet peace and beauty. My life was now much more closely involved with climbing and expeditions and it seemed ridiculous to live in a place whose sole advantage was that it was easy to get away from and fairly accessible to London. And so we started the long, laborious task of making our cottage large enough not only to take a family, but also to act as a place of work where I could organize my expeditions and write. Thus, that spring of 1974, Everest only occupied part of my mind.

When I set out for Changabang at the end of April the cottage still wasn't finished and I left Wendy and the children ensconced in a small caravan at the bottom of our field. We had reached Delhi and Doug Scott, Dougal Haston and I were staying at the Indian Officers' Club before setting out on the final stage of our journey to the Garhwal Himalaya when the telegram arrived. We had permission for Everest in the autumn of 1975.

2   It's the South West Face

Doug Scott came into my room later on that morning. He told me that he and Dougal had been talking about the opportunity that had been given us and suggested that I might reconsider my decision to make a lightweight push by the South Col route. He asked me how we'd all feel if we arrived in the Western Cwm and conditions seemed suitable for an attempt on the South West Face, and yet by the very nature and size of the expedition we were forced to pursue our plan for making a lightweight push by the South Col. We should always be aware of the South West Face towering above us with its intriguing unknowns of the Rock Band and the upper stretches of the mountain. This was the real challenge and until it had been met and overcome any other route or style in climbing could only be a second best.

I shared their feelings, but knew all too well that it was I that would have to spend the next year putting together the strong expedition that we should need to give us the slightest chance of success, with all its accompanying problems of raising funds, co-ordinating another large team and taking the ultimate responsibility for all our decisions and acts. This time we would have over a year to make our preparations and anyway, here in Delhi, on the way to another mountain, the romance of the challenge was stronger than my own practical doubts or memories of the months of worry and hard work which the last expedition had brought with it.

Even so, I was cautious in my reply, insisting that we must first find a single sponsor who could cover the cost. We had only just succeeded in raising sufficient funds in 1972 from several different sources, and most of my energies had been spent in fund-raising instead of planning how best to climb the mountain. It was obvious that to have any chance of success we were now going to need an even stronger and therefore more expensive expedition. We should also have to take into account the effects of inflation and the fact that many companies and certainly the entire media were feeling the pinch of the economic crisis. In other words, we needed more money, but there was less of it around.

We left Delhi that night for a rackety journey in the back of an open truck, across the moonlit Indian plains, on our way to the Garhwal Himalaya. On the approach march to Changabang, and even on the mountain itself, we often talked of Everest, analysing the reasons for our failure in 1972 and looking for the means of improving our chances in our next attempt. The key problems were the cold and high winds of the post-monsoon period. Somehow we had to get into position to make a summit bid before the arrival of the winds which seem to come at any time from early to mid-October. An obvious way would be to start earlier, but here one was limited by the monsoon, which continues until towards the end of September. By starting too early in the monsoon, however, quite apart from delays caused by bad weather, there would also be much greater danger from avalanche. The critical question, therefore, was just how early in the monsoon did one dare start? The Japanese had reported fine mornings followed by snow most afternoons when they established their Base Camp on 25 August. This, therefore – three weeks earlier than we had started in 1972 – seemed a reasonable target to aim for.

Having established Base Camp early, the next essential would be greater speed in climbing the mountain. Inevitably this meant a larger team would be required to give greater carrying power. In 1972, with eleven climbers and forty Sherpas, there had been several occasions when we had had to delay our advance on the mountain in order to build up supplies at one of the camps. Once again I had to find a balance between a sufficiently large team to ensure that we could maintain our speed up the mountain and yet, at the same time, avoid becoming unwieldy. We needed better tentage which could stand up to the high winds, the heavy snowfall and the stones that raked the Face. By the end of the previous expedition, hardly a tent remained undamaged and we had even had to cadge some box tents from a neighbouring expedition.

Finally, and perhaps most important of all, we needed to find a better route. The feature which had defeated all expeditions so far was the Rock Band. In the autumn of 1969 the Japanese had ventured onto the Face for the first time reaching the foot of this wall of sheer rock stretching across the Face, its base around the 27000-foot mark. They approached it at the left-hand end where a deep-cut gully seemed almost to lead off the Face and a narrow chimney stretched up more towards its centre. They favoured this chimney as the best line when they returned in the spring of 1970 with a very strong expedition, but failed to climb the South West Face partially because there was practically no snow covering the rocks immediately below the Rock Band, thus making it difficult to establish Camp 5. Also, as a result of the scarcity of snow, there was heavy stone fall. Another reason for their failure was probably their decision to attempt two routes at the same time. It is all too easy to concentrate on the easier option once the going becomes rough on the other and the Japanese, turning back below the Rock Band, then climbed Everest by the South Col route.

The International Expedition made their attempt the following spring. Although weaker in numbers than the Japanese expedition, they also went for two routes – the South West Face and a direct route up the West Ridge of Everest. This was over-ambitious and many of the arguments which bedevilled this expedition resulted from the almost inevitable abandonment of one of the routes, in this instance the West Ridge. Don Whillans and Dougal Haston, who were out in front on the Face for almost the entire climb, found similar problems to those the Japanese had faced the previous year. They used the tent platforms constructed by the Japanese at Camp 4 but, above it, almost having failed to find a suitable camp site on the left-hand side of the Rock Band, they were attracted towards the right by a well-protected ledge in the upper part of the Great Central Gully. This channelled them onto a long snow rake which stretched across the foot of the Rock Band towards the right-hand end of the Face. Here they established their sixth camp at a height of 27300 feet, just below a chimney that seemed to lead to the top of the Rock Band. But by this time they had been at altitude for too long, their supplies had thinned down to a trickle and they were forced to retreat.

The following spring Don Whillans, with Doug Scott and Hamish MacInnes joined Dr Karl Herrligkoffer's European Everest Expedition. This time they concentrated on the South West Face as a single objective, but the expedition was poorly equipped and, more serious, disunited from the start with the large Austro-German group distrusting the British element. Don Whillans had recommended by-passing the Rock Band by skirting its right-hand corner and crossing the relatively easy slopes towards the South East Ridge just below the South Summit. The British party withdrew from the expedition when it became evident that they were not even going to be given the chance of making a second ascent once a German pair had made the first summit bid. Felix Kuen and Adolf Huber did reach the top camp but after a night there were driven back down, having done little more than look round the corner.

In our turn, in 1972, I had planned on making a determined attempt on the right-hand chimney, since Dougal had assured me that it had been filled with snow in the spring of 1971. In the event, the snow had been blown away. More serious, however, the chimney did not even lead to the Upper Snow Field which had an exit up a gully leading to the South Summit; on close examination it could be seen to lead onto the crest of a buttress between the South West Face and the South Face, leaving a lot of hard climbing before reaching the summit.

It is surprising that the Japanese, in 1973, followed the same line as ourselves and previous expeditions, particularly since the first Japanese expedition had been confident that there was a route through the Rock Band over on the left. They had decided, however, that the Rock Band was too difficult for a first ascent and favoured the tactics of the German expedition, by-passing the Band on the right, with a seventh camp on the way across to the South East Ridge – or even perhaps on the

Ridge itself. In fact they were unable to establish their sixth camp.

Whilst planning the autumn 1972 trip, I had come to the conclusion that it would be impractical to think of a seventh camp on Everest since it would inevitably place too heavy a burden on the lines of supply. It is advisable to sleep on oxygen and, of course, to use it for climbing and load-carrying from about 25 500 feet upwards to ensure that the team can maintain their effort to the top on a mountain as high as Everest. Camp 5 is at around 26 000 feet and it seemed possible to service only one camp above this point, however strong the expedition.

Examination of our own performance in 1972, and that of all the other expeditions to the Face, seemed to show that the right-hand route was a blind alley. Both Doug Scott and I were very attracted to the deep-cut gully which appeared to penetrate the left-hand side of the Rock Band. You could not see all the way into the back of it, but a tongue of snow led into it and there seemed a good chance that this could continue a good way up. The problem might be to find an escape from the gully out onto the Upper Snow Field, but it was thought likely that the difficult climbing would be for a comparatively short section.

Another advantage of attempting the Rock Band from the left was that we should be able to tackle it from Camp 5, ensuring that our lines of communication would be that much shorter, with the climbers sleeping lower and, therefore, going more strongly. If successful, we should be able to have our Camp 6 above the Rock Band – admittedly, with a long traverse across the Upper Snow Field to the foot of the South Summit Gully – but this seemed acceptable since the main difficulties would then be over. Most important of all, the successful ascent of the Rock Band would provide a considerable morale boost to the team. I suspect, one of the reasons for a retreat had been the demoralizing realization that in spite of having reached 27 000 feet and establishing Camp 6, the hard climbing was still in front.

By the time we returned to Britain, heartened by our success on Changabang, I had mapped out the general principles for our new approach. I still had to find our single sponsor, however, and that looked as though it could be difficult. The day after we got back I went to see my literary agent, George Greenfield, to present him with the problem. He knew all about my lightweight Everest project and was confident that he could raise the money for this without too much trouble, for it would only have cost about £12000. Now, though, I wanted to raise over £100000. He winced as I told him of the change, but after I described the discussions that Doug, Dougal and I had had during the Changabang expedition, I succeeded in convincing George that we had a chance. The next problem was to find our single sponsor. George suggested that we might approach Barclays Bank, especially as we had a mutual friend, Alan Tritton, who was a director.

George arranged an appointment and I prepared a paper on why I thought we had a chance this time and the probable cost of the expedition. A week later we were ushered into his office in Pall Mall. He was sympathetic but non-committal. He had to put it in front of his Board. I sat it out for a fortnight, living in the confusion of a small caravan at the bottom of our field as the builders still worked on the cottage. Now – back in Britain – the prospect of master-minding yet another huge expedition was terrifying. It was hard enough writing an article to help pay for our Changabang trip, sorting out all the pictures and supervising the alterations to the cottage. Why the hell did I have to complicate everything!

And then I learnt that we were over the first hurdle. Barclays were prepared to sponsor the expedition. In taking this bold step they made our effort on the South West Face possible for I suspect that there were very few, if any, other major companies which would have given this level of support. Although Barclays had sponsored other sporting activities in the past, usually through their International arm, they had never undertaken such a major commitment. In effect, they were going to underwrite the expedition for although their sponsorship was given on the strength of the budget I submitted they were accepting the responsibility of having to foot the balance if I went seriously over budget.

B

For me, it removed the greatest worry that any expedition leader can have. Now I could concentrate on organizing the expedition, secure in the knowledge that we could select the very best possible equipment, that we would not have to take second-best, just to save money.

I shall always be grateful to Alan Tritton for putting our case to the Board of Barclays Bank International with the conviction and enthusiasm necessary to get their support. In the final analysis, however, it was Anthony Tuke, the Chairman who had to give his consent. Over the last few years I have approached many organizations for help in equipping or organizing climbing ventures and have become increasingly convinced that very rarely is this support given for purely commercial reasons. In almost every case, the potential sponsor or supplier has had his imagination caught by the venture in question, has decided he would like to back it and then, and only then, has he started to try to justify it to himself and his board in commercial terms.

Barclays' support for the expedition was announced on 18 October 1974 at a press conference at their Head Office. I suspect they were slightly shaken by one aspect of the response by some of the media and their customers. Although many acclaimed their initiative, a number of people asked how they could possibly justify spending so much money on a pointless venture which seemed to have little chance of success, at a time of grave economic crisis. Even the mountaineering press questioned the wisdom of the expedition.

Ken Wilson, who edits *Mountain*, and had been with us for a short time in 1972 helping to look after Camp 1 and then staying at Camp 2, felt he had to question the viability of the forthcoming attempt, writing in an editorial:

Does the forthcoming Everest South West Face Expedition stand any chance of success? This is a question that many British climbers are asking themselves, as Chris Bonington and his wealthy sponsors, Barclays Bank Limited, crank that whole tedious media bandwaggon back into action after a two year break . . .

There are however a number of ancillary considerations that should be given greater weight on this occasion. Many people in the climbing world and a growing sector of the press are becoming increasingly sceptical about the value of the project. Is such a route really worth the expenditure of £100 000 and should climbers remain so completely oblivious of this point, when the country and indeed the world are in such dire economic straits? To state that the money could not be diverted elsewhere is to avoid the issue. The fact is that involvement in such an extravagant project at this time of austerity lays the expedition, and indeed the entire climbing world, open to the charge of irresponsibility and frivolity in relation to the world about them . . .

A successful conclusion (a remote possibility) would please everybody, but a more likely outcome would be an embarrassing rehash of the 1972 affair with a few hundred feet gained and some ticklish explaining to be done to an increasingly sceptical press.

A Member of Parliament, Mr John Lee, Labour Member for Handsworth, even announced he was going to ask a question in the House. 'I have great admiration for mountaineers,' he said, 'but frankly, the banks surely have better things than that to finance at the moment – like the regeneration of our economy for instance.'

Perhaps most daunting of all for Barclays was a flood of letters from angry customers who had, perhaps, just been refused overdrafts, asking how the bank could justify refusing them when they had just given a mountaineering expedition so much money.

Alan Tritton remained splendidly imperturbable – at any rate to all the expedition members – and continued to give us unstinting support. We got on with the business of organizing the expedition, but the questions needed answering. After the 1972 expedition I had been shaken, even hurt, by the criticism of a number of mountaineers whose opinion I respect, both of the value of the route and the size of the expedition we had used to tackle it. For instance, David Cox, an ex-President of the Alpine Club, in a review he wrote of our 1972 attempt, expressed his regret that we had abandoned the concept of a lightweight push by the South Col for a siege of the Face.

The fundamental question was whether the South West Face could be considered a worthwhile objective. I think it was. There is a natural evolution from attempting a mountain by its easiest route; on Everest, the South East Ridge; then tackling other, perhaps harder facets such as the North Ridge or the West Ridge and then, finally, the steep walls embraced by the ridges. This same evolution has taken place in the mountains of the Alps, on the Matterhorn, the Eiger and every other mountain and the steps forward onto harder ground were often accompanied by controversy over new techniques used or risks taken. The South West Face of Everest was not 'The Ultimate Challenge' of mountaineering (the title used for the American edition of our 1972 book) – there is no such thing, for no sooner is one 'last great problem' solved than another is found. It was, nevertheless, an intriguing problem which would continue to nag mountaineers until it was solved and man – perhaps especially, climbing man, being a very competitive creature – would be even more attracted to it, the more his fellows failed to solve it. It is this very instinct of enquiry linked with competitiveness which has accounted for much of man's progress as well, of course, as his aggressiveness.

There was no doubt in my mind about the worth of the route; inevitably I did wonder about the means we were going to use to climb it. My own philosophy is that one should use the minimum force or number of climbers necessary to give some chance of success. Lito Tejada Flores has explored these ideas in a magnificent article called 'Games Climbers Play', first published in an American magazine called *Ascent* and subsequently reproduced in *Mountain*. He has taken the various types of climbing, from bouldering, through short rock climbs to Alpine face climbing and Himalayan mountaineering, and examined the various unwritten rules which climbers have imposed upon themselves to maintain the element of uncertainty that is such an important feature of the sport. In other words, there would be neither risk nor uncertainty of success if one used a top rope on a short but difficult boulder problem in Derbyshire, or used pitons for aid on all the difficult sections on a rock-climb in North Wales. These self-imposed rules change in time, usually becoming more rigorous as the sport develops and frontiers of the unknown become more limited. A large number of rock-climbs in Britain and the Alps which were first climbed using pitons for aid, have since been ascended completely free, using only what the natural rock offers. This is not necessarily a reflection on the pioneers who originally climbed the route, but merely a mark of the development of climbing skills and changing ethics.

In the Himalayas there has been a growing trend towards very lightweight expeditions tackling increasingly difficult problems, often using an Alpine-style approach, abandoning the concept of set camps, high-altitude porters and fixed ropes, for a continuous movement up the mountain, carrying everything on the backs of the party and bivouacking each night. This is an exciting and very satisfying concept – one which Haston, Scott, Boysen and I followed on Changabang in 1974. Another pleasing feaure of this approach is that the entire team can go to the summit together, thus all share in the climax of the expedition.

On the South West Face of Everest, however, there could be no question of such an approach. In a way, one of its most pleasing features as a problem was that no matter what steps we took in our attempt to solve it – size of team, improved equipment, better food – our chances of success still seemed very thin. I found the sheer immensity of the problem fascinating. To be successful on any kind of major climb, whatever the size of party, requires meticulous planning. This in no way diminishes the essential romance of the adventure – indeed, it heightens it – for any venture can turn sour very quickly if the basic planning is faulty. Everest South West Face needed a whole set of new concepts in planning, equipment and timing to give any chance of success at all. Perhaps I am a frustrated Field-Marshal, my passion for war games and my early military career providing a clue in this direction, but I both enjoyed, and at times was frightened by, the scale of the responsibility I had undertaken – to form a sound plan and then to make it work in practice in terms of people, the wind, the cold and the thin air of the upper slopes of Everest. This was every bit as intriguing as tackling a smaller mountain with a more compact team.

It could be argued that we should have waited, or even allowed some future generation with improved equipment, or

longer necks, to make a lightweight push straight up the
Face. I have a feeling, however, that if each generation just
sat back, abandoning the challenge of the moment to the
people of the future, we would never make any progress at all.
In the climbing sense, though this probably also applies to the
entire range of human discovery, each generation blunders
forward, using the resources and concepts it has at its disposal to make an advance which at the time seems supremely
difficult but which, in the course of time, could appear comparatively easy.

The team members were certainly satisfied that the South
West Face was a worthwhile objective and there is little
doubt that very few mountaineers anywhere in the world
would have turned down an invitation to join an expedition
to attempt it. If uncertainty of success is one of the prime
attributes of an unsolved problem, the Face certainly rated
very highly. None of the team gave more than a fifty-fifty
chance of success and some of them – especially at the
beginning – gave us no chance at all, yet could not resist the
invitation to join. Their attitude mirrored that of the majority
of mountaineers.

But could we justify spending so much money on the
venture? As climbers without large amounts of money of our
own, we have to justify our financial needs to the people we
ask for sponsorship. I have succeeded in covering the cost of
my expeditions in the past through the sale of magazine
articles, the expedition book and film rights. The Annapurna
South Face Expedition, which was fully sponsored by the
Mount Everest Foundation, actually made a profit which was
then recycled back into the Foundation funds for use in
helping other expeditions. But Everest was a bigger proposition
altogether and there was no prospect of financing this expedition on the same basis. If we were to go ahead we needed an
outside sponsor.

Barclays' decision to back us, inspired though it no doubt
was by enthusiasm for what we were attempting, was based
nevertheless on a commercial judgement. We were not
receiving charitable help; Barclays Bank International backed
us from their advertising budget in order to help promote

their name and identity. They were certain to have a huge number of mentions in the press and, of course, provided we were successful, would show that they knew how to back a good investment which brought prestige not only to themselves but to the entire country. At this stage, when we had barely started to organize the expedition, however, it was a very bold step for it was becoming equally obvious that, should we fail, they could pick up a great deal of counter-publicity. But this was the chance they were prepared to take. Only they, at the end of the expedition, could say whether their association with it had been worthwhile.

£100000 is a lot of money by mountaineering standards, but set against the magnitude of the problem we were tackling, the size of the team we needed, the quantity of specialized equipment required, our budget becomes quite modest. But £100000 is still a lot of money. There is no commercial value in climbing a mountain, and no simple answer to the question of whether such expenditure can be justified. In the end, this is something about which we must each make up our own minds. I do know, however, that we gave many people a great deal of enjoyment – and perhaps even a little inspiration as well – as they followed our story in the newspapers and on television.

3 Picking the team

Even before the press launch of the expedition I had put in a great deal of work, deciding on the basic plan on the mountain and, from this, determining the strength of the team and our programme over the next year. These were the foundations of the expedition; get these wrong and the entire edifice could collapse later on. It was only after completing this initial work that I finalized the selection of the team.

In a series of conversations whilst climbing Changabang, we had already determined our basic strategy and it was almost inevitable that Martin Boysen, Doug Scott and Dougal Haston should become members of the team. I had known Dougal since 1966, when we had both taken part in the First Ascent of the Eiger Direct with John Harlin, a brilliant American climber whose meteoric climbing career tragically ended when a fixed rope was cut by a falling stone. Since that time Dougal and I had made a number of winter ascents in the Alps together; he had been with me on the South Face of Annapurna, when he reached the summit with Don Whillans, and had also taken a leading part in the 1972 Everest expedition. He knew the South West Face well, for he had been there in 1971, as a member of Norman Dyhrenfurth's ill-fated International Expedition. With Don Whillans, Dougal had been out in front most of the time and had, of course, selected the right-hand line crossing below the Rock Band as the ideal route through this barrier.

I have never come to know Dougal closely – I doubt if anyone ever could, he has so strong a reserve – but throughout our years of climbing together he has proved a loyal friend, always giving me a quiet support on expeditions. With a finely developed mountain sense and considerable determination, he seems to know exactly what he wants from life and quietly, but resolutely pursues his own course.

I had known Doug Scott for a much shorter period and, although having met him on the climbing scene from time to time and given a few lectures at Nottingham for his local climbing club, in which he has always taken a very active part, we had never climbed together before our autumn attempt on the Face. He had already been to Everest once that year, with Dr Herrligkoffer's European Expedition. Out of the 1972 expedition had grown a friendship which had been further strengthened by our experience on Changabang. Doug and Dougal form an interesting contrast – Dougal, self-contained, with a carefully ordered mind, developed perhaps in the years spent at Edinburgh University studying philosophy, his mind reflects his appearance – clean-shaven, casually, but carefully dressed – he is economic in thought, effort and movement. Doug, on the other hand, is a great, shaggy bear with shoulder-length hair, beard and eyes that peer through wire-framed spectacles. His dress, and at times his thoughts are untidy, though his creative capacity is every bit as strong as Dougal's – less disciplined, perhaps, but more broadly-based, for as well as being a good writer Doug is a superb photographer. Like the traditional picture of the bear, he has a latent strength and violence in his make-up but, at the same time, is very lovable with a warm emotional spontaneity. I have never known anyone with such an appetite for climbing. For instance, in the early part of 1972 he went climbing in the Alps, then took part in the European Everest Expedition in the spring, went to Baffin Island in the summer and joined me on Everest in the autumn. He had been away from home for over three quarters of the year.

Martin Boysen, the fourth member of our Changabang team, was another obvious choice for Everest. He is one of my oldest climbing friends; we had both started in the same climbing area, on Kentish sandstone, and had known each other from the early sixties, when Martin had just left school and had already become the climbing star of south-east England. He went on to Manchester University, chosen because of its proximity to the crags, and quickly emerged as an outstanding rock-climber. He may not have the single-minded drive of Haston or Scott, but he has a broader love of the mountains, born from a passionate interest in their fauna and flora which led him to study botany at university. His is a complex personality, combining the competitiveness and ego-drive of most successful climbers or sportsmen hidden beneath an easy-going, indolent exterior. He was with me on the South Face of Annapurna, sacrificing his own chances of going for the summit in the work he did in support of the lead climbers at a crucial stage of the expedition. I had invited him to join us on Everest in 1972 but his wife, Maggie, had been pregnant at the time and he had therefore reluctantly refused.

Graham Tiso and Nick Estcourt were already involved in my plans for a lightweight push on the mountain. Nick Estcourt is one of the few top-class climbers I know who combines a considerable talent for climbing with one for organization. By profession a computer-programmer, he brings a well-trained, analytical mind to bear on every mountaineering problem, often coming up with sounder solutions than climbers like Doug Scott or Dougal Haston who, perhaps, have greater élan and drive. Both on Annapurna South Face and to an even greater extent on Everest in 1972 he fulfilled important roles. In the latter expedition he kept our accounts straight as Treasurer and led some of the key sections of the route almost all the way to our high point at 27300 feet, just short of the site of Camp 6 below the right-hand chimney through the Rock Band. Nick Escourt welcomed my change from a lightweight push to a full-scale attempt on the South West Face, but Graham Tiso had different feelings.

Having organized all the equipment in 1972, he knew the vast amount of work entailed by another full-scale attempt. A canny, forceful businessman, he runs a very successful climbing shop in Edinburgh and is used to working out the odds dispassionately. Viewed with cold logic, our chances of success to him did not seem great. He did not feel inclined to put in all the grinding, repetitive effort of getting our equipment together for a trip which seemed to have little chance of success and in which his role would have been identical to the one he had fulfilled in 1972. Then, he had worked magnificently in support, staying at Camp 4 for a long period and carrying up to Camp 5 without the use of oxygen. He had been enthusiastic about my lightweight push, for this might have given him a chance of going for the summit. Graham would not claim to be a brilliant mountaineer but he has sound judgement and, in 1972, had shown that he also had a fine pair of lungs. When he decided against coming with us I was seriously disturbed, for good administrators who can also climb are in much shorter supply than brilliant mountaineers.

Now I had a nucleus of five whom I had invited to join the expedition. In my initial planning I had decided a stronger team would be needed to fulfil the lead climbing role and also the support. In 1972, with six good climbers who took turns out in front, and five, including myself, in support, we had been desperately short-handed. I juggled numbers around and finally decided on sixteen, with eight lead climbers and eight in support. Later, we were to increase this number to eighteen.

The next place to look was obviously amongst the other members of the 1972 expedition. Hamish MacInnes was a natural choice for deputy leader. He was one of my oldest friends; we had first climbed together in 1953, when I was a young lad on my first winter climbing trip to Scotland. We had met up with Hamish and climbed with him, making the first winter ascent of Agag's Groove on the Buachaille Etive Mhor. My more experienced companion had then returned home and Hamish, also on his own, then decided to use me, a young novice at winter mountaineering, as a portable belay on a couple of hard winter first ascents – one of them on Raven's Gully, which retains its reputation even today. We went off to climb together in the Alps, making an abortive attempt on the Eiger North Wall in 1957, for my first Alpine climb, and climbing the South West Pillar of the Petit Dru. Hamish, at forty-six, five years older than myself, was an immensely experienced, very sound mountaineer who had made his life in Glencoe and become a world expert on mountain rescue. This would be his third trip to the South West Face, for he had been on Dr Herrligkoffer's expedition as well as my own. He accepted my invitation with some reservation, being doubtful about our chances of success, but unable to resist going to Everest once again.

Mick Burke's reaction was much the same, at first. He did not think we had much chance but could not resist the challenge. When asked why he was going to Everest again, he said: 'I don't think the whole business allows much choice. If you've been once and you didn't get to the top then, when the opportunity comes again, although you might not want to go, you don't really have a choice – you've got to go. I mean, just think how ropey you'd feel if someone got to the top this time and you weren't mixed up in it. It's as straightforward as that.'

Mick's role, however, was not entirely simple, for besides being an ambitious and forceful mountaineer, he had become a professional cameraman and was now working full-time for the BBC. I asked him whether he wanted to come along as a member of the climbing team or to concentrate on being a cameraman and, presumably, be paid for doing so. After quite a bit of thought he decided he would like to be a full member of the team and then film as much as he could at altitude. This was a very similar role to the one he had held both on the South Face of Annapurna and on Everest in 1972 when he had taken a cine camera to our highest point on the last day of the expedition.

I also asked Kelvin Kent who had been with me in 1970 and 1972, running Base Camp and organizing the porters. A serving officer in the Army, he had been with the Gurkha Signals and, as a result, spoke fluent Nepali. His military career had by now reached a crucial stage, however, and he decided he had better sit this one out.

I could easily understand the decision of the support climbers not to go on another trip to the South West Face. They have all the hard work and very little of the exhilaration of making the route out in front. As a result, even if we were successful, their own experience would be very similar to what it had been in 1972. The lead climbers, on the other hand, had the lure of the summit and, even if they failed to get there themselves, the prospect of making the route over new ground. I was surprised, therefore, when Dave Bathgate decided against another trip. He had played an important part in 1972 when, with Nick Estcourt, he had made the route out to Camp 6. In doing so they had accepted a role which gave them very little chance of making a summit bid and, in effect, were setting it up for the other lead climbers. Dave is one of the least selfish people I know. A climber of considerable ability, his very modesty and lack of push has stopped him achieving the reputation of some of his peers. He was doubtful of our chances of success, suspecting perhaps that he might find himself in a subsidiary role and, anyway, had plans for a smaller peak and smaller expedition.

As our medical officer in 1972, Barney Rosedale had been ideal. Although not a hard climber, he had spent two years in Nepal working in a hospital His entire medical career had been in out-of-the-way places where he had had to take the full responsibility for medical decisions, even doing simple operations without the back-up of specialists. His maturity, rich sense of humour and work in managing Camp 2 in addition to his medical responsibilities, had been a tremendous source of strength to me. He was now practising in Marlborough, his wife had just had her second child, and I suspect that the heavy, unrelenting responsibility of doctor to an Everest Expedition is something one wants to undertake only once. He therefore regretfully declined my invitation. It was obviously going to be difficult to find anyone to live up to his precedent, but in the event, we did.

Charlie Clarke, the very antithesis of Barney Rosedale, was a keen expedition climber in his own right, having undertaken several expeditions to the Nepal Himalaya and the Kishtwar range in Kashmir. On first meeting he seemed almost too smooth – well dressed, with almost boyish good looks and an elegant house in Islington – very much the public-school product. On getting to know him, however, his enthusiasm proved to be backed by a steady strength of character and on the mountain, in spite of his strong interest in climbing, he always placed his medical responsibilities to the fore as a reliable and very dependable doctor. He described his own reaction to the expedition shortly after I had invited him to join us.

This isn't my style of expedition at all. Previously, I've been on small trips, often without much serious climbing. I'm coming firstly because I've never been to the Everest region, and I've always wanted to, and secondly the lure of the big mountain is absolutely enormous. Though I could turn down most other expeditions without too much heart-searching, I'm sure I could never turn down a chance to go to Everest.

Strangely, it isn't the Face that worries me so much, but I often wake at night and worry about the Ice Fall; I suppose it's the thought of the vast number of people having to go through it the whole time. In fact, most expeditions – however careful they've been – either lose somebody or come very close to doing so. I must say, I think we've the best chance of anybody of getting up the Face. We seem to have the right size of party and, what is most important, we have people who are not prima donnas making up a substantial part of the team.

There was no shortage of advice concerning potential team members and probably very few climbers would have refused an invitation. To me, at this stage, the most important choice was not that of the lead climbers but of the right person to organize all our equipment now that Graham Tiso had decided against coming with us. I certainly wanted someone in the equipment business who would have the right contacts and a businesslike, organized way of tackling the mammoth task which was going to confront him. Then I remembered that an old friend of mine, Dave Clarke, who ran a climbing shop in Leeds, had written just before the 1972 expedition, volunteering his services as an unpaid Sherpa.

Dave Clarke had been on an expedition to South Patagonia in 1962, primarily to carry out a geological survey. The leader of this team and two of its members had later invited Don Whillans, Ian Clough and myself to join them on a climbing venture to tackle the most challening peak of the range, the Central Tower of Paine. Dave was just starting work as a civil engineer at that time and therefore had to stand down from this expedition. We had met again when he came to the Lake District to build a bridge by Backbarrow in 1964. The lure of the Lakes was strong and he accepted a job as a quarry manager in Coniston but in 1967 he moved on to open a climbing shop in Leeds. We had climbed together on several occasions in the Lake District and, in 1968, had both been involved in an attempt to canoe down the upper reaches of the River Inn in Switzerland, Dave acting as support party with myself photographing the venture for the *Daily Telegraph Magazine*. We succeeded in snatching a climb on the 3000-foot-high Laliderer Wall in the Karwendelgebirge in Austria on the way out.

Dave was the only person, I could think of, who had all the qualifications for collecting the equipment. He was a hard worker, a perfectionist in everything he did and yet, at the same time, had a warm sense of humour and a real considera-tion for the people with whom he was working. When he accepted my invitation, however, I doubt whether he realized just what he was letting himself in for. No more did I, for the scale of this expedition was so much greater than anything I had organized previously. Nevertheless he fully justified the confidence we put in him, and it was a great relief that I had found the ideal person for this formidable task.

Mike Thompson was another old friend. We had been at Sandhurst and done a lot of climbing together over the years. On the South Face of Annapurna he was a support climber and had organized the food. His career as an anthropologist had been at a critical stage when I had invited him to join us on Everest in 1972 and he had decided not to come. He could not resist the invitation this time, however, and once again took on the task of food organizer.

I talked to Mike about the role he expected to fill on the expedition, and he commented:

It's easy for me, in a sense, because I'm going along as a supporter anyway. One says to oneself 'I won't think too much about anything else – just get on with the job in hand, acting as a supporter and keeping an eye on the food.' It all happens naturally; you just get on with that and if other opportunities present themselves that's a bonus. It's ideal, really, because in a support role nobody is expecting anything more of you. On the other hand, if you're expected to reach the top and you do no more than carry two loads to one of the lower caps, that's a disappointment.

Now I started to look round for another support climber, one I hoped would be able to help me with some of the organization prior to setting out on the expedition. I had asked other members of the team for suggestions and one name came up from two very different quarters – that of Ronnie Richards. Doug Scott had met Ronnie in the Pamirs during the summer of 1974, when they had both attended an International Mountaineering Camp organized by the Russians. His steady endurance as a mountaineer, his quiet modesty and the fact the he obviously knew how to organize himself, had impressed Doug.

'We didn't think much of him at first,' he said. 'I suppose he was too much of the public-shool type, but when we got to know him, we realized he was a good bloke.'

A recommendation also came from Graham Tiso, who has climbed Pik Lenin (23 400 feet) in the Pamirs with Ronnie, that he was a first-class, steady, well-organized mountaineer. There was also the extra advantage that he was living at home with his parents in Keswick, close enough to me to be of immediate help. He came over to see me and I took to him immediately inviting him on the spot.

Another vital gap to be filled was Base Camp Manager and Organizer in Nepal. In 1972, Jimmy Roberts had been deputy leader, looking after the recruitment of all our Sherpas. His last job with the Army had been that of Military Attaché in Kathmandu and, on retirement when he had started his very successful trekking firm, Mountain Travel, he used Sherpas to run the treks As a result, he had on his books some of the best high-altitude porters available They were all devoted to Jimmy and this had been a tremendous help to us in 1972.

Jimmy's director was Mike Cheney, who had done so much of the background organizing of the 1972 expedition. An arthritic hip had been giving Jimmy an increasing amount of trouble over the previous two years and so it seemed wise to give Mike his chance. I asked him to act as 'Our Man in Nepal' whilst Jimmy Roberts continued to give us his help and advice.

Mike was not a climber, but would run Base Camp and I felt we needed another fluent Nepali-speaker to look after our Advance Base Camp in the Western Cwm. It is all too easy to have unnecessary misunderstandings between climbers and Sherpas simply through lack of communication. I left this selection to Mike Cheney who suggested Adrian Gordon, an ex-Gurkha Captain who had recently left the army and was now working with the Gurkha Resettlement Scheme in Nepal.

With my full allocation of support climbers, there were still two places to fill among the lead climbers. The problem here was one of over-abundance – there were so many good climbers to choose from. I was aware of the criticism in the climbing world that only Bonington's cronies had any chance of getting on a Bonington expedition. There was, of course, some truth in this since one naturally tends to ask people one already knows and of whose performance and compatability one has first-hand knowledge. At the same time, though, I wanted to broaden the membership of the expedition, but to achieve this through the recommendations of the other members.

Paul Braithwaite, better known in climbing circles as 'Tut', had had, in the last few years, an outstanding Alpine record, making a number of impressive First British Ascents. He had also had some expedition experience in Baffin Island with Doug Scott and then, at greater altitude, in the Pamirs when he reached the summit of Pik Lenin, also with Doug. He had been to art college but gave it up to become a free-lance decorator, finding that this gave him the freedom and money to climb when he wanted. On meeting him, it was difficult to believe that he had the endurance to climb at altitude – he has a slight build which is emphasized somehow by his wispy moustache and long, straggly hair.

There seemed to be a multitude of possibilities for the eighth place and yet, when one started analysing the mountaineering background, experience at altitude and general compatibility of candidates, it quickly thinned out. Tut Braithwaite, Doug Scott and I had gone for a quick trip to the Alps and it was during this holiday that Tut suggested the name of Pete Boardman as a talented young climber who would get on with the other team members He was only twenty-three, but already had experience of one very successful expedition to the Hindu Kush, when he had made bold, Alpine-style ascents of the North Faces of the Koh-i-Mondi and Koh-i-Khaaik. Now he was working as a mountaineering instructor at Glenmore Lodge, the Scottish National Mountaineering Centre in the Cairngorms. I had never met him, and so asked him to come down for a weekend in the Lake District, and was immediately impressed by his quiet maturity. I invited him to join us, at the end of the weekend.

There was just one more place to fill to bring my team up to sixteen. We had agreed to take along a representative of Barclays Bank and since we needed another support climber, this should obviously be the same person. At this stage I was getting suggestions from a dozen different quarters. Ken Wilson phoned me at least once a week with unsolicited advice: 'You've got no sense of politics,' he'd say. 'Your team just isn't representational. You want some of the lads in it from the Welsh scene. Who on earth has heard of Richards or this fellow Gordon.'

I tried to explain that I was trying to build up a compatible team, not a political party.

I was still juggling names when Graham Tiso rang me one night.

'You must have Allen Fyffe,' he told me 'I can't think how you've missed him out! He's as good as anyone on ice, went really well on Dhaulagiri and would fit well into your team.'

From my high regard for Graham's judgement and knowing Allen slightly, having met him in Glencoe several times over the years, I decided – perhaps impulsively – to invite him to join the expedition. In doing so, I undoubtedly complicated things for myself. Allen was very definitely a lead climber and this gave an uneven number, unless I included myself or another member of the team in this category. We now had seventeen members, including the Barclays representative, Mike Rhodes, an easy-going, enthusiastic rock climber from Bradford.

By this time there was also a Committee of Management, chaired by Lord Hunt. Sir Jack Longland, who had been on Everest before the war, Ian McNaught Davis and Charles Wylie were members. I shall always be grateful for their advice and support. Doug Scott was also on the committee, to represent the feelings of the expedition members. At one of their early meetings Sir Jack Longland suggested that with such a large team it might be advisable to have a second doctor. The good sense of this was immediately apparent; I had already received a letter from Jim Duff, a young doctor who was working in Nepal on the Trans-Nepal Highway as medical officer. A friend of Doug Scott and Mick Burke, both of whom gave him a strong recommendation, he seemed ideal and I invited him. This, then, completed the team. In subsequent months I often worried that I might have made the team too large and wondered how on earth I could control them all on the mountain. I had also agreed to taking with us a BBC team of four and Keith Richardson of the *Sunday Times*. But there was little time for reflection in those seven hectic months before despatching our gear to Nepal.

One of my most critical decisions was the date on which to establish Base Camp and start the climb. The monsoon, which brings warm, very wet weather to the foothills and heavy snowfall to the mountains, ends around late September, usually with a violent storm that heralds settled, sunny weather. With this, however, come the constant high winds and bitter cold of the autumn that had defeated our 1972 attempt. I wanted to be in a position to establish our top camp and make a summit bid before the arrival of these winds. This would mean climbing through the monsoon, with the accompanying risk of bad weather and of avalanches. Hitherto the usual practice for autumn expeditions had been to start after the monsoon was over, though some pre-war expeditions had climbed through the monsoon.

The report of the 1973 Japanese expedition, however, was encouraging. They had established their base camp on the 25 August and enjoyed surprisingly settled weather until early October and the arrival of the end of monsoon storm, after which the high winds had constantly plagued them. Up to this date, they had had fine mornings, but snowfall almost every afternoon. Most important of all, there was practically no wind.

I wondered whether to start the climb even earlier than the Japanese, but finally decided against it; I felt that the earlier one started in August, the warmer it would be during the day, and the greater the avalanche risk. I decided therefore to follow the example of the Japanese and establish Base Camp around 25 August. On this basis I planned for the team to leave Britain on 29 July, allowing us just over three weeks to get ourselves organized in Kathmandu and make the approach march.

The key problem then was how to get the gear out. In this respect, Mike Cheney had recommended that we send it out before the arrival of the monsoon, reaching Kathmandu by early May, so that it could be flown from there to Luglha,* the airstrip just a day's carry from the Sherpa villages below Everest. This would avoid the problems involved in carrying all the expedition gear overland, through the monsoon, when rivers are swollen and it is almost impossible to keep loads dry. There were three ways of getting the gear to Kathmandu – by air, by sea or overland. The former was undoubtedly the easiest and most reliable. It was also prohibitively expensive as we estimated there would be at least twenty tons of food and equipment. Having sent the expedition gear out by sea for the Annapurna South Face Expedition in 1970, we had very nearly failed before setting foot on the mountain as a result. Engine failure had caused the ship carrying our gear to be nearly two months late in arriving. I was attracted, therefore, to the idea of sending the gear overland since, even if a truck broke down on the way, we could still do something about it, even if it meant sending a reserve truck. If the gear is at the bottom of the hold on a cargo ship, on the other hand, it is completely outside one's control. The only thing to do is to wait for it to be unloaded.

Someone was needed to organize the overland transport and I approached Bob Stoodley, a friend who is chairman of a large garage group in Manchester and helped raise funds

*The spellings of place names in this book are taken from the 1975 Royal Geographical Society's Survey of the Everest region and present one or two unfamiliar variations of earlier accepted spellings, e.g. Luglha for former Lukla, Khumde for Kunde, Tengpoche for Thyangboche.

for our 1972 trip. He seemed ideally suited for the job and flung himself into it with enthusiasm, persuaded Godfrey Davis to hire us – at an almost nominal rent – two sixteen-ton Ford lorries and coped with the complex tangle of paperwork required to send commercial vehicles from London to Kathmandu. Ronnie Richards took on the job of communications and helped Bob Stoodley with the documentation.

To reach Nepal by early May, the very latest Bob could afford to leave Britain was early April. This meant we would have to have everything ready and packed in Leeds in time for loading. The story of the problems and work involved is told in the relevant appendices, but this represented an Everest in itself!

Mike Thompson had to feed over a hundred people for a period of twelve weeks with three types of ration, for Base Camp, Advance Base and the Face itself, with variety built into each type of ration. He went about the task with characteristic ingenuity and economy of effort, completing the job so efficiently that there was a tendency to underestimate its magnitude.

There is no doubt, though, that the job of organizing the equipment was probably the most complex of any expedition to have left Britain. Dave Clarke had to equip not only the eighteen climbers, but a BBC film team of four, a *Sunday Times* reporter, thirty-eight high-altitude porters, thirty Ice Fall porters and various Base Camp personnel. There were the problems of getting all the correct boot and clothing sizes, ensuring that there were sufficient reserves and steering a number of prototypes through their development. In this respect he was helped by Hamish MacInnes who not only organized our oxygen system but also designed a completely new series of very strong box tents for use at Base and Advance Base Camps, on the Face and for the summit camp. In 1972 our tentage had not been strong enough to withstand the wind, avalanches or stone falls. These were probably the strongest tentage ever designed for an expedition and are described in Appendix 5. It was interesting to see how his attitude to the expedition developed from initial pessimism to growing optimism and then very real enthusiasm as a

result of both his involvement and the confidence he had
in the equipment he had designed.

I shall never forget that week in Leeds when, in a chilly,
dusty warehouse we packed the myriad of gear required for a
major expedition. At first glance it was difficult to believe it
could all be fitted into two trucks. Not only did we have to
pack it, we also had to keep an accurate record of the contents
of each box. I wanted to pack it all into loads which would
either be left at Kathmandu, sent through to Khumde a
Sherpa village near the foot of Everest to be opened on our
arrival, or carried straight through to Base Camp. Each load
had to be weather-proofed, fragile items packed safely and
then, to make life even more complicated, each load had to
weigh roughly sixty pounds, the standard weight for a porter,
as well as fitting into our two standard-size boxes.

We worked for eighteen hours a day, helped by a group of
volunteer Scouts. Bob Stoodley brought the two vehicles over
in April and we spent two days loading them. We only
just managed to fit everything on board, thanks to careful
packing by Bob, his secretary, his four teenage children and
the drivers, but each truck was two tons overweight, rolling to
a frightening degree on the easiest bend. Another night spent
by my long-suffering secretary, Louise Wilson, typing the
manifests and we were able to collapse, thankfully, the first
phase of the expedition over. The bulk of the gear and food
was now on its way to Kathmandu.

Bob Stoodley had with him Ronnie Richards and three
professional drivers, Alan Riley, Allen Evans and John
O'Neill. They drove night and day with only three scheduled
night stops at Ankara, Tehran and New Delhi, making the
7000-mile journey in twenty-four days, a remarkable achievement considering the size of the vehicle and the degree of
overloading.

I couldn't resist remarking to Dave, just after the gear had
left Britain, 'Well, if it's all hi-jacked on the way out, you'll
still have more time to replace it than we had to organize the
whole expedition in 1972!'

Dave did not think this was funny. On the contrary it
brought out a very real fear that I had, that in choosing this

overland route we were taking risks not just of hi-jack but also of accidents. At least we had plenty of time in hand, though; if the worst happened and the gear was delayed for some reason – for anything up to eight weeks – we should still have been able to hire porters and carry it from Kathmandu to Base Camp when we flew out at the end of July. Even so I was immensely relieved to get Bob's telegram, that they had arrived safely in Kathmandu.

The vehicles reached Kathmandu on 3 May and were unloaded in Mike Cheney's garden. The next three weeks were spent in shuttling the loads to the airport, waiting for the right kind of weather to fly the planes to Luglha and, from there, ferrying them by Sherpa porter to the home of Nima, one of the Mountain Travel Sirdars who had agreed to store everything in his house in Khumde, one of the Sherpa villages.

Mike Cheney was employing several new approaches; instead of controlling everything himself he had come to an agreement with the Sherpa Co-operative (which he had recently helped to form) to pay them 5·50 Rupees per kilo of baggage from Kathmandu to Khumde, leaving them responsible for the contracts with the light aircraft, organization and payment of porters from Luglha to Khumde. It was more than just a modern, more effective way of doing things, it was also a demonstration of trust in both the integrity and – more to the point – the management ability of our key Sherpas. This was to prove one of the corner stones of the eventual success of the expedition.

Jimmy Roberts had suggested Pertemba as Sirdar, or Head Sherpa, of the expedition. Although he had been one of our outstanding high-altitude porters in 1972, he was still very young at the age of twenty-six for such a responsibility. I had been very impressed not only by his performance but also by his personality, however, and was very happy to agree to Jimmy's suggestion. The Deputy Sirdar, Ang Phu, was a year younger than Pertemba and had also put up a good performance in 1972. Like Pertemba, he was typical of an emerging generation of Sherpa, educated at one of the schools founded by Sir Edmund Hillary and accustomed to Western ways.

Mike, having consulted his Sherpas closely throughout the planning phase of the expedition, wrote to me on one occasion:

The Sherpa Co-operative (which includes Mountain Travel staff and Sherpas as well as expedition Sherpas) should be treated as full partners in support of the expedition. I now hold regular meetings with Dawa Norbu (head of the Co-op), Pertemba and Lhakpa Thondup (to be Base Camp Sirdar) and discuss everything with them. I trust them in the same way that you trust Nick, Dave, Ronnie, etc.

This is something new and very valuable. To a large extent it looks after the security of gear problem. The staff of the Sherpa Co-op are looking after the gear of *their* expedition, not just the gear of a lot of foreign climbers.

In spite of bad weather which sometimes prevented flights to Luglha, the Sherpa Co-operative completed the airlift of our stores by early June. Everything was crammed into Nima's house.

It was good to have our last-minute rush three months before we were due to set out for Kathmandu in the luxurious comfort of an Air India 747. Inevitably, a few items had not been delivered on time and there were lots of loose ends to tie up, but the bulk of the organizational work had been carried out. This gave most of us time to relax a little before the expedition. Doug Scott, with his insatiable appetite for climbing, went off to the Karakorum to climb in the Biafo region, Ronnie Richards joined him from Kathmandu; Martin Boysen went to the Trango Tower; Tut Braithwaite went off to the Alps and had a very successful season.

With time to concentrate on some detailed expedition planning, I endeavoured to work out the exact logistic pattern we might encounter on the mountain. Ian McNaught Davis, an old friend and member of our Committee of Management, runs a computer firm in London and he made available Stephen Taylor, one of his programmers, to write a programme to help plan our logistics. Quickly, I discovered that it was impossible to get the computer to do it all for you; rather, it represented a quick check on one's own planning ideas, telling whether the logistic plan would work out or not. We made a climbing game in which I gave the order for movement and load-carrying, and the computer would swiftly calculate the finish at the end of each day. We played this through three times but always reached a logistic bottleneck around Camp 4. As a result of this, I developed a formula for planning the most effective distribution of manpower in the early and mid stages of the expedition, which seemed to solve the problem. Not only did this work so well that we followed it almost exactly in practice, but also – when we changed the siting of our camps in the later stages of the expedition – I found I was able to adapt mentally to the changing situation quickly, even at 25500 feet. I prepared a programme for the climb which would, in theory, enable us to make a summit bid towards the end of September. At the end of July 1975, however, when we flew out to Kathmandu, I did not dare believe that we could possibly achieve these targets; there were so many unknown factors; the weather, performance of the Sherpas, the state of the snow, our own ability to acclimatize in a very fast ascent.

On the eve of departure, even our best friends gave us no more than an even chance of success – these were the odds quoted by John Hunt at our press conference. Some members of the team felt even this to be optimistic.

4   The approach march

(2 August–16 August)

The path winding up the hill past small mud houses, under the spreading branches of the Peepul tree, was just the same as it had been three years before; it was just as humid, just as hot with the sun glaring through billowing clouds, which would shed their load of monsoon rain well before dusk.

The start of another Everest Expedition approach march; the ride in Land-Rovers from Kathmandu to Lamosangu, along the winding Chinese-built road; the seeming chaos of the start with cursing Sherpas distributing loads to a mob of porters; three or four local photographers from the news agencies darting about getting pictures of each other, of the porters, of the gear; pictures that could be transposed with those of so many other expeditions.

It was the same, and yet unique. Those of us who had been there before were three years older, had learnt more about ourselves and each other; for the rest it had the freshness of a new adventure about to start. There was excited anticipation, tempered I suspect in every case by some apprehension.

Just before leaving England our doctor, Charlie Clark, had written in his diary:

There is, of course, that awful empty fear, with so many men passing through the Ice Fall for so long, how can we avoid a serious accident and even a fatality or two. I know we can probably take no real precautions; selfishly I pray that it won't be me, but I have got myself into the position that I am prepared to take the small risk – no more work, no more Ruth, no more little Rebecca; tears, anger, hardship, widow, fatherless child – these are very horrid things to think about. To justify them is easy by saying, 'Well, I've always climbed and I've always accepted the risk of a fatal accident – Ruth knew it before we married', and so on. It doesn't bear thinking about too much. Even though I have just walked over to see little Rebecca in bed, I know that I really do

The walk in from Kathmandu to Base Camp

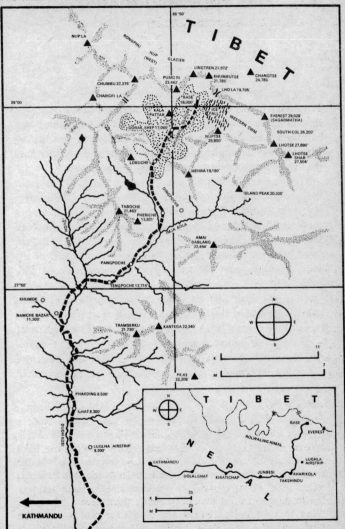

want to go, I know that I will actually enjoy myself for a large part of our trip in Nepal, it doesn't stop me being frightened. What I wish for is what it could be worth in terms of that lovely feeling as we turn our backs on Base Camp for the last time and walk back to safety. I want men to do these things and I want one of those men to be me, second-hand isn't any good and I just hope all is well because I really think we deserve it.

The expedition no longer seemed quite so big and un-manageable, for we were walking into Sola Khumbu in two separate parties. All twenty-three of us would have been too many to pack into one of our mess tents at a single sitting and we should even have had trouble in finding enough space at the camp sites on the way to pitch everyone's tent. Mike Cheney was going to look after our first party, which con-sisted of Nick Estcourt, Dougal Haston, Allen Fyffe, Dave Clarke, Ronnie Richards, Charlie Clarke and myself. The complete BBC team had wanted to travel together with us, so that they could get used to each other as a team within our team, but, unfortunately, Ned Kelly, the co-producer had fallen sick in Kathmandu and as a result had to wait for the second party. We therefore had with us Chris Ralling, the producer, Ian Stuart the cameraman, Arthur Chesterman the sound man, and Mick Burke, who was fulfilling his two roles as a full team member and BBC high-altitude cameraman. We also had with our first party Keith Richardson, the *Sunday Times* reporter, and our liaison officer, Lieutenant Gurung. We could just fit round our camp tables in the mess tent each night and, because of this, could start to become a cohesive group.

Dividing the party had worried me, however. The second group had been due to leave a day behind us but on the evening of our first day out I learned over the Racal HF radio we carried with us, that they were going to be delayed at least another day.

That night I commented in the tape-diary I kept throughout the expedition:

The news that they haven't set out is a bit disturbing because I definitely don't want the groups too separated. It's always a problem separating at all, because all kinds of implications are read into how

I divide the groups and, of course, I haven't taken the names of the members of the groups out of a hat. I have tried to break up really close pairings; for instance, Pete Boardman and Allen Fyffe know each other very well, and it seems a good idea to break them up, so that they have a chance to get to know other members of the team. I suppose also there's a feeling of the possibility of a strong, small clique developing, which might have ideas of its own that could conflict with mine; it's not a bad idea to try to avoid this as well. I think this is most unlikely to occur, though. But, there is no doubt about it that a second group, especially if it's two or three days behind us, is going to feel slightly more uncertain of itself, just because it is so far behind; and therefore it could become more defensive in its discussions and thinking, when it eventually joins us. The other real danger, if it's about three days behind us, is that they could find it difficult to catch up with us on the Ice Fall because I certainly am not going to delay for the second group. I'm going to push through as fast as I possibly can.

Chris Ralling, who travelled for a time with each group, was able to observe their different character objectively, writing in his diary:

It's interesting, what a different character Group·B has to Group A. I've dropped back to Group B now, so that I can do the sound with Ian because Ned is still two or three days behind us until he gets better. In Group A Chris Bonington more or less sets the tone and they are all rather keen to get on with the climbing; in the evening they play cards like mad; you can see chess, pontoon and poker all going on at the same table. Group B are much more relaxed; they stop at every chang house they can find for hours at a time and when the evening comes no one wants to play cards at all, they just want to go out and find yet another chang house. They are a more amusing group but I think Chris will be well advised to mix the two up quite soon. Probably it'll happen automatically when we get to Base Camp.

To Pete Boardman everything about the walk in was a fresh experience, as he recorded in his diary:

Not at all like the monsoon I imagined. A clear sunny hot day, umbrellas up to keep us in the shade. Much tea drunk, much sweated out and a little shed as fairly undiluted urine. . . . A day of fireflies, lizards, leeches, swallows, kestrels, vultures, kingfishers, crickets, grasshoppers and other noisy insects, of water-buffalo, goats and carefully nurtured cows, of chortens passed on the left-hand side, of gompas, prayerflags, chang and rakshi. We round a corner and there is the British Raj in all its glory neatly lined up erected tents, crowds kept at a distance and we sit down at tables in the mess tent and are brought steaming kettles full of tea. For a mountaineer surely a Bonington Everest Expedition is one of the last great imperial experiences that life can offer.

8.00 p.m. and an early night. One of the great things about this trip is the relaxed atmosphere it had lent to it by it being such a gathering of hard and experienced travellers. The Hindu Kush trip [Pete's only other Himalayan expedition, made whilst an under-graduate at Nottingham University] was such a trip in the dark and we never met anyone who had been there before or could make it any easier for us. But being on an Everest Expedition you meet more people. Mike Thompson, Ned Kelly, Hamish MacInnes, Adrian Gordon, Doug Scott; they've been all over the world and tell good travellers' tales about their experiences. This evening we ate chicken and heard all about lions, tigers, elephants and spiders; of Africa, South America and the Himalayas; all of vital fascination. I am the cub in the wolf pack and sit in the background on the edge of the light, listening to the stories as they are related; but also I am the camera with its shutter open, quite passive, recording, not thinking. The time for evaluation comes later I suppose. Tut and I share a joke, 'I'm not here to criticize, I'm here to learn.'

Yet at the back of my mind lies a worry; I haven't climbed with any of them and as they all seem to know each other and each other's relative abilities, I sometimes feel I have yet to prove myself so that I can talk with ease and confidence like I do to somebody I have climbed with over a longer period.

11.45 p.m. The dreams before the seriousness of Everest; so distant and yet such an undercurrent. Tut and Doug confessed with gallows humour, 'I keep getting stranded above the Rock Band' and 'Dougal got severe frostbite last night' . . .

8th August. I slowly gain confidence within the group, but am daunted into a fawning chameleon by the background experience and anecdotal powers of the others.

9th August. After eating a bizarre meal of chicken, potato and spaghetti to the dramatic background of Beethoven's Fifth we discuss penal reform and then the new dance, doing the Hillary Step to the music of the Rock Band; Bonehead on trumpet, Mick Burke on skive, Hamish on fiddle.

Expeditions are good spacers – time and distance for weighing and evaluating life back home as well as beginning to understand somewhere new.

Everyone read a great deal, paperbacks being passed around the team. Reading tastes varied from light thrillers, through the classics to historical works. I titillated myself with *Couples* by John Updike and then studied the *Origins of the Second World War*, with A. J. P. Taylor. Conversation was also varied, rarely sexual or bawdy, very often political and inevitably quite a bit about climbing in general, but comparatively rarely about the climb we were about to tackle. Our own group had a broad spectrum of political opinion, from Keith Richardson, the *Sunday Times* correspondent, who was prospective conservative candidate for Hemel Hempstead, to Mick Burke who was a strong socialist.

The routine of a Himalayan approach march is always much the same. This one was particularly relaxing because of the superb organization master-minded by Mike Cheney. Once again he had delegated all the authority to the Sherpas who were looking after us, in our case to Pertemba, our Sirdar, who supervised the porters, loads and setting up of the camp each night, and to Purna our cook, who fed us better than I have ever before experienced on a Himalayan expedition. Purna was a great character; he was Mike Cheney's personal cook and protégé and had been with him for several years, ever since Mike had been working on a tea plantation near Darjeeling. One night he had been driving into the town and a group of youngsters had hitched a lift. He had been impressed by the appearance and brightness of one of them and had offered him a job as cookboy. Purna had accepted and has been with Mike ever since. He can neither read nor write and has the additional disadvantage of being only half Sherpa. His mother was Tamang. In spite of this, through his powerful personality he has captured the respect of the Sherpas and on the expedition was a natural leader who automatically became the major-domo of every ceremony.

Thanks to Pertemba and Purna, we climbers had nothing to do but pack our rucksacks each morning and walk on to the next stopping point. The day started at about 6.00 a.m. and with a cheerful 'Chiya, Sahib', from Changpa, our cookboy, and a plastic mug full of tea would be thrust through the entrance of the tent. By the time one had wakened fully and downed the tea, a little group of Sherpas and porters would be standing round, ready to take one's load and collapse the tent. It was necessary only to pack a porter load and a day sack and amble over to the mess tent, which on a fine morning would already have been taken down, to have breakfast of porridge, cereal, sausages, fried potatoes and egg, washed down with more tea. By the time breakfast was over our overnight home would have vanished, the porters would be on their way and it just remained for us to pick up a rucksack and stroll along in their wake, overtaking them through the day for they were carrying anything up to seventy pounds, whilst none of us carried much more than twenty.

Pete Boardman couldn't help being worried by the contrast, commenting:

I sense a tinge of guilt about this expedition. Nobody ever thinks that it is right that a foreign power subjugates another; and so it is that I feel guilty about being waited on by the Sherpas and having all the appendages and contrivances of the Western world carried on the backs of a string of Tamang porters; sunglasses and 'Vaponas' for keeping out insects, changes of socks, tables and foam mattresses . . .

The porters have a smell like the Afghans, that drifts to my nose as I tumble up the trail amongst them – a mixture of sweat and woodsmoke. I expect Europeans have a smell too; apparently the Chinese think we smell like corpses.

The only ones amongst us who had to work hard were the BBC team, for Chris Ralling wanted to film the approach. He is a big man of forty-six, over six feet in height, who has made a series of very successful dramatized television documentaries of the discovery of the Nile and, just before our expedition, on slavery. I had immediately taken to him when I first met him in London some months before. He had a combination of a strong personality and considerable sensitivity; the quiet self-confidence that fulfilled creative ability can give. His role in making a documentary of our expedition and at the same time becoming an integral part of the team, which was necessary if their venture was to succeed, was not easy and it is a tribute to the personalities of both Chris

Chris Bonington

Jim Duff

Allen Fyffe

Mingma

Nick Estcourt

Dave Clarke

Hamish MacInnes

Mike Rhodes

Phurkipa

Ang Phurba

Pete Boardman

Ang Phu

Ronnie Richards

Dougal Haston

Mike Cheney

Pertemba

Doug Scott

Mike Thompson

4

1. The South West Face through monsoon cloud, from Kala Pattar.

2. The twenty-four tons of gear and food were unloaded in Mike Cheney's garden in Kathmandu before being flown into Luglha.

3. The camp site at Yarsa.

4. Looking up the Imja Khola from Tengpoche at the South Face of Nuptse, Lhotse on the right, and the top of the South West Face of Everest behind.

5. 180° wide-angle lens view of the Khumbu Glacier, with the Everest massif in the background, from Kala Pattar.

6. Ceremony to consecrate the Sherpa altar at Base Camp.

Ralling and Ned Kelly that they were indeed so successful. I also found in Chris a useful confidant with whom I could talk over some of my problems, with the certainty that the confidence would be respected. I could talk to him in a way that I could never have talked with the members of the expedition, even though some of them were among my oldest friends, because they were too closely involved.

On the approach Chris Ralling tried to set up one or two filmed sequences each day. He was very aware of the dangers of irritating the team members so that once we got on the mountain he might lose some of their co-operation. But, at the same time, making any kind of film takes a lot of work and inevitably sequences have to be set up and repeated. Even with the comparatively little filming that he did on the approach there was some grumbling within the team. It also meant that he and his film crew had to rush ahead each morning, set themselves up with their cameras and sound recording gear, film us as we passed and then, if they wanted another sequence, overtake us and set up yet again. And we just wandered from tea house to tea house, very rarely in a group, sometimes two or three climbers together, but as often, each climber on his own, travelling at his own pace, wrapped in his own thoughts. Jim Duff, our doctor with the second party, caught the mood in his diary:

9th August. Clear dawn. Up at 5.15 and way up the trail – not going so well up 3500 feet of ascent – at least it was shady. Walking along behind Doug and Pete listening to their conversation. Thread of thought much less choppy in this one foot after the other routine of sweat tired calves and broken breathing. Spent a quarter of an hour drinking tea at the top of the Pass. Small boy with thrush. Then on up to a non-view; cloud gathered as we arrived. Large collection of mani walls – two tea shops; chang, tea and talk. Tenzing off laughing into the mist to fetch cheese from the Jira cheese factory. Easily downhill to camp to pass a deserted gompa. The Lama died last year. Two beautiful stupas and more chang next door. Caught up with Doug bargaining for a musical instrument with four strings and a horse's head.

So into camp by mid-day. Very hot – and after breakfast and camp erection spent three hours playing with ulcers and abscesses.

C

Washing games to start with! What's the point of treating abscesses if you don't dress them every day. Sherpa with a sprained knee, elastic bandage. Porter with a sprained ankle.

A chicken being chopped. An American comes in from the wet and talks about Carolina and medicine.

Chicken and chips followed by apple and Nestlé's milk. So to bed after a windy shit. Spent a lot of time in unstructured thought, roaming the byways of past and present. A bad habit and waste of time.

> Walking up and down
> Through sun-drenched valleys
> Unfolding
> Small houses
> Smaller people
> Green
> Vibrant green
>
> Trees and rice
> Shot through by sun
> Rain green.
>
> A porter
> Bent below his load
> Box or cooking pot
> Snow shoes
> Medicine
> Bare feet
> Tense muscles
> A stop, a whistling sigh,
> Drink of water
> Cigarette of course
>
> Fourteen or forty
> In ragged shorts
> When all the world is on your back
> Smoke on.

But Jim was also aware of the stratification of our small society, where the pecking order was unstated but very important. A little diagram immediately after the lines quoted above shows this awareness.

There are three distinct groups:

There are three distinctive groups:

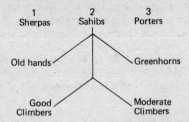

I spent much of my time on the walk balancing out these groups in my mind. Before leaving Britain, I had planned out the expedition in terms of numbers and logistics, was armed with a batch of graphs and diagrams arrived at by a series of formulae taking into account the likelihood of bad weather, the number of days' rest I expected climbers or Sherpas would need, the kind of loads they could carry at different heights and the need, based on hard experience, for a contingency margin against the unexpected. These were the foundation but they were meaningless unless I could fit them to the people with me. Now, with part of the team around me, in the reality of the Nepalese foothills, much of my waking thoughts were directed to this problem, fitting real people, each with his own personality into an overall plan. I had to take into account how different individuals got on together, what kind of role on the expedition they expected, the balance of each particular team.

In 1972 I had gone through the same thought process and resolved on giving everyone a clear role in advance all the way to the summit bid. Climbing Everest using siege tactics is like a ponderous game of leap-frog, each group out in front, usually a foursome, making the route from one camp to the next and then retiring for a rest, thus enabling the lead climbers to remain sufficiently fresh to contend with the challenge of the final two thousand feet of the mountain and at the same time to maintain the momentum of the ascent. I had had three teams, each of two climbers and two Sherpas. I had given Nick Estcourt and Dave Bathgate the invidious job of making the route from Camp 5 to Camp 6, Doug Scott and Mick Burke the task of climbing the Rock Band and putting in the first summit bid, Dougal Haston and Hamish MacInnes, that of making the second summit bid. The advantage of this approach was that once everyone had accepted their role, they automatically made the best of it and since everyone knew their position, in theory there would be much less stress and manoeuvring for a favourable position to have a chance of making a summit bid. In practice, however, it did not work out so well, since it presupposed that everything would go to plan, a most unlikely eventuality on a mountain the size of Everest. Having given team members a role expectancy they inevitably become very possessive about it, and one of the few serious rows we had in 1972 was when I was forced to give Hamish MacInnes and Dougal Haston the role I had promised Doug Scott and Mick Burke. The same problem had arisen on Annapurna in 1970.

This time, therefore, I resolved to avoid committing myself to giving individuals a specific role within a climbing team any earlier than absolutely necessary. But because of the leap-frog principle, the initial grouping of team members could determine their position on the mountain in the final vital stages, thus affecting the logical choice of the summit pair. I consequently spent many hours, as I walked up and down the winding paths of the foothills, fitting together the different combinations of lead climbers and also trying to formulate my own response to the challenge of leadership of this tremendously talented, strong-willed group of mountaineers. My thinking changed and developed with the days. This time, however, I managed to keep most of my thoughts to myself. In the past I have often made life difficult both for myself and my team by thinking out aloud, plunging into speech when thoughts have only been part formed. This has inevitably led to what has seemed like changes of mind, upsetting everyone concerned.

One obviously wanted to have at least one experienced person with each of the three lead teams to make quite sure there were no stupid mistakes about siting camps, or other delays. One also wanted to have each group fairly equal in ability. And there were bound to be some groups who would be used in a support role in the later stages of the climb, but who wouldn't be involved in a summit push. But nothing was certain. Everything depended on the weather and it would be a matter of seeing that whichever group was in a position to make a summit bid had a pair fully capable of doing it.

In the end I decided to delay making a decision on the composition of the three lead teams until our two groups had been reunited and we had climbed the Ice Fall. I also wanted a chance to sound out the old hands – Nick Estcourt, Dougal Haston, Mick Burke and Hamish MacInnes – in a way that didn't commit me, so that I could get their feelings on how they would like to be split up. On 5 August I commented:

Nobody ever really feels like having a formal discussion and certainly nobody offered any criticism, constructive, or otherwise, at the one formal meeting we have had so far. In the evenings people much prefer to play liar dice, read a book, joke or what have you. I think this is a lot healthier; the fewer meetings I can get away with the better. Obviously we need a few but I prefer to keep them to a minimum, getting the feel of what's going on, and getting my own ideas across by just informal chatting.

Had a bit of this yesterday with Dave Clark. I walked quite a long way with him and we were able to discuss informally how we were going to sort out all the gear and its distribution to the Sherpas once we reach Khumde.

I don't think there's any danger of us ever having leadership by committee. Of course, though, if there is a strong consensus against what I say, this is going to emerge in a troublesome sense later on and I think this is where I've got to be very receptive to the feelings of the team so that I can effectively sell them my ideas and make them feel and believe that these are ideas they have taken part in forming. At the same time I must draw ideas from their combined experience and not be afraid to change my own plans if other suggestions seem better. I don't think the old military style of leadership can possibly work.

I also talked round their potential roles on the climb to Dougal Haston, Nick Estcourt and Mick Burke, on the way to Khumde. After our arrival I recorded their reaction in my tape-diary:

Their various attitudes are quite interesting. Dougal's approach is undoubtedly that of a prima donna; he reckons that he wants to get to the top, that he deserves the top and that he's certainly the best person to go there. I'm inclined to agree with him. At the same time, though, one must be very aware that forcing the Rock Band, pushing the route out above it, might be just as exacting and every bit as vital. I don't think Dougal, if I ever put him in a position where he was forcing above the Rock Band, would agree to drop back and let someone else go for the top.

Anyway, we talked round his role and the one that I had seen for him was one that he's happy to fit in with, establishing Camp 4 and pushing the route out towards Camp 5, as a member of my third lead climbing party, with Hamish MacInnes and two of the others whom I have still not decided upon.

We swapped round some names. Dougal did raise the point – wouldn't it be ideal if he and Doug Scott were paired up. I countered this though, with the fact that I couldn't possibly put the strongest pair together right at the beginning, both from a morale point of view and also because I wanted to even out the abilities of each of my lead-climbing teams. At this stage I think it unlikely that Doug and Dougall will end up climbing together; I think I'd rather use them in successive summit bids, to ensure that a second attempt is as strong as the first.

I also talked to Nick Estcourt. He's a bit uncertain of himself in many ways, can be obsessive over small things, but in many ways, the big important ones, is very unselfish. Nick just said, 'I leave it entirely to you, Chris; you know I'll do anything you ask me to do.' It's great having this kind of support but I can't help worrying that perhaps I end up taking advantage of him, using him for a key role on the way up the climb that I know requires a highly developed sense of social responsibility.

I talked to Mick Burke as well. Last expedition he was much more tense because he hadn't got his own role in life clear. This time he's more relaxed, largely I suspect because he has a secure career with the B B C and even more important his role in the expedition is secure in that whatever happens he's the star of the B B C team; he's got everything to gain and very little to lose. Mick said, 'Just play it along as you see best; I'll fit in with whatever you want.' He then grinned and said, 'You've got one hell of a job; I don't envy you one little bit.'

I still had to talk with Hamish MacInnes and Doug Scott, but my plans were now becoming more formalized. For me the latter stages of the approach march to Khumde were a nightmare. I had begun to suffer from some kind of bug and plodded from one camp site to the next racked with fever and dysentery. I went for three days without being able to hold down any food, and began to worry that this might seriously affect my endurance on the mountain itself.

I wasn't the only one who was sick. In the second party Ned Kelly was desperately weak from something he had contracted in Kathmandu and had to be carried by horse for much of the way. Hamish was also slow to recover from the infection he had picked up in Kathmandu. Most worrying of all, however, was the health of Mike Cheney. He had been in hospital only a few weeks before our arrival as a result of an allergy to penicillin. He had looked very frail when we met him in Kathmandu, but was determined to set out with us. Each day he started several hours before us, but was always the last in to camp, often getting in after dark. He never complained even though it was obvious that he was in considerable pain for much of the time. Charlie Clarke commented in his diary on 6 August:

Mike is toiling along, looking very very grey and ill, with severe girdle pains at mid-abdomen. Very worrying – what he is describing is hideously like spinal cord compression but there is no cough or strain pain. I haven't examined him because he hasn't really asked for advice – I think he is really best left his own way at present. Even if this is his last trip, is there a better way to go?

I sometimes wonder if perhaps I missed some of the fresh beauty of the approach march through my preoccupation with the climb ahead. To the members of the team who were making it for the first time, and who had no such responsibility, it undoubtedly had a special impact which is captured in the pages of Charlie's diary.

Kharikhola – 11th August, 1975: At last we have reached Dudh Kosi; how the scale of the country has changed from the little Beatrix Potter valleys and re-entrants to the vast sweeps of the ridges of Dudh Kosi. No wonder there is the highest mountain in the world at the top of it.

Kharikhola is a horrid little place with people and relics of tea shops. 'You can buy bread and biscuits here', says one sign. But it's still remarkable to me that this main route through Nepal to Khumbu is still so unspoilt.

I wonder what the life-cycle of a leech is?

I still worry about the dangers of the Ice Fall. Enormous avalanches sweeping down off Nuptse; tottering ice towers just waiting for me personally; or the horror of being off-route in mist and hearing the groaning of avalanches and séracs. I have other fantasies about going to the top, but these will shortly be dashed when I find how unpleasant it is.

The bridge below Namche – 13th August, 1975: There is something very special about this valley which still entrances me, entrances us travellers as though we were the first to come here. The majestic scale is impossible to capture on film and it is only by having to walk up the Dudh Kosi that one realizes how enormous it all is. Each little side valley is as large as most main Himalayan valleys and each ridge or re-entrant takes an age to cross.

A delightful chang session with potatoes at lunchtime, marred only by the recurring political arguments about the state of the nation – I do wish I had something original to say about it all, but it does bore me.

Here in camp I watched, I made certain I saw, the slaughter of our dinner – a large, black goat. I've never seen an execution before and one is certainly enough. The squealing creature was dragged over a tree trunk and then with a single blow of a kukri, the head was severed and leapt forward on the rope around the neck, followed by two jets of blood. I was very nearly sick and thought how tenuously the whole of our invidiual lives is held together. I think about death a lot – not my own particularly – but the practical aspects of what we'll have to do. It's rather like being at war, this expedition, with the Sherpas as our mercenaries. I think many of us are scared, but no one will bring himself to discuss it – Chris just turned off it a few days ago. It's so odd how Ian Clough and Tony Tighe* are talked about as though they're still around, and morbidly fascinating to hear Nick discussing Dougal's floppy hat as the one Tony used to wear. I like Dougal very much, in a quiet sort of way. I wonder what he thinks about all the time. Mick has curious effect. Talkative, funny, aggressive. I think he is very anxious about everything and this is his reaction to it. I've never really seen him in this setting before and at home he is very much quieter.

So, to Khumde tomorrow and the action really starts. I realize how important it is to have a reasonably long approach on an

*Ian Clough was killed in an ice avalanche on the Annapurna South Face Expedition. Tony Tighe was killed in similar circumstances at the end of the 1972 expedition.

expedition of this size. Everyone seemed fairly unfit and enough of us were newcomers to need a substantial settling-in period.

I do wonder how enjoyable this expedition will be and, unlike others, I don't think I must look for too much individual pleasure. It will be a collective thing – probably, as Mick said, irrelevant of the outcome, 'It doesn't seem to alter your joy at the end of an expedition whether or not you've climbed the mountain.'

We reached Khumde on 14 August, just twelve days after leaving Kathmandu. Dave Clarke and Ronnie Richards had pressed on a day ahead to start unpacking the gear and by the time we reached the village, the tents were already up and piles of boxes neatly covered by tarpaulins were scattered over the small field in which we were to camp.

Khumde and Khumjung are two Sherpa villages, 12 500 feet above sea level, lying in a shallow valley, cradled by the craggy slopes of Khumbui Yul Lha, an 18 900-foot peak that towers above the villages to their north, and the carelessly flung arm of a tree-clad bouldered ridge line that clutches the little valley on its southern side. To reach it, we walked through one of the most perfect natural rock gardens I have ever seen. The leaves of the trees were already touched by autumn and varied from a dusty green, through shades of yellow to rusty red. The ground was carpeted by an array of exquisite flowers, shrubs and mosses that nestled into the crannies of boulders, some of which were as big as houses. The mist clung to the top of the ridge and hid the high mountains around us, somehow increasing the romance and feel of excited anticipation that we all felt.

At first glance Khumde had not changed at all since 1961, when I first visited it. But then a second look showed differences. Most of the houses still have the traditional slate roofs, and are two-storeyed, with small deep-cut windows. The smoke from the open cooking fire in the corner of the single first-floor living chamber finds its way out though the windows and chinks in the roof. There are very few houses that have chimneys. One house was different; it had a bright green corrugated iron roof and big glass windows. It looked like a badly designed detached house on a modern housing estate and was completely out of character in the village of

Khumjung. It was a symbol of the growing affluence of the Sherpa people; an affluence born from the developing tourist trade and expeditions like our own. It was owned by Ang Tsering, the chairman of the village Panchayat, or council. He had been the Sirdar of our expedition to Nuptse in 1961 and had since taken part in many major expeditions.

There are other signs of change as well. At the top of the village is the hospital built by Ed Hillary; between the two villages is the school which was also opened by Hillary, though is now entirely run by the Nepalese. Hillary more than anyone has helped the Sherpas to help themselves, in starting schools and hospitals, in building bridges, in financing scholarships to secondary schools and universities in Kathmandu and India. External influences are also growing. The Japanese have built a hotel on the crest of the low ridge dividing Khumjung from Namche Bazar. Just below it at Syangboche they have carved out of the hillside an airstrip which Pilatus Porter aircraft can land on. As a result the tourists, who otherwise could never have walked from Luglha, the other airstrip, can now be carried straight in to a height of over 12 000 feet. We met some of them in the lounge of the Everest View Hotel. They belonged to a tour party from the Mid West of the United States. They were all over sixty, and two of them had needed oxygen on the walk up from the airstrip. One lady, dreadfully pale, had a bottle of oxygen beside her and was clutching a mask to her mouth. They were there for only two days and so far had only had a glimpse of Mount Everest. Not one of them had felt up to walking down to the village or through the flower-filled woods around the hotel. Apparently no one has yet died from altitude sickness at the hotel but one can't help wondering when will be the first casualty. For an elderly person to fly up to this altitude is a risky business.

A young American girl who had been there several days and who had visited Tengpoche and some of the neighbouring villages commented, 'What a pity these places have got to change. I suppose they'll have electric lights soon.'

This attitude highlights the problem of a place which wants to acquire modern amenities without losing too much of the pattern of life that both renders the place attractive to the outsider, and, much more important, represents a stable and very balanced society. Running water, sewage systems and electricity make life both easier and pleasanter, but are all too often accompanied by many of the evils of modern develop-ment. The Sherpas, however, are very adaptable and have a background that should enable them to adopt what they want of western ways. They are not a primitive people; living as they do on the watershed of the Himalayas in a region that is barely fertile enough to support them, they have always depended on trade to make a living. The Sherpa menfolk have always travelled far into Tibet and down into lowland Nepal and India on their trading ventures. They were already settled in Darjeeling in the twenties when the early Everest expeditions set out for Tibet and were therefore natural candidates for high-altitude porters. Today, more and more westerners are coming into their home country, bringing with them all the problems as well as benefits of a fast expanding tourist economy. The trails are littered with rubbish; the rate of deforestation is being increased, the Sherpas are having to import more rice and basic foods into Khumbu to help feed the visitors. At the same time, the brighter Sherpas and the families who already have wealth are making a lot of money, whilst the less adaptable are probably only slightly benefiting, thus exaggerating the extremes of wealth and poverty within the villages. It is the development of tourism and trekking rather than that of mountaineering expeditions that is pushing on these changes. Each season many thousands of trekkers throng the trails, while even a massive Everest expedition only involves thirty or so outsiders at the very most.

Very few of the menfolk in Khumde wear traditional dress. Most of them have expedition clothing, breeches, anoraks, down jackets in various stages of decrepitude. The women on the other hand still wear traditional Sherpa dress of long sleeveless tunic of plain dark material, livened by a gaily striped apron and coloured blouse. Very few wear the traditional Tibetan boots, most having plimsolls or basketball boots. The children are just as dirty, just as inquisitive and just as cheerful. It was a time of meeting with old friends, all of whom had bottles of chang, the Sherpa rice beer, to offer us. There was Ang Pema, with his round moon face, who had been cookboy on my first ever expedition to Annapurna II, who had come with me to the summit of Nuptse in 1961 and who had been cook on Annapurna South Face in 1970. There was Pasang Kami, as dapper and smart as ever, very much the modern Sherpa. He had been our Sirdar on Annapurna South Face, but now preferred the trekking game. He looked, and was, a successful businessman, with his smart guide's peaked cap and horn-rimmed spectacles. He spoke fluent English, had been to California and Europe, owned a restaurant in Namche Bazar. There was Kanchha, who had carried an incredible double load of sixty pounds on Annapurna, who had always been so willing. He was the same as ever, grinning through broken teeth. Somehow he hadn't made the grade, was hoping to carry a load for us to Base Camp, and said, without regret or jealousy, 'I'm just a poor Sherpa. I have no yaks, only a little land.'

It was good to see so many old friends. We did no work that night, and went to bed befuddled with chang and talk.

5   From Khumde to Base Camp

(17 August–25 August)

The gentle limbo of the approach was over; there were boxes and piles of gear everywhere, piled high round the field, cramming our big Camp 2 box tents and lying stacked beneath tarpaulins. Dave, millboard under his arm, had a permanent worried frown as he juggled sleeping bags, boots, pen-knives, down suits and the thirty or so other items of personal issue amongst the eighty Sherpas and twenty-five Europeans. Everyone, suddenly avaricious, was looking across at other people's kit.

We had been at work for two days when the second party arrived. We had become used to each other and had felt a small, compact team that was easily managed. Dave had taken complete charge and we all, including myself, did what he asked in making up the individual issues. But then the second party, happily drunk from a series of reunions in Namche Bazar, had straggled in and suddenly I realized just how large a party we were. We could not even all fit into a single mess tent, but needed two. The camp became a teeming village; effective communication was difficult. You needed a meeting to ensure that everyone knew what was going on. I think everyone was slightly appalled by our unwieldy size and it was emphasized by the way each group tended to maintain its own identity, sitting for the most part in different mess tents, accustomed to relaxing in different ways. Each night the gambling school played poker, whilst the second party talked or wandered off to find more chang.

In spite of the frantic rush and the almost inevitable short falls on a few items of kit, we had achieved a lot in those few days. Traditionally, an expedition makes a leisured progress to Base Camp, pausing for the odd week to acclimatize to the altitude and organize itself. I have never believed in this approach, preferring to instil a sense of urgency in the party from the very beginning. In 1975 this was accentuated by the settled nature of the weather. Although it rained each afternoon, the mornings were clear and still – ideal weather for getting started on the Everest Ice Fall. I resolved, therefore, to send Nick Estcourt and Dougal Haston ahead on 17 August to find a site for Base Camp and make a reconnaissance of the Ice Fall. The first party would then set out on the 18th to move straight on up to Base Camp, with the second party following on the 19th. Although I proposed to set up an acclimatization camp at Gorak Shep, a short day's walk from Base Camp, I only wanted to use it for the team members who felt in need of a few extra days' acclimatization. In this way I hoped to get Base Camp established as soon as possible. I also had the chance of talking to Hamish and Doug Scott about their roles on the expedition. In my diary I described the conversation:

Had a long talk with Hamish where I laid out my ideas and plans, and discussed the composition of the lead teams on the Face. I definitely want Hamish to set up the boxes at Camp 4. I think that is one of the most important moves on the expedition, for unless this camp is secure, we won't be able to keep up the flow of supplies on the Face. With a bit of luck he will also be able to site Camp 5 and make sure that's all right. It's really good having his advice and support – he's so wonderfully relaxed about it all and yet, at the same time, very canny.

I also talked to Doug. Doug was very reasonable. I think he likes the idea of having a crack at the Rock Band and would even take on one of the genuinely sacrificial roles – for instance, forcing the route across the Upper Ice Fields, as close to the South Summit as possible, thus putting it on a plate for the next pair through. He just commented: 'There's no point getting uptight about it. You never know – the weather might close in and anything could happen to change the role you think you're going to get.' I think he really means it and that means that he will be relaxed. I must say, he is one of the biggest, most unselfish people I have got amongst the lead climbers.

I still couldn't help worrying about the size of the team. Being big meant we had the reserves we might need, but there were going to be a lot of people sitting around at times, and there's nothing like idleness for making people discontented. This was something I realized I was going to have to watch.

Although the team was so big, at Khumde there was certainly no shortage of work for everyone. Hamish was checking the oxygen cylinders and producing a new invention daily, developing a special rucksack for the lead climbers to use with their oxygen, modifying the platforms, helping team members fit their oxygen masks. Mike Thompson was sorting out the distribution of ration boxes, Adrian Gordon was helping Mike Cheney, and the BBC team were filming, while at the same time trying to get some climbing gear for themselves.

It was a relief to set out for the final stage of our walk to Base Camp, to break away from the big expedition and to form, once again, into two compact parties. Charlie Clarke and I set off together, picking our way along the narrow footpaths that wind through the little drystone-walled fields of the villages of Khumjung and Khumde. It was easy to identify our Sherpas, for most of them were wearing red T-shirts stamped with the legend 'British Everest Expedition'. They were also getting ready to leave home. Charlie described a ceremony we witnessed on our way through Khumjung:

We saw a touching, solemn scene of a Sherpa parting with his family; the sacrificial fire of juniper, his wife and three children standing round – the silent prayer that he would return to them. A soldier leaving for the wars, pointless wars, wars he is fighting for someone else. How happy I shall be if we return safe with as many as we left Khumde.

As we wandered down past the last mani wall below the village, along the narrow path skirting the precipitous slopes above the Dudh Kosi, past a deserted village, terraced fields lying barren and untended, past stunted pine trees and big succulent blue-black cones which oozed resin. A Lammergeier cruised above on great outstretched wings; cumulonimbus clouds towered above Amai Dablang, engulfing its shapely spire, ready for the afternoon storm.

It was easy to forget the size of the expedition, even the ever-present problem of logistics, people, their vulnerable

egos, dreams and expectations. Charlie and I crossed the
Dudh Kosi, feet thudding on the worn boards of a cantilever
bridge, jostling with a small herd of yaks which were being
driven unladen to Pheriche, ready to act as beasts of burden.
The Area Panchayat, or council, had decreed that we could
not use yaks before Pheriche for fear that they might damage
the crop of grass that lay, ready to mow, on every available
flat space in the villages and surrounding fields.

We paused for chang at the little tea house at the foot of the
long hill that led up to Tengpoche and then shouldered
rucksacks and wafted in an alcoholic haze to the monastery.
That night we stopped at Makyong, the other side of the hill
just below the Tengpoche monastery. Our porters, most of
them women ranging in age from thirteen to seventy, were
camped in the open in the woods around us, huddled through
the night round little camp fires, wrapped in a few dirty old
blankets. They seemed to regard their work almost as a
holiday, flirting with the lads, talking and singing far into the
night. The lucky ones shared a tent with our high-altitude
porters.

The following morning, in the dawn, we walked back up,
under the dripping rhododendron trees, to the monastery to
receive the blessing of the Head Lama and to present him
with the expedition's offering towards the upkeep of the
monastery. We were ushered into his reception room where he
was sitting, clad in saffron robe, quiet and impassive. The
Sherpas made three ritual bows, each time touching the floor
with their foreheads in a gymnastic, flowing movement which
had a strange grace, before bowing their heads to receive the
Lama's scarf. We made our Namaste greeting and then sat
round the room, making stilted conversation with the help of
Mike Cheney as interpreter.

The Lama gave us the same advice as he had given in 1972:
'If you work together and do not argue amongst yourselves,
you have a chance of climbing the mountain.'

Outside the ceremony was repeated in the courtyard of the
monastery for the benefit of the BBC. Patiently, the Head
Lama did as he was asked, his little group of Lamas standing
to either side of him at the head of the steps leading to the

great double doors of the temple as I walked up and said my little piece. Even though the cameras were turning and the ceremony had been specially set up, I found it strangely moving. Charlie was less sure, writing that night:

A ceremonial hand-over of 2000 Rs to the High Lama (the Second Incarnation). Film, flash, majesty. The ascetic mysticism of those remote monasteries always seems a thin covering of an empty world. Can there really be all that learning, wisdom and religious thought practised by these monks who fought and giggled in the courtyard. I suppose my disbelief in God makes it very hard for me to accept. Then on to Pheriche. How fabulous is this glacial plain with swirling mists and jangling yaks. Dusty, hooded shadows collecting firewood in the fog, the yak looking out of nowhere. This is like Central Asia.

Pheriche is a summer village, where a few crops are grown and now, with the growing number of trekkers, it has also become a trekkers' stopping-place with four or five Sherpa hotels which are little more than single-storeyed shacks stocked with food bought from expeditions and offering some floor space for anyone who wants to stay the night. The most modern of these 'hotels' was owned by Nima, one of the youngest Mountain Travel Sirdars. He had been with us on the South Face of Annapurna but had then decided that the life of a high-altitude porter was altogether too risky. Now he worked as a trekking Sirdar but was also a freewheeling entrepreneur, owning a small herd of yaks and this hotel, which his wife would look after through the trekking season. He even had bottles of beer and cans of German lager.

Sitting on a rough bench in the single room of the hotel, it was interesting to see the Sherpas together. We had with us two of my former Sirdars, Pasang Kami from Annapurna and Pembatharke who had been Sirdar on Everest in 1972. Both were providing yaks and helping to organize the porters in the carry to Base Camp. There seemed to be no resentment of Pertemba, who had the job of Sirdar this time, even though he was so much younger than either of them. He was assured and dynamic; they were friendly and helpful. They were all united in a struggle with the local Panchayat which had just decreed that no yaks were to be used in the carry to Base

Camp. This was aimed at the yak owners, of whom several were expedition Sherpas, who could make a fair amount of money carrying double loads of gear on their strings of yaks. The idea behind the Panchayat decision was that the money should be spread amongst the ordinary Sherpas – at first glance a very fair principle. Pertemba argued, however, that they could not recruit sufficient local porters to carry our gear and that therefore we needed as many yaks as they could get.

The problem was further complicated by the fact that Ang Phu was, at the same time, trying to negotiate a divorce from his wife with the Panchayat, and was worried that a conflict between the expedition and local council would delay a settlement of his own personal problems. We were fortunate in having Mike Cheney with us, for he counselled us to leave the Sherpas to sort it out amongst themselves and not to become involved. That night, Pertemba raced down to Pangpoche to argue with the Panchayat and the following morning returned with the news that they had agreed to the yaks being used, provided no one supplied more than four of his own yaks. I suspect that the Sherpas paid little more than lip-service to this proviso.

And so we walked towards our mountain in three easy – almost lazy – mornings, up the flower-jewelled slopes below the snout of the Khumbu Glacier to Lobuche, on to Gorak Shep, over the tumbled boulders of the base of the Changri Nup Glacier and, on the 22nd, we walked up the Khumbu Glacier itself to the site of Base Camp.

Our Sherpas had cut out of the ice a track for the yaks. Base Camp was as bleak as ever, the rubbish of the Japanese Ladies' Expedition strewing the rocks just below the site that Nick and Dougal had chosen. There was no more grass, no flowers, not even any moss; dusty granite blocks covered the ice and an occasional grinding groan reminded us that we were on a slow-moving glacier. Wet snow gusted down as the porters trailed in, dropping their loads in careless piles. Young Sherpanis giggled and made eyes at us as we tried to photograph them. A couple of yaks stampeded, trampling over our personal boxes. We sorted out the boxes into ordered piles. Pertemba and some of the Sherpas had erected a tarpaulin shelter and were paying off a shouting crowd of Sherpas and Sherpanis. Purna was building the cook-shelter, other Sherpas and climbers were levelling spaces for their tents.

That day, Dougal Haston and Nick Estcourt were already up in the Ice Fall, making the first reconnaissance. It was 22 August, three days earlier than I had scheduled the establishment of Base Camp. We were starting on the right note in our race against the autumnal winds and cold. We had a total of three hundred loads at Base Camp and the second party were at Gorak Shep, ready to follow on. Pete Boardman was among those who arrived next day. His first impression of Base Camp was of a cold, humourless place, with the freshly scarred unwelcoming character of a working quarry.

It was Pete who recorded an early impression of Allen Fyffe and Mick Burke.

Allen shared a tent with Mick on the walk in and I think they got on very well. Allen sometimes appears a bit distant and dour partly because he is rather shy, but has a very shrewd sense of humour that glows in Mick's company here at Base Camp. I think they feel an affinity for each other both being on the small side. They share a tent next door to Keith Richardson who owns one of those tiny computerized watches on which, if you press the right button the time and date lights up in red lettering. One night Allen and Mick were in bed when Allen said, 'Well, I think I'll get some kip. I won't stay up to watch the date change on my watch tonight.' Mick said, 'I'll tell you what, if we go next door we can watch it in colour.'

In the next three days the rest of the climbing team arrived and the vast bulk of our loads was carried up to Base. No longer did we feel such an unwieldy expedition. There was too much to do, and barely enough people to undertake all the tasks in hand. Each day a group went up into the Ice Fall to push the route out towards its top. Back at Base Camp, there were crampons to fit to boots, all the face boxes to be erected then dismantled and made up into manageable loads, the Sherpas' issue to complete of karabiners and lengths of nylon tape for clipping into the fixed ropes on the way up. There were boots which didn't fit and had to be exchanged.

Dave Clarke worked for twelve hours a day, a perpetual worried frown on his face. Members of the climbing team were doing a morning's work in the Ice Fall and then coming back to Base Camp to spend the rest of the day helping with the hundred different administrative chores. Each day caravans of yaks and Sherpanis carried loads up from Gorak Shep.

The morning of the 24th dawned warm and cloudy. Dougal Haston and Nick Estcourt had intended to go into the Ice Fall, but decided against it. This was one of the hazards of tackling the mountain during the monsoon. It snowed most afternoons but usually cleared during the night, with a hard frost that helped to consolidate the snow. We always set out in the early hours of the morning before dawn, in order to get back down from the Ice Fall before midday, when the fierce heat of the sun softened the snow and brought down huge avalanches. On the occasions that it did not freeze during the night, we had to stay put in our camp the following day and wait for the next night that it did freeze.

We resigned ourselves to a day of administrative chores. I had settled down in one of the big box tents with Dougal, Hamish and Ronnie Richards to alter the Sherpas' crampons. We had ordered a size too big for most of them and to get them to fit their boots we had to shorten the arm linking the heel piece to the main set of spikes. Hamish was the expert at this rough engineering, whilst the rest of us riveted on the straps and altered the screw-on sections. It was about ten thirty when Pertemba came into the tent and told me that I was wanted for a ceremony to consecrate the Base Camp altar. This was the first time any of us had heard about it. Slightly mystified, I followed him out to find all the Sherpas assembled round a pile of stones which had been built up into a simple altar. Purna was the self-appointed master of ceremonies and thrust into my hand a tray on which was balanced a bottle of local rum and around which was heaped rice and tsampa smeared with margarine. A ceremonial scarf was placed around my neck and another around the bottle of rum. Phurkipa was chanting a prayer from a tattered book of Tibetan script whilst the rest of the Sherpas were shouting and laughing. The entire ceremony was typical of the Sherpa temperament, light-hearted yet very serious, all at the same time. The Sherpas were throwing handfuls of rice and tsampa over Pertemba, myself and each other; laughter and muttered prayers mingled, whilst I clutched my top-heavy tray, fearful that the bottle of rum might topple over. I imagined that this would have been a terrible omen.

A fire of juniper shrubs had been lit on the altar and its aromatic smoke swirled into a grey sky dusted with snowflakes. Other members of the team had gathered around to watch the spectacle, but were yelled at to get to one side. No one was allowed to come between the altar and Sagarmatha, (the Nepalese name for Everest) to whose guardian gods the offering was being made.

A flag pole, decked with prayerflags, the expedition flag and that of the BBC Television show 'Blue Peter' was pushed and heaved into position on the altar; Pertemba then placed his offering onto the altar and I followed suit, making, at Pertemba's bidding, a Namaste, bowing with hands held in prayer to the altar and Sagarmatha. Phurkipa's chant rose to a climax and the rest of the Sherpas shouted, laughed and yelled, hurling fusillades of tsampa over everyone. I felt tears in my eyes as I walked over to the others and secretly prayed that our Sherpas would be protected through the expedition.

Every morning before setting out into the Ice Fall, the juniper fire was lit and each Sherpa made an offering of a little tsampa or rice on the altar. On the way through the Ice Fall many of them muttered prayers, particularly in the danger areas threatened by avalanches. The ceremony over, we had to come to terms with an increasingly worrying problem.

The previous evening it had been reported that one of the porters who had set out that day from Gorak Shep had failed to return. He was a young deaf and dumb lad called Mingma, whom Doug Scott had befriended. At that stage none of the Sherpas was worried, thinking that perhaps he'd missed the path on his way back and had spent the night out. The following morning, however, he still hadn't turned up and it was obvious that something could perhaps be wrong; being deaf and dumb, if he had only strayed a little distance from

the path and had sprained an ankle, he would have had no
means of calling attention to himself. Perhaps because he was
particularly vulnerable this young lad had a rather special
relationship with the expedition. I had noticed him at Khumde,
bare-chested under an old, torn, plastic motorcycle jacket, his
intelligent face often wearing an anxious grin. As long as he
was with us we were responsible for his safety, but being
intelligent, and yet unable to make himself understood, he
was rather unpredictable. The Sherpas seemed to feel the
same and were quite happy to let him go his own way.

Doug Scott, however, felt more involved, for he had first
befriended the boy in 1972 when he and Don Whillans and
Hamish MacInnes had stayed with Mingma's family in
Pheriche. Now he saw quite a bit of the lad on the walk in,
on one occasion even helping him with his load. At Gorak
Shep Doug and Tut Braithwaite had climbed to Kala Pattar,
an 18000-foot shoulder of Pumo Ri which gives wonderful
views of the Khumbu Glacier and the Everest massif, and
they had taken Mingma along to help carry some of the heavy
camera equipment, which had meant extra money for the boy.

By the time Doug and Tut got back down from Kala
Pattar, most of the porters had already left for Base Camp.
Doug asked Ang Phu if he could find a load for Mingma so
that he also could earn a day's wage for the carry. Ang Phu
agreed and Mingma set off just behind some yaks that were
being driven across the glacier. There was a constant coming
and going of the yaks and Sherpanis along the trail across the
glacier. This was the last time he was seen alive.

Gazing over the rocky wilderness of the Khumbu Glacier, I
was appalled by the extent of the area we should have to
cover in our search. I divided the team into six parties of
climbers and Sherpas, each equipped with a walkie-talkie.
The occasional figure that came into view, a tiny dot in the
vast expanse, only emphasized the magnitude of our task.
Dougal Haston wandered over the lower limits of the Ice Fall,
Tut Braithwaite was among the ice fins and ridges just below
it. Charlie Clarke scoured the rocky debris below Base Camp.
Doug, because he was the last person to employ the boy, had
an unwarranted sense of guilt, records what happened next:

We took a section each and fanned out down the valley, all in radio contact with Base Camp. I felt very much alone with my three Sherpas and grieved that the lad, unable to shout might be trapped under moraine debris or a fallen sérac. I scrambled along like a madman until Adrian [Gordon] reported sighting clothing and then a body in a stream.

I went down to him, lifted Mingma out of the icy stream and put him on his side. His face was just like it had been around the camp, set firm, withdrawn into his silent world. I sobbed uncontrollably for him.

Chris appeared, having run the two miles down from Base and put his arms around me and wept. He spoke of Conrad, his first child, who had been drowned whilst playing by himself on the banks of a stream in Scotland. He was able to put the situation in another light, one of accident and not of fault – and yet how can I absolve myself? I don't think I ever can. Adrian also showed compassion, pointing out that I had brightened up his life for this short spell and how bleak would have been his prospects for the future. On our return to camp, the ever-pragmatic Mick Burke pointed out that the Sherpas were not unduly troubled because they could shrug it off with a thought that his time had come and he had gone to a better life. I hope I can finally accept it as they did.

Next day we pressed on. Yet I could not help asking myself, once again, whether these climbs were worth the loss of life that so often accompanied them. I have no answer. People die climbing in Britain too, and few outdoor sports are entirely without some element of risk. But a climber can assess the risks, and can accept or reject them. Mingma was not a climber, and can have had no thought of danger. His death was an accident which might have happened at any time, but he was carrying for us, and we are responsible.

And yet everything went on; the drive to climb the mountain was as great as it ever had been and on this expedition there would be good moments, happy moments, wonderful moments and perhaps there would be some very sad moments as well. We could only pray that there would be no more accidents.

6 The Ice Fall

(22 August–27 August)

The Ice Fall, gateway to Everest from the south, is also one of the most dangerous sections of the route. It is a frozen cataract, the solid river of ice being broken up into huge blocks which are thrust inexorably downwards by the force of the glacier slowly flowing down the Western Cwm. One can never make a route that is completely safe through the Everest Ice Fall, but merely try to avoid as many of the dangers as possible. Inevitably though there are places where the route must go under a tower or ice wall which sooner or later is going to collapse. One can only rationalize the risk; the fact that one is only in the danger area for a few minutes at the most, whilst the tower will stand for weeks, or even months before it falls. The trouble of course is that climbers and Sherpas were moving through the Ice Fall daily for however long the expedition was going to last. We had learnt to our cost in 1972, when Tony Tighe was killed on the last day of the expedition, just how random the risk could be.

We had already completed two days' work in the Ice Fall before Mingma's death. On 22 August, the day the main party reached Base Camp, Dougal Haston and Nick Estcourt succeeded in climbing halfway up and on their return reported that it seemed as safe as it ever could be. On 23 August Allen Fyffe, Ronnie Richards, Mick Burke, Arthur Chesterman and I went into the Ice Fall to consolidate the route. Dougal and Nick had left no ladders or ropes in place and our aim on 23 August was to build a road through the Ice Fall as well as to press the route beyond their high point. For this purpose eleven Sherpas, led by Phurkipa our Ice Fall Sirdar, were going with us, carrying fixed rope, bamboo markers and ladders. Phurkipa, at fifty-four, was the oldest member of the team and our most experienced Sherpa. Having probably been through the Everest Ice Fall more often than any man alive, he had become an Ice Fall specialist. In both the spring and autumn expeditions of 1972 he had taken charge of the Ice Fall Sherpas earning the title of 'Roadmender' for his efforts in repairing the route and building bridges over crevasses. He was to have the same job this time.

Setting out just after dawn, we followed the tracks made by Dougal and Nick. For half a mile the route weaved round piles of rubble and low ice ridges on the way to the foot of the Ice Fall. Some of the Sherpas had set out earlier and we overtook them where the angle began to increase; they were putting on their crampons and seemed to be having some kind of argument, with Phurkipa talking very vehemently and pointing over to the right. Quickly I gathered that he did not like the route to the Ice Fall chosen by Nick and Dougal. I could see his point. The existing route, although certainly the easiest and most direct – going straight to the foot of the Ice Fall – crossed the glacier immediately below the Lho Lha Pass into Tibet and the great Western Shoulder of Everest, both slopes being the spawning ground for huge avalanches. Phurkipa preferred to make a long dog-leg to the right to avoid this risk. I was quite happy to follow him. After all it was the Sherpas who would be going through the Ice Fall most often and it seemed only right, therefore, that the ultimate choice of approach should be left to them.

We met the tracks of the reconnaissance party at the foot of the Ice Fall itself and followed them up, placing marker flags at close intervals, anchoring in fixed rope wherever it seemed necessary and bridging the few crevasses which were not covered. After all the months of theorizing and the past three weeks' walking, it was profoundly satisfying work and by nine o'clock that morning we had reached Nick and Dougal's high point, just below 19000 feet. So far the route had been both straightforward and very safe; it ran up an ice spur on the left-hand side of the Ice Fall and was not threatened by any dangerous sérac towers.

Now we were venturing into the centre area, where the Ice Fall flattens out for a short section, just before its final climb into the Western Cwm. This is one of the most unstable sections of the Ice Fall, being prone to cataclysmic icequakes caused by the pressure of ice from above. Mick Burke and Arthur Chesterman had come along to film, and here they set up a short climbing sequence with Allen Fyffe leading out up a snow slope above the previous pair's high point. It was indicative of Mick's divided loyalties between filming and climbing that, as soon as he had completed his stint of filming, he abandoned his camera and joined Allen and myself in pushing out the route into a region of unstable ice blocks, lavishly covered in snow. The crevasses seemed deeper than they had been in 1972, and we had to advance very cautiously to find a route through them.

The sun had by now struck the glacier and within a matter of minutes it was like an inferno, its dazzling light reflected by the snow around us; the air temperature was in the seventies. Everest is a place of extremes, of violent changes from bitter cold to blazing heat, sapping one's energy and changing hard frozen snow to a soft morass in a matter of minutes.

Although having climbed only a few hundred feet beyond the previous day's high point, we were well content with our progress. Not only had we made a little new ground we had also consolidated our route, ready for the next thrust forward into the upper reaches of the Ice Fall.

The next day had brought tragedy and had been spent searching the Khumbu Glacier for Mingma, but on the 25th we returned to the Ice Fall. By the time I got up, Nick Estcourt and Pete Boardman were already high ahead, two tiny black dots dwarfed by the towers of snow-clad ice which, in their turn, were dominated by the soaring walls of Nuptse and the West Ridge of Everest. Dougal, also having set out that morning, in the dark had stepped onto an ice-covered glacier pool and fallen through into the icy water, up to his waist. He had had no choice but to return to Base Camp.

Hamish MacInnes and Mike Thompson, with twelve Sherpas carrying ladders and rope, had also gone into the Ice Fall to consolidate the route pushed forward by the leading group. Hamish, in spite of suffering from severe dysentery, put in a fine morning's work, laddering the section immediately beyond the high point reached by Mick Burke, Allen

Fyffe and myself on the 23rd. The ladders were in six-foot sections which could be bolted together to form a ladder of any desired length. These were used either to scale walls, or as bridges over crevasses.

Climbing the Ice Fall is a cross between a medieval assault on a fortress and crossing a dangerous minefield. The first time through, everything seems to be full of lurking threats, of toppling séracs and hidden chasms, but once a trail has been broken, with all the obstacles laddered, one can quickly be lulled into a dangerous illusion of security, for the risk is always there, as we had learned so tragically in 1972, right at the end of the expedition.

Nick and Peter, out in front, were savouring all the fresh joy of discovery as they picked their way up a long, shallow ice valley and then tackled a line of ice walls that barred their way across the Ice Fall. Pete Boardman, telling the story, said:

Route finding through the Ice Fall has a very creative feeling – plodding through guttering gateways of ice, looking in all directions for the snow bridge that will not collapse, moving on the horizontal, backwards and forwards as a team, a roped entity, to find the way – not only for us but for the future.

Such is the power of the media myth-making machine, I have lurking thoughts that all the Big Names gain superhuman qualities when they set foot on a big mountain. But Nick Estcourt gasps with the altitude just as I do. It's just Nick and me, and now I feel I'm doing something I understand. I enjoy climbing with Nick; he treats me with respect and encouragement – always willing to hand over the lead, give praise where it's due.

We arrived at the foot of a short overhanging ice wall – 'It's your turn,' said Nick. 'I led the one lower down!'

I started front pointing, straight up it. It was overhanging and towards the top, about twenty feet up, it domed out with softer snow. I rested on my terrordactyl (a special ice hammer designed by Hamish MacInnes) and got Nick to pass up his axe. I clipped the terrordactyl in as a runner then attacked the top, but my arms felt drained and fingers were opening so I left one axe firmly embedded at my high point and came down to rest on the terrordactyl. Suddenly, I found myself in an undignified heap, gasping and wheezing in the snow next to Nick. Feeling a bit ridiculous, with a small cut on my forehead, a distant quote from an American guide book drifted into my head: 'A climber is like a bull, wandering around tormented and confused who, when he sees the red flag of a cliff, all he can do is charge!'

Nick took over and I learnt a lot watching him lead the pitch. He seemed to pace his breathing as he carefully cut steps and hand-holds all the way up so that he could gain the maximum rest. Slowly, he moved over the top – but at least he did stop there for five minutes, unable to speak and feeling ill!

We had been watching their progress through our binoculars back at Base Camp and had been slightly perturbed to see that they were following a shallow valley that led up towards the left-hand side of the Ice Fall. This looked a certain channel for any major avalanches from the West Ridge of Everest. A few minutes after they got back, hot, tired, but jubilant from their morning's climb, a huge avalanche curled down the flanks at the West Ridge into the shallow valley that they had just descended, a cloud of powder snow hiding their tracks. We were all badly shaken by the threat, but Nick Estcourt – ever rational – pointed out that the three avalanches were more visually impressive than truly dangerous, for the tracks were still there, once the snow cloud had drifted away; he reaffirmed the relative safety of the route which Pete and he had pioneered. I temporized and left the choice of line the following day to Dougal Haston and Doug Scott.

Our minds were taken away from the threat of avalanche by the arrival of Martin Boysen. His expedition to the Trango Tower had lasted longer than he had anticipated, and he had only got back to Britain on the same day that we had flown to Kathmandu. I had left him a note advising him to make sure he gave himself sufficient rest before joining us, but at the same time urged him to try to catch us up before we were fully embarked on the climb. Naturally, I had been worried about his late arrival, whether he would be too tired or stale, coming straight off one expedition to join another.

His wife, Maggie, had arranged to go on holiday camping in the French Riviera and so he joined her there for a fortnight and then flew out to Kathmandu arriving on 12 August. He had hoped to get a light plane to Luglha but the monsoon was still active and so he had to walk, making the journey to

Base Camp in the very fast time of ten days. He looked lean, fit and pleasantly relaxed as he strolled into camp just before lunch. It was very good to see him and he quickly became absorbed into the life of the expedition.

Each day I had to make a difficult decision – to stay put, because the weather was too warm or there was too much snow, or to push on with the day's work. We were racing against time but under no circumstances did I want to risk another accident. On 26 August, having set reveille at two a.m., I woke automatically just before our early-morning call, to find it was snowing lightly and that we were in a dense mist. I decided to delay the decision to move, dropped off into a light sleep to wake at three a.m. The mist had cleared and it was freezing hard. The sky, jet black, was encrusted in stars that shone with the brilliance only seen amongst the mountains. Rolling out of my sleeping bag, I went down to wake Changpa, the cookboy. The fire in the corner of the cooktent was still smouldering, a huge kettle already filled with water.

The previous night we had heard a great commotion in the cooktent, which was also the meeting place of the senior Sherpas. Purna, forever the natural leader, was organizing the funding of the Sherpas' end-of-expedition party. Each Sherpa had to pay a certain amount into the kitty for every Sherpani he had slept with on the approach march. This was a sure way of making plenty of money, for very quickly the Sherpas were having to pay for their boasts of sexual prowess.

Now, in the quiet of the dawn, Changpa was hunched over the cook fire, waking the smouldering embers into a blaze. The other cookboys were still fast asleep, wrapped in their sleeping bags. I felt a warm feeling of satisfaction in just being there, and one of anticipation for the day in front of us. Doug and Dougal were going to press on ahead, to try to extend the route all the way to the top of the Ice Fall whilst I, with Allen Fyffe, Ronnie Richards, Mike Rhodes and Charlie Clarke – with sixteen Sherpas carrying ladders and rope – was going to consolidate the route behind them. The Sherpas had made up their loads the previous night and now, in the glimmering of the early dawn, were starting out in little groups, placing their offerings on the altar and muttering prayers as they plodded up the well-worn trail.

That day I got no further than the middle of the Ice Fall, into a region we named the 'Egg Shells', because of the complexity of the crevasses and the seeming fragility of the blades of ice which were holding up a roof of snow. We had to fix an almost continuous track of ladders and fixed rope to ensure that if the entire area collapsed, any climbers or Sherpas passing through at the time would have a chance of survival through being clipped into the line of rope.

Whilst fixing the ladders in place we very nearly lost Mike Rhodes, the Barclays Bank nominee. This was the first time he had ever been in an ice fall of this complexity. I called him back to help Ronnie Richards bridge a particularly wide hidden crevasse. Automatically, he should have clipped into the safety rope we had already stretched over the snow, but through inexperience it never occurred to him. Walking across the innocent-seeming snow towards Ronnie, he suddenly dropped through, up to his shoulders, only saving himself by flinging his arms out to either side. We pulled him back and cautiously gazed down the hole he had made. It was like looking down into the nave of St Paul's Cathedral from the top of the dome! The crevasse looked at least two hundred feet deep, vanishing into blue-black shadows which opened out into a giant abyss. I think I was even more shaken than Mike by his narrow escape, and told him:

'For Christ's sake, always clip on to the rope if there is one. We bloody nearly lost you just now.'

By this time the sun had crept over the West Ridge of Everest and was pounding down onto the Ice Fall. We had fixed roped and laddered the entire middle section and had run out of ladders. I wanted to get the Sherpas back before the mid-day avalanches and so we turned back in the enervating heat, to skid and slide back to Base.

The previous evening I had paired Doug Scott with Dougal Haston. At this stage I had no particular thought of putting them together for a summit bid and their pairing was largely a matter of temporary convenience. Doug described his reaction:

Every decision Chris made from start to finish was scrutinized minutely. This was only natural with such a close-knit bunch, where everyone would be affected in some way or another. When Chris paired me with Dougal I was conscious that I was with someone special, for everyone knew that Dougal was summit material. Then I wondered what Tut Braithwaite would think of this arrangement, for only recently I had spoken to Tut about Chris's intimation that he wanted me to lead the Rock Band and I had asked Tut if he fancied doing it with me. Now, here I was, out of the blue, paired with the star of our show. All I could do was to go along with the flow and see what turned up next. There was no telling at that stage of the game and no point in thinking it was Dougal and me for the top.

After a 4 a.m. breakfast I left Purna's kitchen; following marker flags I stumbled and clattered across the moraine to the snow path winding up and round Ice Fall hummocks. I noted my heavy breathing with some concern but comforted myself that I was going better than in 1972. I knew, however, that I was in for the usual 'little bit of suffering' of acclimatization. Dougal came by, gliding along the trail effortlessly, whereas I sweated and staggered in his wake – perhaps in a week's time I would move with the same economy as he.

We rested at the avalanche debris that had scoured Nick's route and veered right through knee-deep, virgin snow, sharing leads to the base of a two-hundred-foot ice cliff. I led up to mid-height and Dougal came through to lead the steeper top section. By now, Pumo Ri was all lit up behind us in a bright, white show of light, in complete contrast to the cold, dark Ice Fall. As Dougal led up, he had to chop off slender icicles that tinkled down past my stance, he then traversed right, on hands and knees, along an ice shelf just below the top cornice.

Our concentration was interrupted by shouts from below. Mick Burke and Arthur Chesterman had arrived to film the climbing. It wasn't the place for Dougal to hang around and so he continued inching his way across and up through the cornice, much to Mick's annoyance, for he had no chance to set up his hefty camera gear. Dougal climbed on to the top of the ice cliff and disappeared way back to belay. I scrambled up, listened to Mick's light-hearted abuse and gave him as good as I got. We always did this whenever we were together.

'Why did you let him lead it?' he asked.

'Because he's better than me,' I shouted, for want of a better answer.

'You're not doing very well, are you?' he said, as I squirmed my way along the gangway shelf and out on to the top.

'Cheeky little sod,' I said to Dougal, who was oblivious to such jibes. 'Seeing as how you got up too late to film, you may as well make yourself useful and ladder this section,' I yelled down, sarcastically.

We left Mick, Arthur and their Sherpas to the difficult task of anchoring ladders to the vertical and slightly impending ice cliff. The sun was now skimming across the snow, bringing life and colour to the dead, cold ice. Mushrooms of fresh snow sparked like cushions of sequins; ice walls glinted back the light from their wind-scalloped surfaces and icicles everywhere hung down, twinkling light, as we moved along. It was good to be back. We moved faster, knowing that the day would be hot and the powdered snow would turn into a mire.

By ten a.m. we had scrambled across the last of the crevasses and up the remaining snow slope to the top of the Ice Fall; we found ourselves at the entrance to the Western Cwm. As luck would have it, we had arrived at a perfect place for Camp 1. It was a flattish area, completely surrounded by crevasses that would absorb the biggest avalanches which might topple down from Nuptse on the right and Everest on the left. We left our rope fixed from the site and slid down to meet the climbers and Sherpas, everywhere laddering up the route.

Back at Base Camp, there were plenty of problems to be solved. That afternoon, I had a meeting with Pertemba, Ang Phu, Adrian Gordon and Mike Cheney, to decide on the loads the Sherpas would carry and the numbers of rest days they would need at different heights, the payment of bonuses and other incentives to ensure maximum co-operation. We already had an excellent spirit between climbers and Sherpas. They were happy with their equipment and impressed by the organization of the expedition. They certainly seemed to believe that we were going to succeed this time. I wanted to make certain, however, that they also felt that they were going to reap the rewards of this success.

I promised a generous bonus scheme, therefore, where Sherpas were to receive 50 Rs. (£2), for each carry from Camp 2 through to Camp 4, 100 Rs. for every carry from Camp 4 to 5, and 200 Rs. for a carry from Camp 5 to 6 – this, in addition to their daily pay of 30 Rs. I promised, also, an additional baksheesh, to be divided amongst the entire Sherpa team, of £1000 over and above the standard baksheesh of approximately ten per cent of their total regular wage if the expedition proved successful. This might sound very mercenary, but then it must be remembered that in helping the expedition in return for payment, the Sherpas are no different from any other employees on a daily wage, though – in common with an ordinary factory-worker in Britain – they need more than just money to command their enthusiasm as well as obedience. They need to feel that the job is worth doing; they need to develop friendship with their employers and to feel that their efforts are fully recognized. In this respect Pertemba and Ang Phu were especially important, for I was employing them as 'managers' in the very fullest sense of the word. I consulted Pertemba at each step, occasionally irritating my lead climbers by accepting Pertemba's advice on what he felt the Sherpas could do, or even on route selection, in preference to their own. He was left entirely to his own judgement on the choice of individual Sherpas for different roles.

I offered both Pertemba and Ang Phu some very real incentives to make the expedition successful, promising each of them a trip to England in the event of success, and promising Pertemba that I would try to get at least one Sherpa (which, in all probability would be him), to the summit. Very strongly, I felt that we owed the Sherpas the opportunity of putting one of their number on top. Admittedly, they were getting their material rewards in return for helping us but then, in many instances, so would the members of the team. If anything, the Sherpas took greater risks than we did and certainly tended to work harder, having only one rest day in four below Camp 2, whilst the climbers usually rested every other day. They too deserved to share in the ultimate satisfaction of standing on the top of Everest.

It was this feeling of sharing, and the care that every single member of the climbing team took for the Sherpas working for us, that was as important as the money we paid them in creating the spirit of co-operation which contributed so much to our success.

D

I was getting increasingly worried about the route through the Western Cwm. Climbing this early through the monsoon increased the risks of avalanche, and it was beginning to look as if the Western Cwm could be even more dangerous than the Ice Fall. I resolved, therefore, to send Dougal Haston, Doug Scott, Hamish MacInnes and Allen Fyffe, with Mick Burke to film them, up to Camp 1 as soon as the route through the Ice Fall was secured. This still left the question of how I was going to deploy the climbers on the Face, and the next two days were spent in finalizing this, talking it over with Hamish MacInnes and one or two of my old hands.

On 27 August we consolidated the route up to the site of Camp 1, Nick Estcourt, Pete Boardman, Tut Braithwaite, Ronnie Richards, Jim Duff and seventeen Sherpas moving up, into the Ice Fall. One of the advantages of having such a big team was that it could be split into small working groups, each bridging a section of the route, all at the same time. Back at Base we could follow them through our binoculars as the long line of dots snaked its way across to the far right of the Ice Fall and then disappeared completely into what seemed a narrow corridor leading back to the left. Dougal was convinced they had taken the wrong route, and we were all getting rather heated about their incompetence when, suddenly, a little figure appeared at the top of a massive squarecut tower at the very head of the Ice Fall. Whichever route they had chosen, they had reached Camp 1 and, more important, had marked and consolidated the route.

We had climbed the Ice Fall in just five days, had consolidated the route on the sixth and would be ready to move into Camp 1 on the seventh. So far, so good; we were ahead of schedule, but I was still worried about the Western Cwm. The weather pattern was as settled as we had hoped, with clear mornings every day, but the snow build-up was considerable and the avalanches across the Cwm from the walls of Nuptse and the West Ridge of Everest were frightening.

7   The Western Cwm

(28 August–1 September)

There were queues of Sherpas at every ladder, sixty-eight
people in the Ice Fall that morning, plodding up through the
gloom of the pre-dawn, shouts and laughter mingling with the
muttered prayers of the fearful or very religious. Charlie
Clarke caught the excitement in his diary:

28th August. The day we established Camp 1. A swift 3 a.m. start
in mist, though with the brilliance a moon still bright enough to
march by. A crisp route, reasonably safe, and for once I felt terrific.
Up at Camp 1 by 7 a.m. and back down by 9.30 to an enormous
breakfast. Chris Bonington, Keith Richardson, Adrian Gordon and
I set off together, Keith going very poorly from the word go, slow,
breathless, vomiting. It was clear that he was still very unacclima-
tized and privately I wonder whether he will ever become properly
fit. Adrian going well, but diarrhoea defeated him. I felt strong and
confident, having left behind my fears of several days ago.
The Western Cwm was everything I had not expected. It should
have been straight, wide, vast. Instead, it was so narrow with the
walls of Nuptse and the West Shoulder barely making room for it;
certainly the route through this defile is hardly attractive.

I, also, enjoyed that early-morning climb through the Ice
Fall, was able to revel in being able to carry a thirty-pound
load without undue fatigue, talked and joked with the
Sherpas who were resting as I passed. I tried to remember
names, asked them about previous expeditions; some had
been with me in 1972, others had been to Everest three, four
or even five times with various expeditions. Some youngsters
were there for the first time. I felt an ebullient love for this
whole, massive enterprise, this group of people who, although
with widely differing motives, were so united in a common
purpose. As I passed one group I yelled out 'Likpadello' (a
Sherpa sexual boast). My remark was received with roars of

laughter and accompanying calls of 'Likpadello' and other sallies in the Sherpa language.

That morning there was a great atmosphere of dynamic, unified movement. But there were also worries. A particularly bad pile-up of climbers and Sherpas occurred as they waited to climb the big sérac wall which was breached by a series of ladders. The entire sérac was dangerous. You could see where it was beginning to peel away. Shouting and yelling at the Sherpas to stay well back, I resolved to work out a programme for a staggered start so that we could, in future, keep the groups of Sherpas climbing the Ice Fall more separated.

The site of Camp 1 was on top of a huge ice block, poised on the very brink of the start of the Ice Fall. Eventually it would be thrust over the brink, but it looked as though it would survive the expedition, and was out of the line of avalanches that could come down from either wall of the Western Cwm. It was further protected by a deep moat, described by a broad crevasse that barred the way into the Cwm.

Leaving the little force who were going to push the route into the Cwm, I dropped down to the ladders on the sérac wall. Phurkipa was already there and we spent an exhausting but satisfying hour making improvements, joining together four more sections of ladders, to engineer the route up the wall clear of a potential collapse. In spite of all this work, I was still able to get back to Base Camp by eleven a.m., and collapsed into my sleeping bag for a couple of hours' sleep before getting up for lunch and the next crisis of the day. This one was rather different from the normal.

The one person on the team who had not become completely accepted was Keith Richardson, the *Sunday Times* correspondent. He was a big, slightly clumsy man who, one felt, had almost cultivated a blunt Yorkshire manner as a protective shell. We had climbed together many years before, when I had spent a short period working in London and he was a junior reporter with the *Financial Times*. He had stayed with the business world and, at the time of the expedition, was Industrial Editor of the *Sunday Times Business News*. Impressed by his balanced reporting of industrial problems, I had felt that a fresh approach to climbing reporting could be interesting. Although I got on well with him myself, I had been worried by the very defensive stance he had adopted in not being prepared to show the expedition members what he had written before sending his reports back to England. Perhaps this was unwise, since he could have allowed people to see his copy with the proviso that he had the final say on what went out under his name, but he was not prepared to do this. Several members of the team had complained to me about his approach and I decided, therefore, to bring it out into the open, and raised the topic at lunchtime.

Nick Estcourt advanced a very rational argument in favour of Keith showing us his copy, making it quite clear that we would not expect, or want, any kind of power of veto. In this way, we could at least ensure that what went out was correct, free from the errors which any observer, however expert, could easily make. Keith countered this with the argument that he would feel inhibited in what he wrote, if he had to show it to everyone, and that this could lead to even more acrimony. I tried to remain neutral but felt obliged to back Keith up, emphasizing that once we had elected to take a journalist with us, we had to respect his professional judgement and accept his methods of reporting. I could sympathize with Keith, having been the journalist of the Blue Nile Expedition of 1968, and knew something of the problems. In that instance, however, I had followed a policy of showing the expedition the reports I was sending back.

His attitude had undoubtedly antagonized most of the rest of the team and, in doing so, he was making it harder for himself to gain the confidence of individual members. Charlie Clarke commented:

In the end it will be Keith's loss, I know; he seems to make no effort to penetrate the fascinating lives of the individual members and, in his words, 'stands back from the expedition'. It would be so nice if he was a member of the expedition who could share the joys and arguments and the tragedies.

It is possible that, through working with the rest of us, carrying loads into the Western Cwm and high onto the Face, he might slowly have relaxed his stance and become a member of the team. Sadly, this was not to be the case, as Charlie described in his diary:

On the 29th, the day after Keith's speech, I felt he was not very well and asked to see him in the evening to look at his retinae. In chatting, it transpired that he really had deteriorated over the week at Base. 'Disproportionately breathless' is the key to it all. His respiration has never settled to that regular compensation for either exercise or altitude. He has puffed and panted up small, low hills – was very unfit (but no more than me) at the beginning – and now puffs on minimal exertion. It's so easy to miss this. There were no abnormal signs in the chest, though his blood pressure was a little high, at 140 over 100. I could see a flame haemorrhage at three o'clock in the left fundus, but the discs were flat. Clearly, he was in incipient pulmonary oedema, and with his horrid, hacking, un-productive cough, I worried about what to do. I had not really expected this confrontation with serious illness at all and had no prefixed remedy for its management. Slowly, it became abundantly obvious that he must go down at the earliest opportunity and, in his present state, that a doctor should go with him. Pheriche seemed the only place to aim for.

I struggled with the emergency oxygen and couldn't get it together until it seemed midnight – but it was only 9.30 p.m. I hardly slept. I was worried about the case, faintly annoyed that I hadn't jumped on it earlier, but a little proud that I had done so at all.

A foul night, sleepless almost completely, but as Mum says 'the best thing to do is lie still', so I did. Big breakfast at 2.10 a.m., then another at 7.15 and we were off with Pemba Tsering, the smiling kitchen boy, two porters and one Mountain Travel Sirdar. The descent to Gorak Shep, three hours, was anguish with frequent stops and Keith gulped the oxygen I was carrying. It was clear that he was moderately anoxic when his colour changed for pink, and equally clear that he would only have had to have been slightly worse to have needed a stretcher. For this, our thanks. He improved gradually, but steadily, throughout the descent and, even though exhausted, he was good and didn't stop too often. We were down by four. I was very, very tired myself and had been carrying a good fifty pounds all the way. Still, we were down and we were happy.

The problem of the day is what to advise. Keith is Cheyne-Stokesing now – or at least his respiratory pattern is very irregular. Clearly, a good look in his fundi is essential to make sure there is no macular haemorrhage. However, I really do feel that if anything happened on a re-ascent I would be very much to blame. Reluctantly, I spelt out the news and, in an odd way, he seemed relieved. He said he had half thought it all along. We wrote our letters, packed and were away by two for Tengpoche.

At about 3.30, past Pangpoche, we met the returning Pertemba. [Pertemba had been down to Khumde to buy more ladders.] Keith was going well – it seemed clear that my job was done. Three hours march to Khumde on the following day; he would be fine by then.

So, back the weary way to Periche and a ribald chang session – a delicious dinner of spud and buckwheat curry, flavoured with chives and curd and two bottles of beer. I'll take one up for Chris tomorrow.

I had been tremendously impressed by the way Charlie had handled the crisis, both in taking the action he did and in so willingly volunteering to accompany Keith down to Tengpoche. This brought home to us how fortunate we were in having two doctors, for I should have been very unhappy at the prospect of losing my only doctor, even on a temporary basis.

The strain of taking an active part in the climbing, as well as coping with all the administrative problems of the expedition was beginning to tell. At the end of a session in the Ice Fall, carrying a load and improving sections of ladder or fixed rope, one felt like spending the rest of the day relaxing. Things were getting easier, however, with the organizational structure sorting itself out – largely due to the work of Dave Clarke, Adrian Gordon and Mike Cheney.

By now, Dave was going from strength to strength. At the beginning, with the pressure and horror of getting everyone kitted out in correctly fitting gear, and the discovery that he was short of some items, he had been rather tense. Now he was very relaxed, pleased with the really superb job he had done. Dave, Mike and Adrian were sorting out the equipment and everyone was getting stuck into all the work that needed to be done. I felt that there was not a single 'slacker' in the team.

But I still had to finalize the composition of my three lead climbing teams. Juggling names, I played just about every permutation possible, wondering whether it would ever work out right. In combining each team it was essential, also, to bear in mind the role each would play on the mountain. Group 1 would be making the route from Camp 2 to 3 – not a particularly interesting or exciting job, but one which would put them into the logistical position of going up to Camp 5 eventually. Group 3 would establish Camp 4 and make the route to Camp 5. Group 2, who would have the long push from Camp 3 to 4, could then be in a position of finishing off the Rock Band later on – or perhaps even pushing the route across above it.

It was on the afternoon of the 28th that I finally made my decision. Doug Scott and Mick Burke were obvious choices for the 2 to 3 run – Doug to force it, Mick to film it. They also got on well together. Nick Estcourt seemed ideal for 3 to 4, a long, interesting stretch which he could get his teeth into, making him available for some of the vital work towards the top. It occurred to me that Nick and Tut Braithwaite would complement each other; Nick, very conscientious but sometimes tense and anxious. Tut, easy-going but, at the same time, very ambitious with a tremendous appetite for hard climbing. I knew Dougal and Hamish were happy about their proposed role in putting up Camp 4 and pushing the route to 5, thus putting Dougal in a good position for the summit while Hamish could ensure that the platform boxes at Camp 4 were really secure.

For sheer skill in climbing there was no one to touch Martin Boysen and I should have liked him to have had a go at the Rock Band. Not the most methodical of souls, the logical place for him would have been with Doug or Nick, but he had only just caught up with us and seemed in need of a rest. I decided, therefore, to send him up to Camp 4. This left Pete Boardman with the third party, and Ronnie Richards and Allen Fyffe in the first.

Finally, I felt it would be sensible to use two Sherpas in the run from Camp 3 to 4. It was one of the longest stretches and the Sherpas would probably be able to carry better loads than the climbers, without oxygen.

These were the combinations I announced at lunchtime the following day. Meanwhile Doug Scott, Dougal Haston,

Hamish MacInnes, Mick Burke, Allen Fyffe, Arthur Chesterman and Mike Rhodes were up at Camp 1, ready to force the route through the Western Cwm. I had decided to send Mike Rhodes up to the camp so that he could act as camp manager, receiving and sorting the thirty or forty loads which would arrive each day through the Ice Fall, leaving the others free to force the route. Allen described their arrival at the site of Camp 1 in his diary on the night of the 28th:

Got here, sat about for a time and then put up one of the big box tents which will be permanent here. It was worth working, just to get out of the sun. We then lay in the box and had a couple of brews, when the Sherpas who are going to stay up here arrived after a late start. They got their own bell tent and cook area organized.

Doug had one of his tunnel tents up, so Mick and I, with Arthur, helped him put up another. Hamish and Dougal immediately installed themselves in the big box and didn't move. Eventually, it turned out that I was in a tunnel, as was Arthur, Mick and Doug indulged in a bit of squabbling, but both settled in the box. There seems a real division here as to the 'old timers' who know the score, and the new mugs like me, who get left working alone if they are not quick enough!

This kind of situation was probably inevitable; the important thing was that it never got out of hand, never provided more irritation than the odd, healthy grumble.

The following day Doug Scott and Dougal Haston went forward to find a route through the labyrinth of crevasses that barred the way up the lower part of the Western Cwm, while the rest of the group, under the supervision of Hamish MacInnes, concentrated on the initial part of the route. It was here that Hamish really came into his own, applying all his skill in engineering and his enthusiasm for building complex structures. He writes:

It was Dougal who told me there was the daddy of all crevasses just past Camp 1. He and Nick Estcourt had just come down from there and assured me it was thirty foot across and no way round. 'You'll be able to use some of that fiendish gear you've been working on,' Dougal said cheerfully. Everybody seemed to be finding the prospect entertaining, and Mick Burke was determined to film the bridge-making episode. When I saw the pleasant little Rubicon we were going to have to span, I wasn't overjoyed myself, and suggested, in vain of course, that Mick wait until it was finished.

Next morning Ang Phu had already started sorting out equipment by the time we emerged from the super box after breakfast. The scene resembled the siege of Troy – ladders, ropes and stakes littered the snow. Sherpas enjoy constructing things and have an amazing aptitude for mechanical innovations, so building a burra bridge appealed to them enormously, and I found that they had to be restrained in their zeal, as one six-foot section after another was bolted together with haphazard abandon.

Mick already had his camera going, But Allen Fyffe and I soon forgot him as we became absorbed in the task on hand. There were two deadmen anchors secured on our side of the crevasse. Looking over the lip, there was a vertical thirty-foot drop to a shaky snow bridge which connected with the far bank at a lower level. I suggested to Allen that he nip across and field the ladder when we lowered it. The ladder had by now grown to about forty foot. 'I always like to volunteer for these less dangerous ploys, Hamish,' he spoke resignedly, and disappeared from view, crossing the tremulous snow bridge with the celerity of an Aberdonian avoiding a charity collector. When he was safely over I threw him one end of a coil of corlene rope and attached the other to the ladder. While Allen fixed more deadmen belays on his side of the crevasse, I was bolting on three ladder sections at right angles to the centre of the main span, using special triangular alloy plates for the purpose, and baffling the Sherpas completely. When I fixed tensioning ropes from each end of the main spanning ladder and over the top of the upright sections, even Ang Phu began to lose faith. I assured him I was merely bringing some science to Ice Fall thinking and told him to find two more six-foot lengths and send one over to Allen. They would act as doormats at either end of the bridge and prevent it sinking into the ice.

Ten minutes later the bridge was ready to lower into position, but first it had to be raised upright. This was accomplished by the combined manpower of fifteen Sherpas, aided by several guy ropes. One end was placed close to the lip of the crevasse and the structure was lowered slowly, drawbridge fashion, down to Allen who guided it with the corlene tail rope. We brought it to rest with the right-angled section uppermost and the main span bowed downwards by the tension of the double ropes from the bridge ends.

'Hey, MacInnes,' Mick Burke had stopped filming for a moment, 'how the hell can we get across that contraption? That other ladder in the middle is blocking the bloody way.' Another one who didn't appreciate Ice Fall science. I bade him have patience, while I mustered the Sherpas for the last move. The whole shooting match was then rotated on its major axis, so that the right-angled section now hung below and the main span rested, snugly tensioned, over the crevasse. We lashed the bridge ends and rigged parallel ropes from the four deadmen, one on either side of the ladder and finally tied off short lengths of cord from the ropes down to the ladder rungs to form a handrail cum safety net. The bridge was complete.

We called it the Ballachulish Bridge, in honour of the bridge over Loch Leven that had nearly been completed near Hamish's home in Glencoe. There was one difference between the two bridges, however. Hamish built his in a day, keeping well up to schedule, whilst the Ballachulish Road Bridge was then a full year over deadline!

It took Doug and Dougal just three days to make their way to the site of Camp 2. The initial stretch was much more complex than it had been in 1972, with a network of wide, deep crevasses. They had hoped to keep to the middle of the glacier all the way up, to avoid the risk of avalanches from the flanks, but about half-way up the centre is barred by a series of broad crevasses, and they were forced into the Nuptse flank. We were running out of ladders, even though we had brought out half as many again as we had used in 1972, and Pertemba had already been sent back to Khumde to purchase more, some of which were ones salvaged by the Sherpas from the Ice Fall in 1972. We were also rescuing as many ladders as possible left by other expeditions both from the Western Cwm and the Ice Fall itself. Allen Fyffe describes digging one out:

Took us about four hours, but after a lot of hard digging ended up with about forty feet of Japanese ladder. It was a three-section job, and we must have dug about twenty-five feet of it out of an overhanging sérac face. The contrast between sun and shade is enormous. Down in the crevasse, digging out the ladder, it was like an ice box and I was cold even in my orange jacket, windsuit and silk underwear. But then the sun crept round the shoulder and my cold hole suddenly became an oven. The heat is incredible.

Whilst my lead party were pushing out the route up the Western Cwm, between thirty and forty Sherpas were shuttling loads to Camp 1 through the Ice Fall each day. Dave Clarke and his helpers were doing a magnificent job, packing and listing the loads as they left Base Camp. One of the most awkward problems was that of the MacInnes face boxes, which had a dozen different parts ranging from tiny wing bolts to the complex frames and special flooring of honeycombed plastic. These had to be made up into easily carriable loads of thirty pounds each, so that they could go straight to their destinations on the South West Face without having to be unpacked. Mike Thompson, with characteristic thoroughness, had solved this problem.

Ronnie Richards moved up to Camp 1 on 30 August. In a letter home he caught the romantic beauty of the Ice Fall and Western Cwm in his first impression:

Ghostly white, sugar mountains clustered round the other side of Base – Pumo Ri, Lingtren, their exquisite summit slopes contrasting with the debris-coated avalanche slopes of their lower flanks associated with the gigantic rumbling fusillades which alarmed excited, and then caused little comment.

As the dawn approached, the sky changed from deep blue-grey to a lighter shade and the grey-white summits became golden, ribs of rock and ridges casting deep black shadows. The gold turned to yellow, extending further down and soon the mountains reflected a dazzling white. By mid-day, mist and cloud would usually creep in and snow or sleet could be expected.

Arthur and I followed Hamish and his band, bound for higher up the Cwm. As we walked up the Cwm, the valley sweeping round to the left became visible. First Lhotse and the massive Lhotse Face presented themselves more fully than can be seen from Camp 1: an emphatic full stop to a remarkable valley. On the right the huge expanse of buttress, snow and rib that goes to the top of Nuptse was a constant companion; and then the South Col of Everest came into view and finally a ridge going up and up to the Summit of Everest itself, so often obscured by lesser mountains. A spiral of windblown snow was pluming from its summit and the South West Face was now fully visible, falling continuously to the Western Cwm. The sun was up and we had no more work now, so wandered back to our camp.

Closer acquaintance with the Western Cwm revealed other aspects, not all of them romantic cinerama. September the first was spent resting at Camp 1, which was no loss since there was a bright mist and sleet all day, with very mild conditions; a possible trigger to avalanches from Nuptse. In fact, rumbling avalanches were heard all day, and it was good to know that the camp site was so safe; as long as Hamish's contention was ignored that the camp site, perched on the brink of the Ice Fall where the Western Cwm starts its dive downwards, had moved four feet in the night. This was a parting shot as he, Dougal and ten Sherpas disappeared towards Base for a rest. We reckon it's his ladder (the massive cradle by Camp 1) which has sunk four feet, due to traffic and soft snow, and not to the crevasse widening that amount – but professional pride is reluctant to admit that. Others say that Camp 1 is only held from a downward shuffle by old Japanese ropes tautly spanning the last crevasse.

Doug Scott and Dougal Haston reached the site of Camp 2 on 31 August. That night, on the radio, Doug asked to talk to me:

'We've found a safer site than last time; it's further up the Cwm, on a rounded hummock which should keep it clear of any avalanches. It won't be so far to walk to the foot of the Face, either. There's another thing – we think we've found a better and more direct route up the lower part of the Face which'll by-pass the old Camp 3. We'd like you to have a look at it when you come up.'

I instinctively liked the idea, for, as Doug pointed out, it would give us an almost completely fresh route up the Face, but that night I began to think about it and decided to ask Nick Estcourt to come up a day early, so that he could join in the discussion on the proposed route change. I have always had a great deal of respect for his mountaineering judgement.

We were well ahead of schedule, with one hundred and fifty loads now dumped at Camp 1. Dougal and Hamish were on their way back to Base Camp for a rest, while Doug Scott, Mick Burke, Ronnie Richards and Allen Fyffe were to move up to Camp 2 to start work on the Face itself.

It was tremendously satisfying to leave Base Camp on 1 September and set off for Camp 1, in my own case knowing that this was probably the last time I would see Base Camp until the end of the expedition. I went up with Nick Estcourt and Adrian Gordon, who would now take over the camp from

Mike Rhodes. Camp 1 was now a small village, with the big Camp 2 box which the old hands had promptly seized, the bell tent for the Sherpas, and a scattering of smaller tents and boxes round it. Our stockpile of gear and food had reached impressive proportions and it had been all Mike Rhodes could do just to keep it neatly stacked, digging it out each day after the afternoon snowfall. I helped the Sherpas put up another bell tent, erected a tunnel tent for myself and settled down for the rest of the day.

It had started clouding over early that morning and now we were in a brilliant, white rainsoaked mist.

If it didn't freeze that night, there'd be no way we could go up the Western Cwm next day. It must have been conditions like these that destroyed the expedition of Chamonix Guides who attempted to make a route up the West Ridge of Everest, starting from just above Base Camp, in the autumn of 1974. Two of their camps on the flanks of the West Ridge had been swept by a huge avalanche, with the tragic loss of the expedition leader and five Sherpas.

I was longing to get up to the site of Camp 2, longing to look at the route and then face that tremendously exciting, important decision – should we take the left-hand route, or stick to the original one? Temperamentally, without having seen it, the new one appealed to me, and I had a great deal of confidence in Doug and Dougal's judgement. In the meantime, we had superb morale at Camp 1; the Sherpas were singing in the tent next door, and I could hear the lads talking in the big box tent. I felt supremely content to be there, and proud to have the team I had.

8   Avalanches and debate

(2 September–6 September)

The high-pitched call of the alarm buzzed me into wakefulness at two a.m. on the morning of 2 September. I lay for a couple of minutes, snuggled in my sleeping bag, nerving myself to open the tent door. Rain had been pattering down onto the tent roof when I dropped off to sleep the previous night but now it was still and silent with the moonlight filtering through the thin walls of the tent. I looked out to see the steep walled canyon of the Western Cwm glimmering under its myriad of stars set in an opaque black sky; fog crystals, like tiny fire flies danced in the light of the moon.

I switched on the radio for we had agreed to have a two o'clock call to Base Camp to decide whether the Ice Fall was safe enough for the Sherpas. The weather now seemed settled and so I gave the go ahead to Dave Clarke down at Base. This was always a nerve-racking decision, for if an accident had occurred after I had declared the route safe, I should always have felt guilty. The trouble was that one could not possibly be a hundred per cent certain the route was ever safe; it was just a case of balancing relative risks.

I then crawled out of the tent and walked over the crisp hard snow to the Sherpas' bell tent to wake our cook; it was difficult to find him for there were twelve Sherpas crammed into the tent, lying like a heap of dark slugs in a careless pile. After prodding at a few heads buried in sleeping bags, I found the one that I thought was that of Kanchha, our cook, told him to start breakfast and returned to my tent. I lay back in my sleeping bag and started to think out the problems of the next few days. We were maintaining our momentum on the mountain, but just keeping track of the huge mass of supplies was now a major problem. Adrian had to ensure that it flowed in the right order from Camp 1 to 2, so that we had everything we needed for the initial stages on the Face. I anticipated the first sight of the Face as we walked up the Western Cwm, wondered whether the new line might work, and then thoughts and plans merged into a deep sleep and it was daylight when I next woke to the call of 'Chiya Sahib'.

I looked at my watch; it was 5.30. Why the hell was it so late; surely the cook couldn't have taken three and a half hours to make a cup of tea. I was worried about getting up to Camp 2 and back to Camp 1 before the great powder-snow avalanches started trundling down the steep flanks of Nuptse. I rushed out of the tent in a nervous rage to ask Kanchha why he had been so long, only to discover that the Sherpa I had woken in the night hadn't been Kanchha at all and must have rolled over and gone back to sleep. There was nothing more I could do, but try to get everyone off as fast as possible and by 6.30 we had set out from camp. In my haste, I was one of the first to start and found myself breaking the trail, plodding the zigzag route through the initial network of crevasses. Twenty minutes' walking and I was still only a hundred yards in a direct line from the camp, so intricate was the route.

I was quite relieved when Doug Scott and Nick Estcourt caught me up. They were deep in discussion over the relative merits of the routes they had picked through the Ice Fall. I decided that if they had enough breath to talk they might just as well break trail, and stood aside to let them pass. I was going slowly, definitely feeling the altitude, but at the same time was able to enjoy the walk as I plodded on with a load of ropes on my back. That day we had with us eighteen Sherpas, forming a long snaking tail winding back along the track up the Cwm. The path took us inexorably towards the walls of Nuptse. The debris of a huge wet-snow avalanche had spilt over it, covering the marker flags for a stretch of over a hundred yards. Anyone caught in the holocaust would have had little chance of survival.

And then the Face came into view. I made this an excuse to sit down and rest, examining the lower slopes for the proposed new line. It was obvious enough, working its way up a series of snow arêtes on the left-hand side of the Face, just opposite the site of Camp 2. It was much more direct, and therefore would probably be much quicker. It was also more open to avalanche risk.

After the dog-leg which crept under the flanks of Nuptse, the track swung into the centre of the Cwm and stretched, long and steady up a shallow depression towards the site of Camp 2. I met Nick Estcourt on his way back down. He didn't like the new line at all.

A few minutes later I reached Camp 2 to find Doug, Ronnie, Allen and Mick Burke who were going to stay the night already erecting one of the big box tents. I had intended to return that night to Camp 1, partially to ensure that the flow of loads was being organized correctly and partially because I preferred to keep out of the way of my lead climbers so that they could make their own tactical decisions without any kind of interference from me. But this time, however, I was worried about the proposed new line on the lower part of the Face, was still quite attracted to it, but wanted to have a much closer look before committing myself to one line or another. I therefore decided to stay the night, borrowing a down suit from someone and having my gear sent up the next day.

That night I squeezed in between Mick Burke and Doug Scott and shivered through the dark hours. The Face was hidden in cloud in the dawn and we therefore decided to delay a reconnaissance till the following day.

But the weather didn't improve and we spent another day around the camp. There was a continuous rumble of avalanches, a kind of shooshing thunder, like a distant train rushing through a tunnel. It would have been suicidal to have tried to get through from Camp 1 to Camp 2. I felt my policy was being borne out, for though the avalanche risk was high, by being careful in siting the camps we could sit out the storms, free from avalanche threat. We just had to make sure there was enough food and fuel at each camp.

That day there had been some activity in the Ice Fall below Camp 1. The crevasse a short way below the camp had opened out and the Sherpas coming up the Ice Fall that day had dumped their loads below it. Hamish had come up with some ladders to rebuild the bridge over it. Nick Estcourt had also dropped down below the camp to give a hand.

On the morning of the 5th, I set my alarm for 3.45, woke up and called Camp 1 for the prearranged call at four a.m., but got no reply. Cursing them for oversleeping, I dropped off to sleep only to wake up again at 7.30 that morning. Adrian must have missed me at 4 a.m. and had been calling on the quarter hour ever since. Unfortunately he had let the Sherpas set off at about 5.30, a decision that both Nick at Camp 1 and I at 2 were unhappy about. In fact Nick, on waking, had raced after them to bring them back, before they got into the dangerous bottleneck, but had been unable to head them off. He had then followed them up to find out what had gone wrong with the communications at our camp.

We still hadn't set foot on the Face and had spent the entire morning gazing at the lower slopes arguing the pros and cons of the two routes.

I must confess I was uncertain which was the best choice, but the argument was tending in favour of the new direct route, when a series of good-sized avalanches came straight down it. This seemed a fairly conclusive argument against the route but even then we didn't reach a final decision. Nick, who had arrived about one o'clock, the one person consistently against the left-hand line, pointed out how it was in the natural fall line of avalanches from the Great Gully, while the right-hand route worked its way up to one side of all the avalanche runnels. Mick and, to a lesser degree, Doug argued for the left-hand line, pointing out how we could easily lose all our fixed ropes on the original route to the right whenever it snowed heavily. But everyone, almost imperceptibly, came back to the original right-hand route and we finally settled on it.

Looking back at the argument that night I wondered about my own role as leader. Perhaps I should have been more positive, but I wasn't, and I think the way we all changed our points of view and argued round the problem to reach a democratic decision was, in this particular case, the best way we could have done it. We were very closely united by a decision that everyone helped to make. Many months later I was bemused to discover how our consultations had looked to other members of the party. Doug Scott recollects:

Chris suddenly ended the debate with, 'We'll go the old way; I've made my decision.' It wasn't exactly democratic. He had listened to us rather like a prime minister might consult his civil servants before making his decisions. But here it worked and we were all relieved that a decision had been made.

Doug is a passionate believer in a climbing democracy where all decisions are made through group discussion. What he perhaps isn't fully aware of is how strong his own personality is, and how often it is his decision that is adopted. At the same time, though, he understood my side of the problem and always gave me the fullest support, even when perhaps he was unhappy about the way I had gone about it.

The discussion had dragged on through the afternoon. We still had to sort out climbing gear for the following morning and store the loads that had come up that day. We spent the rest of the afternoon doing this, and then, in the early evening I decided to pick up the flags that Doug had placed the previous day to mark our proposed direct route. I wandered along the tracks he had left towards the Face. It was a tantalizingly short way to the foot of the Wall; little more than a quarter of an hour's walk with hardly any height to gain, but sitting by the flag, with the Face soaring above me, I did not regret our decision. It looked rather grim and evil, shoals of black rock sticking out from the snow. A powder-snow avalanche boiled over a rocky outcrop and poured down onto one of the avalanche cones, a grim warning of more to come. I turned back without regret and plodded back towards the camp.

We didn't have any Sherpas with us and while I had been away Doug had prepared a magnificent high tea of sausages, mashed potatoes and peas. Afterwards he and Allen decided to go up and mark the route to the foot of the Bergschrund and set out clutching a handful of flags. We were all relieved that the decision had been made and that we were going to push forward once more the following morning.

Earlier in the day I had sensed some tension in Doug. He

had been rather quiet and moody, almost pointedly seeming to exclude me from the plans for the next day. He and Mick Burke were going to push out the route to Camp 3 and I had suggested that Nick and I might go along to give them a hand. What I didn't realize properly at first was that Mick saw this innocent offer as a threat. He felt that I was interfering with their freedom to be a climbing group out in front on their own, making their own decisions and, for that short time, being autonomous within a huge expedition. For Doug, my policy of keeping roles fluid was slightly worrying. He wrote:

From my own personal point of view I must admit to having been at that time uneasy about my overall role on the trip. For I was now teamed up with two climbers who had no previous experience of Everest and with Mick who was primarily there to film. I kept quiet about my restlessness, as Chris was so wound up with more important problems, and I continued to hope that weather, route and team fitness would determine mine and, in fact, everyone's role. I knew anyway from previous experience that Chris, whose actions were dictated by the overall strategy, often seemed mercurial at a personal level, for he would swop and change his job allocations frequently. We did, however, talk out the making of the route to Camp 3 and, in fact, as it turned out, Nick decided not to go up, but to rest, and Chris himself said he merely fancied a day out load carrying in support. I felt really mean for having been so possessive about our bit. It was just what he needed, a day out front to enable him to clear his head of all the logistical problems and other worries.

That evening I walked a short distance from the camp, just to be alone. In a way my role, I realized, was similar to that of an admiral in a flagship who has to be terribly careful not to interfere with the tactical day-to-day decisions of the ship's captain.

Escaping from my fellow team members, I was able to savour the mountains. From where I sat I could just see one tent, a soft ruddy glow from the lamp inside somehow emphasizing the beauty of the great cirque of ice around us, which was so peaceful and yet held such menace. The threat was lurking the whole time and yet the beauty and challenge of the place were as fresh as they had ever been.

It froze hard that night and we set out in the dark, following the tracks Doug had made the previous evening. I took with me a heavy load of ropes and deadmen. These are small alloy plates which are dug into the snow and act rather like a fluke anchor, digging deeper the harder they are pulled. I didn't bother to bring my crampons because I only intended to go to the foot of the Bergschrund so that I could leave the others to the job of making the route and get back to start planning the push up the Face itself. The route swung far into the centre of the Cwm, to keep it well away from the threat of avalanches from the Face, and then took a slope of fresh avalanche debris at the bottom of the Face as direct as possible, to reduce the period we should be exposed to the risk to as short a time as possible. An old rope and some wire emerged from the ice in the Bergschrund as a reminder of the 73 Japanese attempt. Doug had already tied a rope round his waist and was somewhere up above, cramponing up the hard frozen snow. Mick Burke was scouting round for an easier way over the Bergschrund itself.

Well content, I heaved up the fixed rope onto the start of the Face, dropped my load at the first belay point and wandered back down in the cool shadows of the dawn. I was going much more strongly than I had done in 1972, when it had been all I could do to reach the foot of the Face on my first attempt. This time I felt I had plenty in reserve.

Doug continued up the long slope stretching towards Camp 3; it was at a steady angle of around forty-five degrees, with a covering of twelve inches of soft, unstable snow on top of ice. This was where we started the continuous line of fixed rope that I hoped would stretch as close as possible to the foot of the South Summit Gully, prior to the summit bid. At this stage the angle was still easy, the climbing technically simple, but any kind of movement at nearly 23000 feet is slow and cumbersome. Going very strongly for the altitude, Doug led out all the way. He used the method we were to follow for the rest of the climb, tying on one of the 8 mm non-stretch terylene ropes, which we had unwound from large drums the night before, to make up coils of approximately 200 feet each. He then led on up the snow slope, belayed by Ronnie Richards or Allen Fyffe, while Mick Burke filmed them at work. He plodded up the long slope, kicking cramponed boots into the soft snow, digging in ice axe and terrordactyl; five steps, pause for breath, another five, and on it went to the end of the rope. Doug then anchored the rope, securing it to a special type of ice piton called a wart hog.

The other members of the team then climbed up the rope, that had now been used, using their jumar clamps to fix on to the rope. The clamp easily slides up the rope, but, working on the ratchet principle, bites into the rope, as soon as it is pulled on, giving the climber both security and a handle to grasp, as he plods up the slope. Whilst leading, even up an easy snow slope, there is the thrill of pioneering that engulfs fatigue, but climbing the fixed ropes is a slow monotonous business, of making targets, ten steps without a rest, and all too often failing to meet them, sinking back onto the safety line from jumar to harness at the seventh or eighth step just short of the magic ten. And then another rope length to run out, another rope to follow up.

They climbed the 1200 feet to the foot of the rocky buttress that guards the site of Camp 3. From there the view began to open out, with Pumo Ri jutting out of the swelling ride of cloud at the end of the Western Cwm, framed by the fluted walls of Nuptse and the steep slopes of the West Ridge of Everest. Camp 2 was little more than a cluster of dots, dark against the brilliant snow; the trail up the Western Cwm wound, serpent like, through the crevasse systems from Camp 1, and beyond Camp 2 towards the Face. Even smaller dots, moving imperceptibly, marked the teeming activity that was bringing our supplies to the foot of the Face. The scale of the Cwm was so vast. Those dots were so minute against its gigantic scale, so vulnerable to the huge billowing powder-snow avalanches that swept from either wall, seemingly at any time of day or night. It was a sight that was unbelievably beautiful, peaceful, yet full of menace to us tiny humans who did not belong there; whose fate seemed of so little conse-quence amongst these massive, changeless mountains.

But we were full of confidence, poised ready for the fast push up the South West Face to the foot of the Rock Band, still ahead of schedule. It was 6 September. Tut Braithwaite had joined Nick Estcourt at Camp 2. Martin Boysen and Pete Boardman had also moved up with six Sherpas and a cook to relieve us from the chore of doing our own cooking. At Camp 1 Adrian Gordon had everything under control. Whatever I asked him, however infuriating the request, he remained imperturbable. Down at Base Camp Dave Clarke had very nearly finished all the loads that were needed on the mountain and was ready to leave the day-to-day supervision of the start of our supply line to Mike Cheney.

9   A new site for Camp 4

(7 September–10 September)

Tut Braithwaite and Nick Estcourt were going to move up to Camp 3 the following morning on 7 September to start pushing the route out towards Camp 4. That night Tut experienced the doubts and worry that nearly always precede a major climb. This was to be his first time on the South West Face itself. That day he had watched the avalanches pour down the Great Central Gully and the rocks on either side, had decided that the entire Face was dangerous and yet at the same time was keyed up and excited at the thought of being out in front, making the route. He wrote:

Evening apprehension and morning lethargy soon wore off. Felt good; don't think I'll ever get used to those nights; Nick right on my heels, reassuring, Chris following with Pertemba and his Sherpa team. First fixed rope; clipped into it, pulled over the Bergschrund. I had at last set foot on the Face, and then the silence was broken by what was to become a familiar cry from Nick, 'I've simply got to have a shit' – one of the two things that Nick takes great delight in telling you, the other being when he has just had one.

I carried on, moving quickly up the endless line of fixed ropes. Occasionally, momentum was broken by the odd section of rope which had been frozen into the snow during the night and pulled free under my body weight; I slipped back down for what felt like a lifetime, though usually it was only a few feet. Looking back down I could see Nick, Chris and the Sherpas follow up behind me; across to the right was the South Col. This really was the South West Face; finally the short traverse to the site of Camp 3. It was still early with the sun high over Nuptse. Nick and I decided to carry on and push some ropes out towards Camp 4.

How much rope should we take? always a problem. I was excited and wanted to get to grips with the Face above, possibly to convince myself that I was strong enough to break the trail in the tiring and unpredictable snow conditions. I thought, if I can prove it to myself today, I might at least get some sleep tonight.

I led off, traversing under the shattered rocky buttress that protected Camp 3, out towards the centre of the Face; ran out the hundred and fifty foot length of rope, but couldn't find a crack in the rock in which to hammer in a piton; the snow was too unstable to put in a snow anchor, so yelled to Nick to tie on another length of rope and just carried on. I would stay on the surface of the crusty snow for a few feet but would then go crashing through into the deep powder, up to my knees or even deeper. Finally found a rock spur where I could belay. I had made my first contribution to the expedition, three hundred feet of rope fixed in place.

Nick Estcourt and Tut Braithwaite worked through the morning, taking turns to lead each pitch, slowly running out the lifeline of rope towards the great gully that split the centre of the Face. As they worked, they could see the dazzling line of sunlight slowly work its way down and across the face of Lhotse as the sun, still hidden by the South East Buttress, crept up into a cloudless sky. They were still in the shadowed cool, until the sun reached the crest of the buttress, then within moments they were exposed to its full strength-draining force. Their progress reduced to a spasmodic crawl, they turned back to Camp 3 where Pertemba, the six Sherpas and I had been busy digging out the site and erecting two face boxes.

It was like an archaeological dig, for we quickly began to unearth the relics left by the 1973 Japanese expedition. There was a complete tent that had obviously been left pitched; it had filled up with snow which in the subsequent two years had turned to ice. Embedded in it was some food and various belongings – an old anorak, a down boot, an ice axe, an oxygen mask and various bits of climbing paraphernalia. It was as if the tent had been left for the day and its occupants had never returned. I wondered what interpretation an archaeologist discovering the tent in a thousand years' time, might make. More to the point, we were all interested to see if the Japanese food was still edible. There were little plastic bags of seaweed, boiled sweets and tins of fruit, all of which provided a welcome change from our diet and which proved perfectly edible. We hacked through the relics of the Japanese expedition, salvaging as much as possible, and then came across the ruins of one of our 1972 box tents. No doubt, had we dug deep enough we should also have found reminders of all the previous expeditions. By this time the sun had come round to us and we took progressively longer rests between digging and erecting the tent. Tut and Nick returned and we left them and two Sherpas ensconced in their new home and went back down the fixed ropes. The snow below the camp was now an ugly sight, littered with the newly excavated rubbish, but I was able to console myself with the thought that it would soon be covered by the afternoon snowfall.

Back at Camp 2, we whiled away the hot afternoon discussing the problem of where to put Camp 4. The site used by all the previous expeditions was exposed to avalanche and stone fall from the Rock Band. This was the reason why Hamish had designed such a strong box tent, but it seemed preferable to find some way of avoiding the dangerous camp site altogether. Hamish suggested that perhaps Dougal and he might go up to the old site of Camp 4 with one of the lightweight summit assault tents to try to find a better spot. We talked around the problem but didn't come to any conclusion. I was tired anyway from my day's work at Camp 3 and went to bed early.

I often woke up in the early hours of the morning and would mull over the problems of the moment. This was one such morning and an idea, which was to change the entire logistic balance of the expedition, began to germinate. So far, each expedition had followed its predecessor in siting Camp 4 and had then accepted not only the inherent danger of its situation but also the fact that it was in the wrong place logistically in relation to the other camps. The trouble was that Camp 3 was much too low, too short a day from Camp 2, and Camp 4 was too high. In 1972, the Sherpas had preferred to stay at Camp 2 and then every other day had done a very long day's carry up to Camp 4, a height gain of 3000 feet from 21 600 to 24 600 feet. The climbers had been unable to manage this and had always staged at Camp 3 on the way up. This is what we were planning to do this time. I had always been a little unhappy, however, about the principle of the Sherpas obviously undertaking a very much harder carry than the climbers.

The solution suddenly occurred to me. Bring the site of Camp 4 much lower, to a point just a thousand feet above our existing Camp 3. There was a convenient spur running down from the retaining buttress of the Great Central Gully that looked as if it would give the new camp site some protection from avalanches and at the same time would be a reasonable day's carry for climbers and Sherpas alike from Camp 2. Hamish was immediately enthusiastic, as was Dougal when he returned from a long solitary walk up the Western Cwm to try and spy out the route through the Rock Band. I then put the idea to Pertemba, for his reaction was the most important of all, and he was also in favour.

We could see Nick Estcourt and Tut Braithwaite, two tiny dots on the Face, making slow but very steady progress. That morning of 8 September they had already passed the proposed site of Camp 4 so I decided to let them have another day, pushing the route out as far as they could into the Great Central Gully. They would then drop straight back to Camp 2, so that Hamish and Dougal could move up into Camp 3 that night ready to move into Camp 4.

I spent the morning making the detailed logistic calculations that the change of site for Camp 4 made necessary. I had to discuss with Pertemba the number of carries without a rest day he thought the Sherpas would be able to make. We decided on two carries and then one day off; much better than if we had had Camp 4 in its original position. I then had to explain the change of plan over the radio to the rest of the team at Camp 1 and Base Camp, in a mammoth radio call. Charlie Clarke described his reaction to my activity in his diary:

Chris is in a state of hypermania at Camp 2 in the Western Cwm, drawing charts of stores, oxygen, men, being uncontrollably effusive down the radio and Mick has christened him the 'Mad Mahdi'. He is desperate that the master plan unfolds smoothly and above all that the route from Base to Camp 2 is safe, for it is here that the Sherpas go alone and much can go wrong.

He really is a great leader in spite of all the criticism levelled at him. Nobody else has the personality to command us and deep down we respect him. I have a very good relationship with him particularly as I, thank God, am not in the raffle – i.e. the great decision of who goes to the top. This sadly alienates him from most of the lead climbers. Even a little is enough and it's just beginning to show itself. No splits, no factions, no nastiness, but it's all there in their hearts.

This was written by Charlie just after Mick Burke, Doug Scott and the rest of the first lead party had got back down to Base Camp. For all our mutual reassurances at Camp 2 it was inevitable that tensions should remain on an expedition as large as this, with so much at stake, particularly as the climb progressed and small groups became scattered in different camps up the mountain. Members of the team, and for that matter I myself, needed to express worries and fears either to each other or, in my case, to the confidence of my tape-diary. These, with the odd outburst, provided the vital escape valves that enabled us to go on working together in amazing harmony through the expedition. Certainly, that sunny day of 8 September, there was a feeling of relaxed excitement as we discussed the implications of the decision to change the site of Camp 4.

Up on the Face, Tut Braithwaite, Nick Estcourt and the two Sherpas were absorbed by the challenge of making the route up into the Great Central Gully. Tut describes it:

Strange that I should be climbing with Nick; we both live in the Manchester area and I must have known him for about ten years, yet it was this expedition that brought us together to climb for the first time. I remember it very well; Orion Face, Ben Nevis, March 1975. Nick, whilst tackling a pitch in the upper section, dislodged a large piece of ice which came smashing down into my face and broke five of my front teeth. He did apologize, but what impressed me in those dazed and painful hours that followed, he never suggested retreating; kept on insisting that it cost too much these days to drive to Scotland and not get at least one big route done per day. I remember at the time thinking, well if he feels like this about £10 and a couple of days, there would be no stopping him on Everest.

We left camp at about 6.30 and an hour later reached the previous day's high point. We'd decided against using oxygen. I started off, conditions desperate, heading slightly leftwards into the centre of the Face. Constant streams of avalanche poured down on either side of us. I was feeling extremely fit but at the same time incredibly nervous, even to the point of constantly telling Nick not to pull too hard on the fixed rope, afraid he might at any moment drag out the very insecure deadman anchor belays. At every step above I was frightened the three-inch crust of wind slab would break away, taking all four of us with it. After six or seven rope lengths, sharing the lead and the tension all the way, we at last reached the rock step that had beckoned to us all the way up. We littered it with rock pitons, at last feeling secure. I remember saying to Nick, what a pity it was so low since it would make a good site for Camp 4.

In fact this was the site that I had planned that night. Tut and Nick succeeded in pushing the route out a further three pitches before the enervating strength of the sun drove them back to their camp. They spent the rest of the day dozing and cooking in their tent, and that night, for the first time, Tut took a sleeping tablet. He described the result in his diary.

September 9th. Woke feeling terrible; I'd tried a sleeping tablet, never again. It was to be my first day on oxygen. Nick in his normal very precise informative way, was explaining every detail of the equipment, and all I wanted to do was to stay in my sleeping bag. I had wanted to make that last day out in front really count, but there was no chance, I felt so sick. Started off very slowly, feeling depressed at the thought of wasting one of those precious days out in front, disappointed for the expedition, but even more for myself personally.

Nick came steaming past, then the two Sherpas, and they weren't even using oxygen. God, was I sick. I finally caught up with Nick at our high point and had to offer him the lead all the way. He jumped at the chance, commenting, 'You should try sleeping pills more often.'

Streams of avalanches a constant reminder of the danger of leaving the descent too late; we finally started back down after reaching a point a couple of hundred feet below and to the right of the 1972 site of Camp 4. The actual climbing at this stage on Everest isn't technically difficult or even interesting, but the big overriding factor is that it is on Everest. My thoughts are constantly in the upper section of the Face, the Rock Band, the unknown section above, and, dare I even dream it, the summit itself.

Tackling this lower section in its present condition is what I imagine the trenches were like in 1914. Throw yourselves at it for a few days, then drop back and let another bugger have a go. I feel satisfied with our performance these last few days and pleased that by chance or design I've teamed up with Nick.

It is sometimes difficult to conceive how many different things were going on at different levels of the mountain, all at the same time; each incident of vital importance to the expedition as a whole and to the individuals concerned. The same morning that Nick and Tut pushed up towards the old site of Camp 4, whilst Hamish and Dougal made their leisured way to Camp 3, I had to deal with a minor, but potentially serious, crisis lower down on the mountain.

On the night of 7 to 8 September it had snowed heavily with a fall of eighteen inches at Camp 1 and even more at Base. The morning was clear however and at the four o'clock early morning call I told Adrian to send the Sherpas up the Cwm. I decided however to break trail for them by dropping down to meet them. Mike Thompson very kindly volunteered to join me and we left Camp 2 at about six a.m. wading down through the deep fresh snow, picking our way from one almost submerged marker flag to the next. It was exhilarating walking down in the crisp cool of the morning, good to get away from the crowds and pressing decisions of Advance Base for a few hours, to give oneself a simple, almost mindless role.

But it wasn't to be. It never was. As we dropped further down the Western Cwm, I became increasingly worried for there was no sign of the Sherpa party from Camp 1. We reached the bend in the Cwm, where the route was forced into the side. Still no sign, and it was now nearly 7.30 in the morning, the sun already loosening the heavy piled new snow on Nuptse. We hurried along the track where it curved into the side, uncomfortably aware of the proximity of the avalanche-prone slope. It was all very well, going down, for you could run, but on the way up, weighed down by a forty-pound load, you could do no more than plod, and hope that no avalanche came your way.

Still no sign of the carrying party. We dropped down into the crevassed area, zigzagging away from the threatening wall of Nuptse, and then, in the distance, seemingly only just beyond Camp 1, I saw the vanguard of our Sherpa carrying party. By this time I was in a fine rage, raced down to meet them, and asked Ang Phu, who was in charge, what the hell he thought he was doing starting out so late. Back in the decision-making game. It was now eight o'clock; it would take them three hours to reach Camp 2 and then they had to get back. I decided to call the carry off and told them to stack their loads and return to Camp 1. The Sherpas were sceptical; Ang Phu obviously thought I was being a bit of an old woman. An avalanche, the first of the morning, curled down from the upper ramparts of Nuptse, reinforcing my decision. I raced on down to Camp 1, running all the way to try to catch the eight o'clock radio call before it came to an end, but arrived just too late.

Camp 1 now had the BBC team in residence. Mike Thompson and I lazed the rest of the day, planning to return to Advance Base the following morning, and retired to a tent on the edge of the Camp quite early. I had dropped off into a deep sleep, when suddenly I woke to the feel of an icy wet powder on the small portion of my face that protruded from my sleeping bag. It was pitch dark, but I was vaguely conscious of being shaken, someone, presumably Mike, struggling to get out of the tent, and a flood of powder snow pouring in. Mike shouted something about 'avalanche', but I just snuggled deeper into my warm sleeping bag, clinging to comforting sleep. He had been unlucky in being awake at the time, had heard the giant swoosh of the avalanche coming down, struggled out of his sleeping bag and had dived for the door, hoping to get to safety, wherever that might bave been. At the same time he had shaken me to give me a chance to escape. As a result he got covered in the powder snow, which poured into the tent and had filled his sleeping bag. What we had been hit by was the snow-laden air blast that is driven in front of a large avalanche, though that night we couldn't see its extent. At least none of the tents had been damaged and no one at Camp 1 was hurt. Mike spent a bitterly cold, shivery night in his snow-plastered clothes, eventually moving into the big box tent to find a spare dry sleeping bag.

The following morning of 10 September dawned fine and

at the early morning call I decided that it was probably safe enough to make a carry up to Camp 2 and for the Ice Fall Sherpas to make a carry to Camp 1, on the assumption that the worst of the avalanches had already been spent. Mike and I made an early start from Camp 1 to get up to our Advance Base well before the sun hit the Cwm, so that the Sherpas could get back safely. Down at Base, they were less happy about the order to carry up the Ice Fall. They also had been hit by the windblast of the avalanche, and they were worried about the state the Ice Fall might be in. On a show of hands they decided it would be wiser to send a lightweight repair party, headed by Phurkipa, to reconnoitre the damage and declare whether the route was safe. This was undoubtedly the wisest decision, and one that I was relieved had been taken when I heard of their step on the afternoon call. I was fortunate in having a group of highly experienced mountaineers in the team who were fully capable of taking their own decisions, and on the occasions when I made a directive by radio which seemed impractical to the party at the camp concerned, they would assess the situation for themselves, obviously discuss it with me if this was practical, but if it wasn't, take action accordingly. In the event, no further avalanches swept the Ice Fall that day, but a huge avalanche had earlier come pouring down the feature we had given the name 'Death Valley', crushing and collapsing the broken crevasse region at its foot. As a result a section needed re-laddering and a new line had to be made alongside the valley. It was just as well we had not sent in heavily laden porters that day.

By the time that Dave Clarke, who had come up from Base and Jim Duff, Mike Thompson and I reached Camp 2, Martin Boysen and Pete Boardman had followed Hamish and Dougal to Camp 3. The following day, on 11 September, they were going to move up to Camp 4.

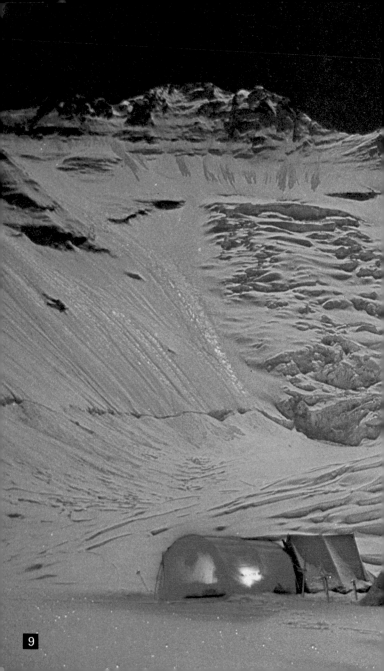

9

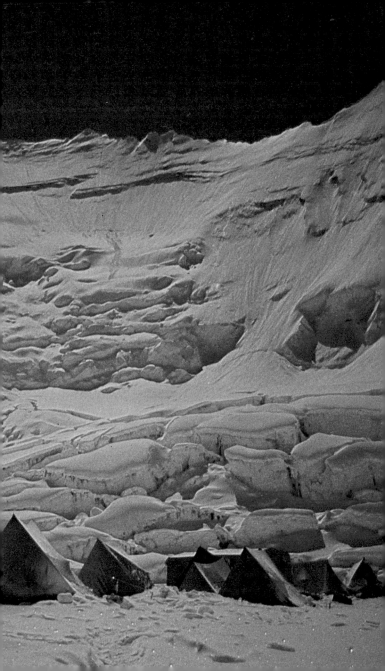

10

11

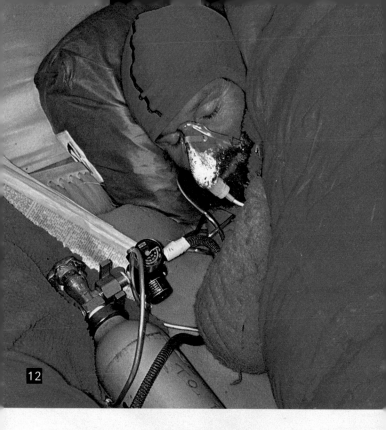

12

7. Camp 1, protected by its moat of crevasses, with Pumo Ri in the background.

8. Looking up the Western Cwm from Camp 1. from a wide-angle lens.

9. Camp 2 at dusk, the face of Lhotse in the background.

10. Hamish MacInnes and Pete Boardman erecting the frame of a box tent at Camp 4.

11. Camp 4 in the late afternoon. The tarpaulins stretched over the boxes helped carry powder-snow avalanches over the top of the tents.

12. Nick Estcourt using a sleeping mask which is plugged into a reducer valve on top of an oxygen cylinder.

10   Up the Great Central Gully

(10 September–15 September)

One of the problems of having sufficient lead climbers in the expedition to cope with a sustained siege of the Rock Band was maintaining their interest and morale whilst they waited for their turn out in front. In this respect, the support climbers were more fortunate. They had administrative responsibilities and were able to gain a satisfaction from helping to carry loads that the lead climbers seemed unable to share. Back at Camp 2, just before taking his turn in the lead Martin Boysen had been very depressed:

It's such a large expedition, I just don't feel the necessary sense of involvement. It really doesn't matter if I'm here or not. I have done sweet Fanny Adams apart from dragging my unwilling body up and down the Ice Fall. Worse, it's dangerous, menaced by avalanches and I just don't feel like sticking my neck out for something I just don't feel wound up with.

And yet on the following morning, 10 September:

Amazing how one day's depression dissolves into happiness. At Camp 2 I was at my lowest ebb, yet next day walking up the Western Cwm with Pete I felt light-hearted and gloriously happy for the first time. The morning was so magically beautiful, the Cwm swathed in boiling mists, Everest in dark blue shadow, Nuptse emerging diamond white, a hundred ice crests gleaming.

They spent the night at Camp 3 and the next morning on 11 September set out for the site of Camp 4. Pertemba and I with twelve Sherpas had already left Camp 2 with loads of box tents, food, fixed rope climbing hardware for the push into the Great Central Gully. The Sherpas pulled ahead of me without any trouble, but I kept plodding – slow but steady up the long line of fixed rope. Martin had waited for me at Camp 3 and it was good to see him relaxed and happy. We

E

set out together for the new camp, being hit by the sun before we were half-way up the big snow slope that led across to the base of the Great Central Gully. The heat was immediately oppressive and our upward progress slowed to a crawl. Dougal Haston, Hamish MacInnes and Pete Boardman had already reached the site of the Camp and were hacking out their platforms. It didn't look quite as well protected as it had through our binoculars from below. They were digging their way into a shallow snow arête, which hopefully would divide any avalanches from the very considerable broken snow slope above, and protect the camp from the worst of their force. The powder-snow avalanches had already carved out channels down which a torrent of snow was pouring. This was the first time that the complete MacInnes box, with its platforms, special floor of plastic honeycomb sandwiched between plywood and bullet-proofed tarpaulins, was to be tried out. Hamish was in his element, spanner in hand, erecting one of the boxes.

Martin digging a platform just below, observed slightly caustically:

Pete sits above acting as Hamish's bolt boy. Dougal squats impassively under the rocks. Pete calls incessantly 'Martin could you secure my rucksack? Martin could you bring my camera up? Martin . . .' I told him to stop pissing about, expecting me to run around for him, and come down to help dig out our platform. Am I being unreasonable to be so shirty? I know I am being a bit grumpy, but why should I feel so annoyed? Perhaps it's because Pete is so young, too easily managed by the old stagers. He's such a dreamy bugger and can appear to be so damned helpless. But I like his company and, as for climbing, he's as tough and determined as anyone.

Eventually the boxes were erected and the foursome settled down to the afternoon routine of brewing tea and cooking the evening meal, our own high-altitude rations being titivated with some Japanese tinned food collected from Camp 3.

The following morning Martin Boysen and Pete Boardman, the two newcomers to Everest, were to go out on their own, while Dougal Haston and Hamish MacInnes were going to improve the camp site. They set out at six a.m., jumaring up the line of fixed ropes left in place by Tut Braithwaite and Nick Estcourt. They had decided against using oxygen but were going quite strongly up to the high point about 750 feet above their camp.

Martin Boysen led out up the first pitch, revelling in the experience of lead climbing: 'The climbing was of a low order of technical difficulty but at least I had to think, make decisions, test the bite of crampons, search for belays, not just jumar up a pre-existing rope.'

He led out two rope lengths and allowed Pete Boardman to take over, heading towards the site of earlier expeditions' Camp 4 which was marked by a few crushed aluminium tubes sticking out of the snow. A length of rope, probably left from the 1973 Japanese expedition, was lying clear of the snow and Pete was able to use it, pulling on it very carefully, for fear it was no longer anchored at its top. They reached the site of the former Camp 4 and returned well pleased with their day's work, to find a third box erected with reinforcements in the shape of two of our strongest Sherpas, Ang Phurba and Tenzing, who is the son of Phurkipa. That day eleven Sherpas, accompanied by Mike Thompson, had made a carry up to Camp 4, bringing up a good stock of rope, deadmen, more boxes and oxygen cylinders.

The carrying party had returned, leaving the four climbers and two Sherpas to their own devices for the afternoon. Pete Boardman commented in his diary:

Hamish has designed quite a dramatic loo and produces the auto load (film camera) as I squat. Martin yells at one of the Sherpas, a bit too seriously I think, because they seem to have more yellow foam mattresses than we have; he's also irritated when he sees yet another piece of gear that I have, that he's missed out on through arriving late. But we have a pleasant lunch of mashed potato, peas and roast lamb, followed by fried slices of Christmas pudding with cream. Martin seems to have slotted me light-heartedly as Bramhall middle class. Hamish is friendly and cheerful but Dougal is ever distant.

They were shaken out of their feeling of well-being that

evening when a big powder-snow avalanche swept over the camp. Hamish MacInnes describes what it felt like:

I don't know what the time was when we woke up, but we woke with a start! The whole box was vibrating in sympathy with the motion of snow not so very far away: the Face was avalanching. Suddenly there was a thud. The box shook violently. The overhanging rocks hadn't been such good protection after all. For an instant Dougal and I feared we might follow the debris down the Face. A short time later we were hit by a further salvo. Martin and Peter, some six feet below, were receiving the avalanche secondhand, so to speak, but this was obviously enough to make them perturbed – it was sufficient to make me terrified. The thought of hurtling down the South West Face in a box was not a pleasant prospect, even if the structure did rejoice in the name of its designer/occupant.

Darkness seemed reluctant to leave next morning, but at long last an anaemic dawn spilled from the heights and we peered out cautiously. All was much the same as before, though the camp scene did look a bit snowswept. Despite the fact that the Sherpa village of Namche Bazar is itself precariously perched on a hillside, one 'street' above the next, Ang Phurba and Tenzing, who were occupying a third box, didn't seem too cheerful that morning. Neither was I, for that matter, and I didn't voice any bubbling enthusiasm for blazing a trail to Camp 5. The snow appeared to be in a critical condition. But Dougal and I donned our oxygen equipment and struggled resolutely out into a day reminiscent of the damp Scottish Highlands. Martin and Peter were to follow later.

The rope rose directly above the camp over a steep step. Dougal went first. I turned on my oxygen cylinder, pulled the face mask in place, and took a deep breath. At least I tried to, but there was no oxygen. As the person responsible for the oxygen equipment, I felt unfairly singled out, as in 1972, in possessing a faulty set. Despite coaxing, it refused to work so finally, in disgust, I threw it into the box and set off without it.

I was making good time; Dougal was only a short way ahead. Looking down on the two boxes, snuggled into the slope like Oxo cubes, I could see Ang Phurba and Tenzing coming up, several rope lengths behind. Dougal had traversed left towards the rope which led over to the main gully from the upper face. I was ascending in a shallow runnel, but due to ice on the rope, my jumar clamps were not holding too well.

Then I heard a swoosh like a quiet, fast-moving car above me. The avalanche overtook me and I was engulfed in a maelstrom of snow particles. It was like breathing fine, white smoke. I could feel it crowding my lungs and sensed the agonizing horror of a drowning man. In the last instant before I was hit, I had managed to wrap the rope round my left arm to prevent the jumar sliding down the rope, with the result that my arm was now being stretched unmercifully by the force of the avalanche. I was passing out as the avalanche stopped just as suddenly as it had commenced. I retched distressfully for a good fifteen minutes. My bladder had released involuntarily – not that this mattered, since I was stuffed, inside and out with powder snow. Even my boots, encased in double gaiters, were filled with the stuff.

Eventually my breathing reverted to an approximation of that cacophony more usually associated with the bagpipes being tuned, and I made an unsteady descent. I was totally numbed by the experience and felt an excruciating pain in my chest. A short way down I encountered the Sherpas but was unable to speak to them and staggered past, clutching the rope.

Martin and Peter were standing outside their box when I appeared above them on the slope. I must have looked a wild sight: I had lost a crampon and was swaying dangerously. I explained what had happened as best I could, and crawled into my box. Eventually I extracted the snow which had penetrated to my skin, took oxygen and Martin brought me a mug of tea.

It was the Sherpas' rest day, for they had made carries in the two previous days up to Camp 4. I was very anxious to maintain the momentum and therefore we had a big 'climbers'' carry that day. Doug was the first to set out with a heavy load of rope and some of his own personal gear. He was accompanied by Pertemba, who, even though he was due for a rest, volunteered to help us. They were both going very strongly and pulled out far ahead of Ronnie and myself, who plodded up at a much slower rate. Allen Fyffe and Jim Duff were bringing up the rear.

The last hundred feet or so, in the full strength of the sun, was particularly exhausting and our progress had slowed down to a crawl. Doug and Martin's gesture in dropping down to meet us, to carry our loads the last few yards, was specially welcome. Allen Fyffe reached Camp 4 about an hour later, keeping going through the heat of the day, through sheer perseverance and will power, but he was obviously finding the going very hard. Jim Duff had also tried a carry but was forced to return just beyond Camp 3. It was unfortunate that he was carrying the mail for the occupants of Camp 4.

Dougal Haston, Pete Boardman and the two Sherpas got back just after we reached the camp. They had only been able to run out a single length of rope beyond the previous day's high point, having found that they had left all the snow anchors behind. It had been a day of mishaps, but I was not unduly perturbed for our forward progress was now outstripping our ability to maintain the flow of supplies to sustain further progress. It also seemed probable that the next morning they should be able to get most of the way to the site of Camp 5, though at this stage we were not at all sure of where this was going to be.

On the morning of 14 September they made an early start. Pete Boardman woke up at 3.15, called the others and started melting snow for the first brew for Martin Boysen and himself. After having two brews and some Readibrek, they started the slow cumbersome business of getting ready for the day. They had most of their clothes on already, but had to squeeze their feet into the three layers of footwear, inner boots, the main leather outer, then the Neoprene overboots and finally their crampons. This time Martin ensured that his oxygen was functioning correctly and was the first to get away. Dougal followed, and Pete Boardman and the two Sherpas were only a short way behind. Hamish MacInnes tried to follow them, using a fresh oxygen system that we had brought up, but even with oxygen he was dangerously breathless and weak. Extremely worried about the state of his lungs, he reluctantly turned round and dropped back down to Camp 2. The others pressed on towards their previous day's high point. Dougal reached it first, and while he sorted out the ropes for the day's climbing, pondered about the climb ahead.

What we wanted was a site for Camp 5. We had thought the left side of the couloir would be best but there was a suspicious amount of avalanche activity there. We were already a long way up from the present 4. The Sherpas' optimum functionability had to be taken into consideration. Also we had to be reasonably close to the

Rock Band. The old 5 was too high and too far right. It was then that I began thinking of the ledges on the right where the couloir begins to fan out. I had seen them many times, knew they existed, but had never regarded them with an eye to a camp, as they weren't of any use on the old right-hand route with its prevailing camp settings. But this time maybe? The other two arrived and progress continued steadily with everyone and everything functioning well. Near the top of the narrows there was only one 300-foot section of fixed rope left and the sun had caught us. Martin, oxygen finished, descended. I continued in the lead with Pete, carrying strongly and steadily behind. The last piece of fixed rope was like the last piece of a successful jigsaw. I turned a corner and there were some good ledges on the right, sheltered by overhangs. Ahead a long snow slope led up to the Rock Band couloir. I reckoned we had found our Camp 5 site.

Pete Boardman also had enjoyed his day out in front, writing:

Going well on oxygen as long as I keep on plodding and don't try any major bursts of effort that make me gasp too furiously. Soft slides pour down either side of our rib of snow. The channel on our left is continually moving, giving that uncertain feeling one gets in a railway carriage when the train next to one starts moving. It's a strange sensation to plod upward, the only sound one's own breathing and the thump of the oxygen valve. So much of this expedition is self-preservation, keeping warm and fed, pacing oneself, looking after one's fingers and toes. Today cold toes as usual and Dougal good to follow, despite his self-congratulatory air . . . Back to Camp 4 and warm toes in the sunshine and at last some letters from home – pleasant to read in the late morning sun and strange to think that I'm at Camp 4 on Everest.

Back at Camp 2 we had been able to watch their progress through binoculars. That afternoon at the two o'clock call, Dougal told me of his thinking behind siting Camp 5 on the side of the gully. It made excellent sense. They had now completed their task and were coming back down for a rest. We were in a position to establish Camp 5 in another two days, but the difficult question was who should establish it? I had originally thought of sending Ronnie Richards and Allen Fyffe up to get the camp built and the route started towards the Rock Band, so that then Doug Scott, Mick Burke, Nick

Estcourt and Tut Braithwaite could have moved up to force the left-hand couloir.

Unfortunately, however, Allen did not seem sufficiently acclimatized to move up to Camp 4. He had only just managed to stagger there the previous day. Ronnie was going reasonably well, at about the same rate as myself, but he lacked experience of this kind of climbing. I talked over the problem with Doug Scott. He was obviously worried about going up to Camp 5 too early, especially when it was obviously going to be a very long haul, just to the foot of the Rock Band, on which he had set his own sights. Therefore I decided to go up to Camp 5 myself, get it securely established, start the route out towards the Rock Band and then probably stay there to co-ordinate the flow of supplies for the assault itself.

In this I was breaking one of the rules I had originally set myself, that I should try to be in the camp immediately behind the lead climbers, to keep an eye on their problems without getting involved in tactical decisions. In this instance, however, I felt justified in going out in front. We had changed so much from our original plan, I no longer thought I had the feel of the problem, found it difficult to visualize the site of camps or the distances involved. Another factor was that Camp 5 was obviously going to be a crucial camp site and I wanted to ensure that it was securely established. Dave Clarke at Camp 2 and Adrian Gordon at Camp 1 had the day-to-day running of the camps and movement of porters well under control, so it seemed that I should be able to run the expedition for a short time from the front, while getting Camp 5 established, and even supervise the final stages of the expedition from this position. Also, I must confess, I was itching to have a little session out in front, actually making the route. I decided therefore to move up to Camp 4 with Ronnie Richards and six Sherpas the following day, 15 September.

Pete Boardman and Martin Boysen with Ang Phurba and Tenzing, dropped back to Camp 2 that day, but Dougal Haston had an urge to be alone for a change and elected to spend the night at Camp 4, observing:

I settled comfortably into my sleeping bag, stove melting snow, and read some letters. Drifting, dreaming, and sifting thoughts about our progress to date and to come, the hours meandered gently onwards until the sun settled down, leaving a stronger than usual night wind. Taking a quick look outside I found that it had started snowing. This was not unusual, and I didn't give it too much thought. Slowly I worked my way through the evening meal and about nine o'clock drifted into a dream-filled sleep. My dreams were pleasant but I kept waking into an almost awake state. As the snow fall continued the avalanches started pouring down the central couloir which was one of the reasons for taking Camp 4 out of the couloir. My present box had been erected on as safe a site as we could find but, of course, it is not possible to be one hundred per cent sure of anything in the mountains.

My home was under a rock – I drifted back to sleep again, only to be awakened a few minutes later by big avalanches going past on the other side. A faint glimmering of unease crept into my mind as I worked out where it had come from. It couldn't possibly have come from the couloir, I calculated. From where then? Thinking back to my previous times high on the Face, the conclusion seemed to be that it came from the snow slope going up on the rightward route to the old Camp 6. That also meant that the snow was building up to heavier than normal proportions. Next thing all calculating fled from my head as there was a loud whistling and rushing noise and a few seconds later a great bang on the side wall of the box smashed me in a tangled heap against the other side of the tent. For one instant I felt completely disorientated and vulnerable. Was I still attached to the slope or rolling down towards the Bergschrund? Then a glad realization of being all right as stability and the movement of body and limbs was established.

There wasn't much fear – vulnerability being the predominant emotion as I'd stripped off most of my clothes in one of our very warm sleeping bags. Groping, I remembered a lighter in my rucksack pocket which was still under my head. The ensuing flame didn't reveal an optimistic sight. A huge bulge in the inner wall showed where the avalanche hadn't managed to escape down the slope. All the equipment was mixed up. First thoughts were to get dressed and get off down the ropes as quickly as possible – a straight panic reaction. Movement and getting away from the scene of an accident is often the first thing that comes to mind in situations like this. It almost goes as far as to be instinctive. Then rational processes started again, working it out clinically. I reckoned that I'd be safer sitting in the tent than on the exposed slopes below. Working also on the optimistic premise that it was still a safe site, that it had been a freak avalanche and it was unlikely to hit the same spot again.

Having decided to do this I stuck my head out of the entrance. It wasn't an encouraging scene but it proved one thing. I'd been fortunate in my choice of box. The one opposite was wrecked. There wouldn't have been any survival for its occupants. It was two a.m. and the rest of my night consisted of sitting fully clothed, with boots, overboots and crampons on as well, inside my sleeping bag waiting for another one. It didn't happen. The snow stopped and at first light I was quickly sliding down the ropes and telling an upcoming Chris the not-so-glad news.

11 Camp 5
(15 September–19 September)

I plodded on up the ropes full of forebodings, out of the still shadows into the glare of the sun that was slanting across the lower snow fields of the Face from above the South East Ridge. I was out in front, Ronnie Richards a rope length behind; a puff of snow appeared on the rocks far above, snow crystals glittering in the sun. The puff spread into a boiling cloud, seeming to stretch across the entire wall. There was no sound, and but for memories of Hamish's experience, of the story that Dougal had just told me, it wouldn't even have seemed menacing. I took a couple of photographs of the advancing avalanche, noticed Ronnie huddling into the snow, and then quickly, now fearful, turned my own back to the coming onslaught, tried to burrow my chin into the collar of my silk polo neck to stop the snow flooding down my throat. A wind whipped round me, I was in a turbulent blizzard, the snow plucking me from my stance. And then, as suddenly as it had enveloped me, it was gone.

I had been on the very edge of the avalanche: Ronnie had had slightly rougher treatment and was looking like a snow-man as he shook himself clear of the snow. I was most worried, however, about our Sherpas, who had set out from Camp 2 after us, and who, when we had last seen them, had just been starting up the line of fixed ropes below Camp 3. Unless they had reached the shelter of the Rock Buttress they could have been in the direct path of the avalanche. I was immensely relieved, shortly after reaching Camp 4 to see them coming up round the corner. They had reached the shelter of the buttress just in time, and the huge avalanche had come pouring over their heads. They were obviously shaken by their experience, but could still raise a smile and were fully pre-pared to spend the night at Camp 4.

Camp 4 was a mess with tents and gear submerged in snow. It was easy to see why the damage had occurred. We had brought with us special tarpaulins of reinforced nylon that are used for the construction of bulletproof jackets. We were hoping that these would provide protection against both stone fall and avalanches. To be effective, however, they needed to be pegged out in the slope above the box they were protecting, so that they would act as a chute, carrying the snow over the roof of the box. Unfortunately, Hamish and Dougal had only draped the tarpaulins over the boxes, with the result that the snow had built up against the walls, crushing them inwards, and, in the case of the box on the outside of the spur, actually buckling the frame. On clearing the snow away, however, we saw the damage was not quite as bad as it had seemed to Dougal in the early hours. A conventional tent or box would undoubtedly have been flattened, but the frame of Hamish's box was so strong that it had been bent inwards but had not collapsed completely and had there been any occupant that night, they would almost certainly have survived, but might well have had a few bruises.

Even so, the damage was worrying and we spent the rest of the day digging out the boxes, uncovering the stockpile of gear, excavating new platforms and erecting two further box tents. We placed one above and one below the two that were already erected immediately underneath the little rock outcrop that had saved Dougal the night before. It was hard work at 23 700 feet, and even when the boxes were up, the day's work was not over. I was determined to establish Camp 5 the next day, on the 16th. This meant sorting out the necessary loads. Dougal had told me that there seemed a good snow build-up at the site he had chosen and so I decided to risk leaving behind the platform; the face box still represented three loads. We also needed rope and snow anchors for fixing the route beyond, oxygen bottles, not only for climbing with during the day, but for sleeping and, of course, some food and cooking gear. The frames of the boxes were all tangled together, and Ronnie Richards, ever methodical, patiently sorted them out into their separate sets. By this time the sun was dropping down below the West Ridge of Nuptse, bathing the face in a rich yellow glow that had little warmth in it. We had made up our six loads for the next day, were about to start cooking our evening meal, when Mingma, one of our Sherpas, poked his head into the box and told us that Dorje, one of our youngest Sherpas, was feeling sick and had a bad headache. He had been our cookboy in 1972, always wore a happy smile and was immensely willing, but now, when I slid down the steep alleyway between the tents to see him, he was lying grey-faced in his sleeping bag, very sorry for himself. I dosed him with Codeine and a sleeping tablet, but it seemed most unlikely that he would be able to undertake a carry the following morning. We had stretched our carrying resources to the limit already and now in the gathering dark I had to try to reduce our loads by one. I flung out the summit box, which we had decided to take, just in case we couldn't find a snowy slope deep enough to fit in one of the standard face boxes; I also redistributed some of the ropes and gas cylinders, before swinging up to our own box. One could never relax at Camp 4; one had to be sure to clip into one of the safety lines at all times, the slope was so steep.

By the time I got back into the tent, Ronnie had prepared a meal of soup, followed by corned-beef hash. We gorged ourselves happily, tired but very content at the end of a long yet satisfying day. Camp 4 seemed firmly established, and I was confident that any snow slides that did come during the night would shoot straight over the roofs of the boxes.

I dropped quickly into a deep sleep, no need for sleeping tablets, and woke up at about three in the morning. I have always been a natural early riser. Though the sleeping bag was snug and warm, the panful of water we had left ready the previous night was now frozen solid. Even so, it would melt much faster than snow, and give very much more water. The trouble with snow is that it takes several panfuls to produce a full pan of boiling liquid.

I lit the gas stove and lay back savouring the moments of idleness before we started the day, feeling deliciously liberated from the administrative and organizational worries of the expedition. Today, Ronnie and I would step on to new ground, even if it was only the fifty feet or so that led to the camp site that Dougal had noticed.

The water started to boil and I dropped in the tea bags, stirred in a dozen cubes of sugar and thrust a mug of tea at Ronnie who was just creeping into protesting wakefulness. We nibbled some biscuits and jam, crawled out of our sleeping bags, completed dressing and were ready to set out by five a.m. Ronnie and I were using oxygen, the Sherpas were climbing without. I had often worried whether this was really fair, but on this occasion I certainly didn't. Ronnie and I had been working on the camp and sorting out loads till late the previous night. Once we reached Camp 5, we should have to dig out a platform and erect a box. I should also have to continue running the expedition. The Sherpas on the other hand had no responsibility, were given a load, carried it up to the camp in question and could then return to their sleeping bags and have a good rest. We had agreed with Pertemba that the Sherpas would stay at Camp 4 for four days at a time and in that time each should make three carries, before returning to Camp 2 for a further two days of complete rest. This gave us a reasonable continuity for this vital carry.

That morning Ronnie and I followed the line of fixed rope alongside the raging torrent of powder snow that came pouring down a deep-cut channel in the centre of the gully. I had never seen anything quite like it before. Using oxygen it was possible to take about thirty steps at a time without a rest, even though I had about forty pounds on my back, with all my personal gear, a rope and my oxygen cylinder.

It was about nine o'clock when I reached Dougal's high point; an empty oxygen cylinder was attached to the ice axe he had left in place as an anchor. It was just round a bend in the gully, and the little gully he had noticed was a mere hundred feet away. It was ideal for our prupose. I tied the rope to my harness and set out; it was just a question of kicking into deep soft snow, thrusting my ice axe into its full length; no technical difficulty at all, but immensely exciting. I kicked my way into the base of the little gully, probed with an avalanche probe we had brought up, to find a good site, wondered whether to follow the gully up on to the crest of the

buttress to get us even further out of the fall line of avalanches, but abandoned the idea when I found how steep and
unstable the snow was, and dropped back down to the base
of the gully. It was sheltered from the wind and avalanches,
but also looked as if it might be sheltered from the sun; it
seemed the safest spot. I buried a deadman, attached the rope
to it, and called Ronnie and the Sherpas, who were patiently
waiting below, to come and join me. Camp 5 was nearly
established.

Nearly, but not quite; once the Sherpas had dumped their
loads and left us on our own, in all probability the highest
men on earth that 16 September (the same date incidentally
that we had reached Base Camp in 1972) we still had to dig
out a platform for the box. It took us the rest of the morning,
with frequent rests, to erect a box. By about half past one, we
were able to lay out the foam mats, get out our sleeping bags
and really relax. It was time for a brew; our mouths were
parched dry and furry from breathing in the cold dry oxygen
air mixture on the way up. The sun had now crept round the
buttress above me and had been hammering on our backs, as
as we had finished erecting the box. I searched through one of
the kit bags, found the gas stove and some spare cartridges,
but there was no sign of the cooking pan, plates, mugs or
eating utensils. I was sure I had packed them, searched our
rucksacks, but still no sign, and suddenly I realized what had
happened. In redistributing them the previous night I had
left them behind at Camp 4.

It might seem a very minor inconvenience to be without
cooking and eating utensils, but in fact is was quite serious,
for one needs a large pan to melt sufficient snow to make a
good brew. At altitude dehydration is one of the principal
debilitating factors and experts recommend a liquid consumption of at least seven pints a day. Ronnie rummaged
through our high-altitude packs but the only remotely
suitable container he could find was a corned-beef tin. We
filled the tin with snow, perched it on top of the stove and
waited, mouths dry with thirst for the drink, but the tin was
the wrong shape and most of the flame was wasted to either
side. Ten minutes later there was a dessertspoonful of dirty

water in the bottom of the tin; I added more snow, another ten minutes; added more snow still, and after half an hour we had a quarter of a pint of water to share between us. I grabbed the tin, burnt myself and dropped it. The precious water trickled over my sleeping bag. We tried again, and after an hour had had a small drink each, barely sufficient to moisten our throats. It was now nearly two o'clock, time for the afternoon call, vital not only to get a pan and mugs sent up the next morning, but also to keep in touch with the rest of the expedition, to be able to monitor the flow of supplies up the mountain.

The radio crackled into life; two o'clock came and I called up Camp 4. Mike Thompson was moving up that day to take charge. There was no reply; I then tried all the other camps in turn, still no reply. And then Camp 2 came on the air, called Camp 4 and they started a long discussion on the following day's carry. I waited, frustrated at not being able to get into the wireless conversation, wanting to assume control and make my requirements known. There was a pause and I quickly called Camp 4 again, no reply; then Base Camp came on the air, talking to Camp 2. At last Camp 2 called me. I replied, but they couldn't hear me, and suddenly I realized the awful truth. For some reason, the wireless set was not transmitting. I could hear everything but was unable to communicate with anyone. By this time I'd lost my temper and had begun to bang the damned radio in an effort to make it work. It didn't respond to treatment, and I continued an impotent listener to the pulsing life of the expedition.

Ronnie had been watching me with quiet amusement and at the end of the call, when everyone had closed down, suggested he try to repair it. He spent the rest of the afternoon fiddling with the radio and miraculously by the time of the four o'clock call he had succeeded in repairing the switch which he had discovered was faulty. To make it work one had to poke a finger or pencil into the hole where the switch had been, press a spring with just the right degree of force and you could send a message.

I forgot my irritation and the constant nagging thirst in my relief and in the late afternoon call was able to order the gear we needed for the following morning. Our kitchen kit came top of the list, but then I had to juggle priorities on whether to get up as much climbing gear and rope as possible to run the route out, or to bring up another box tent to start building up the camp. I decided on the latter, since this was my main object in coming up to the front. In addition, with just two of us at Camp 5 we were going to use three bottles of oxygen a day, two for climbing and one for sleeping. In pushing the route out so fast we were now going to stretch our carrying capacity to the limit. I also had to check that the right sequence of supplies was flowing up to Camp 4 from Camp 2, to ensure that we had the tentage and oxygen reserves we were going to need for forcing the Rock Band. I also asked Doug Scott and Mick Burke to set out for Camp 4 the following morning so that they could join us at Camp 5 by the 18th, by which time I hoped to be near the foot of the Rock Band.

After the radio call we spent a couple of hours brewing small quantities of water that barely moistened our throats, before settling down for the night. This was the first time we were to sleep on oxygen. We each had small plastic masks which were joined by a T-junction to a tube that plugged straight into the reducer valve on top of one of the oxygen bottles. This gave a steady flow of one litre per minute. Although the mask quickly became wet and clammy, giving a claustrophobic feeling, the benefit from the oxygen through the night was considerable, helping one to sleep and stay warm; but even more important, enabling one to build up the necessary reserves for the following day's climbing. The low hiss of the cylinder, as well as being strangely comforting, was also a sign that the system was working. We used, as far as possible, bottles that had already been part emptied to save the full ones for use during the day; this meant that we had to change bottles during the night, never a pleasant task.

I woke as usual about three a.m. and started brewing up in our corned-beef tin. I was determined to get in a morning's climbing. The slope, covered in a uniform blanket of snow, seemed to stretch interminably up to the Left-Hand Gully, which we hoped would take us through the Rock Band. We were going to have to run out many rope lengths just to reach the foot of the Band. Would we need another camp at the foot of the gully for our assault on the Rock Band? Could we sustain such a camp, and then place yet another above? These were just some of the questions I asked myself that morning. I took the lead, kicking into the crisp snow with cramponed boots, crossing diagonally left towards the base of the gully, still many hundreds of feet away. A buttress of black rock thrust out of the snow; should we go to the left or right of it? I decided on the right-hand side, and started kicking straight upwards. The snow was getting softer and I was going through to the rock underneath; the angle steepened, the snow thinned; there was barely enough to take my weight; there certainly wasn't enough snow for a deadman. I swept it away, hoping to find a crack in the rock for a piton, but it was smooth and compact, all sloping downwards in a series of tiny ledges. I teetered on in my blinkered world, encased, in oxygen mask and goggles, feeling more and more insecure as I ran out more rope above Ronnie. At last I came to a deeper patch of snow, put in a deadman and brought him up to me; I set out on another rope length. The snow got steadily thinner – I more anxious. 'You're meant to be co-ordinating this bloody expedition, Bonington, not playing silly buggers on dicey snow,' I told myself. Looking upwards, rocks, like treacherous reefs, protruded from the snow. I looked across to the left and realized I'd taken the wrong line; I should have traversed. You don't waste height and effort willingly at 26000 feet, but I had no choice. I hated the thought of trying to reverse what I had just climbed; on the way up it had simply been a question of stepping delicately, but going down, I couldn't see where I was putting my feet, the oxygen mask got in the way. I had no sense of touch; there were too many layers between toes and rock thinly covered by snow.

By the time I got back to Ronnie, I was panting even harder than I had on the way up. And we had another pitch to reverse.

At last we were on the right route, but had wasted two hours; the dazzling line of sunlight had crept down the long slope and now blasted down on us. As we only had the few hundred feet of rope we had brought with us that morning, and no more would be coming up that day, I decided to abandon our effort and return to camp. We could devote the rest of the day to digging out another platform and erecting a second box, ready to run out the remaining rope the following day.

Mike Thompson with five Sherpas did a carry from Camp 4 that day, bringing up another face box and some more oxygen; I was anxious to build up a reasonable stockpile for when we increased the population of Camp 5, to get Camp 6 established. Most welcome of all they brought up a cooking pot so that Ronnie and I could quench our thirsts for the first time in thirty-six hours.

I had made a mistake in not asking for any rope to be sent up, since we only had 600 feet at our high point and none at the camp. Doug Scott and Mick Burke were coming up the next day, and I asked Doug if he could set out early and try to get some rope to us before seven o'clock, so that we could run out as much as possible that day. It took him longer than he anticipated to reach us, however, and there was still no sign of him at seven. I was impatient to start before the sun hit the gully and therefore set out before his arrival. We ran out of what rope we had all too quickly. By traversing across into the centre of the gully we found deep compact snow and were able to make fast progress. There was still a long way to go from our high point to the foot of the Rock Band. Doug had reached the camp a short time after we set out and by the time we got back Mick Burke had also arrived and they were digging out a platform for our third box. It was grand to see them, and the slight tension Doug and I had experienced at Camp 2 now vanished. We were four climbers out in front with a common aim and purpose, to reach the Rock Band, and at this level could reach our decisions together; it was just like being on a climb in the Alps or a small trip on bigger mountains. My own co-ordinating role was not obtrusive within the small group we had at our top camp.

Two Sherpas and Jim Duff had set out from Camp 4 to make a carry; the Sherpas arrived but there was no sign of

Jim. I volunteered to go down and pick up his load, thinking he was probably just round the corner of the gully a couple of hundred feet below the camp. I got there, but there was no sign of him. I started down the fixed rope and dropped about a thousand feet before I saw him sitting in the snow just above the old site of Camp 4. He seemed in a dream, slurring his words slightly, showing no sign of wanting to go up or down. He had been using oxygen on the way up, but it is possible that it hadn't been functioning correctly. I was anxious to start back up the fixed ropes for I had a thousand-foot climb in front of me and had come down without any oxygen. It was a lovely windless afternoon and I assumed that Jim would be all right just sliding down the fixed ropes without a load. I therefore told him to start down as soon as he had had a rest and started the long ascent back up to Camp 5. I was pleased at how strongly I was going, was able to take about fifty steps at a time without a rest. I glanced back occasionally at Jim, but he was motionless, still sitting in the snow.

I got back to camp just before the afternoon call and was very worried to hear that Jim still hadn't returned to Camp 4. Tut Braithwaite and Nick Estcourt, who had moved up to the camp that morning went out to see what was wrong and found him lying semi-conscious a couple of hundred feet below where I had left him. He had taken his crampons off and as a result had been sliding out of control down the ropes until he had collapsed completely. It took them a further two and a half hours to get him back to Camp 4, where they poured hot drinks down him, put him into a sleeping bag with a couple of stoves going full blast in the tent. It is frightening just how narrow are the margins of life and death at altitude. When I had left him he had seemed a little groggy, but perfectly capable of getting back down, and yet, had the weather been less than perfect, it is possible that Jim could have died from exposure before Tut and Nick managed to get him back to the tent.

It hadn't been planned for him to stay at Camp 4. He had gone up on a day carry on the 17th to find that one of the Sherpas was suffering from altitude sickness and needed to go back down. He therefore decided to stay the night to take the Sherpa's place in the carry the next morning, knowing how short of supplies we were at Camp 5. He didn't have a sleeping bag and spent a bitterly cold night in the partly collapsed box, with only a down suit to keep him warm. This probably weakened him for the carry that day. He returned to Camp 2 the following morning. Fortunately he suffered from no after effects and had had the satisfaction of climbing as high as he was capable on the South West Face. I resolved, however, to be very careful with the less experienced members of the team.

Only four loads had reached us on the 18th and as a result we were still short of rope and had only just enough oxygen for the four of us to set out the following day. We were going to have a strong carry on the 19th, however, for I had brought eight fresh Sherpas up to Camp 4. This meant their sleeping three to a face box which was only designed for two. I had consulted Pertemba about this step and he had just grinned and said Sherpas like sleeping close together. This attitude was a token of the enthusiastic support we were getting from them. We wanted to take up as much rope as possible on the 19th to enable us to reach the foot of the Rock Band. I therefore decided to wait at Camp 5 for the arrival of the Sherpas from below so that I could carry a full load of rope, while the other three could load up with what we had already got.

Doug Scott set out from the camp at about six a.m., quickly reached the end of the fixed rope that I had put out the previous day, and supported by Ronnie Richards, began kicking up a long snow arête that led straight up towards the Rock Band. Mick Burke had left just behind them, but was obviously having some kind of trouble with his oxygen set, frequently stopping, taking his mask off and fiddling with the set. He was carrying some spare rope and the cine camera and was hoping to film the first piton being hammered into the Rock Band.

By the time the first Sherpa reached the camp, the sun was already glaring onto the long snow slope leading up to the Rock Band. It was going to be hard work catching up with the others. I loaded six hundred feet of rope and some deadmen snow anchors into my sack and started off. I was pleased to find that I was going strongly and quickly caught up with Mick Burke who told me that his oxygen system had packed in completely. There was no question of him going on, so he gave me another rope to carry and dropped back down to the camp, while I continued up the line of fixed ropes. The snow was soft and deep, giving Doug, out in front, desperately hard work, while I had the benefit of the tracks that he had made and Ronnie had consolidated. I finally caught up with Ronnie about six hundred feet below the base of the Rock Band. He was paying the rope out to Doug about two hundred feet above. I moved through, once Doug had belayed, and took another load of rope up to him, belaying him as he kicked up there last snow slope before the Rock Band.

It was a good feeling, looking down the long slope back to Camp 5, Ronnie coming up towards me, Mick very nearly back at the camp, the Sherpa, who had brought me the load of rope, still by the boxes and then, looking down into the still shadowed gully below, ten tiny figures strung out along the line of fixed rope, a visual demonstration of our momentum up the mountain. Below them was the Western Cwm, patterened with crevasses; Camp 2, little more than a collection of micro dots dwarfed by the immensity of the mountains around it. We were too far above to pick out the porters carrying loads from Camp 1. At the end of the Cwm, the summit of Pumo Ri was now 3000 feet below; we were level with the top of Cho Oyu, massive and rounded at 26750 feet. As we gained height the view had expanded; we could just see over the containing wall of Nuptse, could gaze far to the West at Gaurishankar and Menlungtse, two mountains that were still inviolate. Memories of 1972; I was looking across and down at that bitterly cold windswept site of Camp 5; the long traverse below the Rock Band to its right-hand end was in full view; we were very nearly at the same level as our high point three years before. But it was all so different; we were so much earlier, had more climbers and Sherpas, the gear was so much better.

A shout from above, the bell-like ring of the first piton being hammered into the Rock Band. A few minutes later I plodded up the rope to join Doug. 'Do you want to go on through and lead the next pitch, youth?' he asked, as I reached him.

We were now close to the mouth of the Left-Hand Gully, but were barred from it by a snow-clad buttress that jutted down from the Wall of the Rock Band. As I set out towards it, a powder-snow avalanche billowed from out of the jaws of the gully. I couldn't help wondering how we should have fared if we had been half way up it. There would have been no way of avoiding it and the weight of snow pouring through its narrow confines would have been like the waters of a great river squeezed through a narrow gorge. But there was no time for fears and I kicked on, excited to be in the lead, only just below the Rock Band, ran out my 200-foot length of rope and belayed to a rock spur on the edge of a subsidiary gully which was also an avalanche chute, carrying great lumps of ice, dislodged by the probing rays of the sun from the rocks above.

Doug was about to follow me but found that he had run out of oxygen; Ronnie still had some in his cylinder and with characteristic selflessness, offered to give Doug his cylinder, so that Doug could have the chance of leading the final pitch into the base of the Left-Hand Gully. Doug crossed the shallow gully and climbed a steep little snow wall on the other side, to the crest of the arête just short of the Gully. It was obviously going to be awkward and as Doug had finished Ronnie's bottle of oxygen and we were very nearly out of rope, we decided to return to camp. It had been a good day with fourteen hundred feet of rope run out. Although we had not been able to see into the gully I had my confidence boosted by the sheer momentum of our progress that we should force the Rock Band.

Nick Estcourt and Tut Braithwaite had already pitched another box tent when we returned. Mike Thompson and eight Sherpas had made another big carry to the camp that day and had waited for us to return to learn of the progress we had made. As they set off down, Mike received as fine an

accolade as anyone could have on an expedition, when one of
the Sherpas turned to him and said, 'Now you are a real
Sherpa. You carry as much as we do and go just as fast.' Mike
had not used oxygen for either of his two carries up to Camp 5.

Ronnie was now feeling quite tired and therefore decided
to go back down with Mike and the Sherpas. I wanted to stay
at 5 until the Rock Band had been climbed. I had allowed
myself the personal ambition of making the carry to put the
summit pair in their top camp. I could then feel that I had
done everything possible to give them a chance of success,
and then, of course, it would be entirely in their hands.

I had been giving a lot of thought to the summit push and
had already changed some of my original ideas. While we
had been making our first steps on the Face I had decided
that it would be wise to ensure that the first summit bid was as
strong as possible; we might not get a second chance. In this
respect I felt that Doug Scott and Dougal Haston probably
were the strongest pair. They seemed to get on well together,
were very experienced and determined and for each this was
the third visit to the South West Face. Our progress had been
so fast, however, that I now had them out of phase. Doug was
here at Camp 5 while Dougal was still at Camp 2. It would
have been logical for Doug to climb the Rock Band with
Nick and Tut, and then for Dougal to move through with one
of the other lead climbers to make the summit bid, but I was
not happy about such a concept. Hamish was still badly
weakened by his experience in the avalanche and had not gone
above Camp 2; Allen Fyffe was having difficulty in acclima-
tizing and was still moving very slowly and painfully up to the
altitude of Camp 4. Pete Boardman, although his performance
so far was excellent, was untried and had never climbed with
Dougal before the expedition. I was worried that Martin
Boysen, a strong contender, might still be run down as a
result of his Trango Tower trip. I decided therefore to bring
Dougal straight up to Camp 5, which he would reach in two
days, on the assumption that by that time we should have
forced the Rock Band and be ready to establish Camp 6.

I spent the rest of the afternoon working out the complex
logistics that the proposed assault dictated, to ensure we

should have enough oxygen, rope and tentage, not only for our daily consumption, but for the summit bid as well. To do this I had to take into account the stockpile already at Camp 4, the number of Sherpas and climbers at each camp, and when they were due for rests, which in the case of Camp 4 meant a complete turnover of Sherpas. I felt surprisingly fresh but took the odd whiff of oxygen to clear my brain. Our supply situation was very tight. To get Dougal and Doug into position at Camp 6 with enough oxygen and fixed rope, not only to make the summit bid but also to spend a day running a line of fixed rope across the Upper Ice Field towards the South Summit Gully, we were going to need a carrying party of six. This would mean eight climbers and Sherpas stopping at Camp 5, which in turn would mean four oxygen bottles consumed for sleeping and a further eight used on the move up to the top camp. The day before we made this move, I had to ensure that there had been brought up from Camp 4, the assault box, camp kit, rations, a thousand feet of fixed rope, and three bottles of oxygen for the push above the Rock Band. On the day they ran out the fixed rope I should have to send up a further five bottles of oxygen and more rope for the summit bid itself. It was obvious that they were going to need two oxygen bottles when they went for the top.

I also had to work out our plans for the ascent of the Rock Band. Tut Braithwaite and Nick Estcourt, supported by Mick Burke and myself would go into the Left-Hand Gully and try to force our way to the top. I thought that this would probably take two days, by which time Dougal would have reached Camp 5. It was asking a lot of Nick and Tut, for in solving the problem that had defeated all four previous expeditions they would be giving the summit to Doug Scott and Dougal Haston.

Doug offered to come up the following day, the 20th, to give a hand. I declined, however, for I felt that not only would he need the rest, but that the Rock Band should be left exclusively to Tut and Nick, as some consolation for not making the first summit bid. I had made another departure from my original plan in deciding to give the summit pair the job of putting the fixed rope out across the Upper Snow Field.

I had originally thought of another pair undertaking this task. It seemed too much, however, to ask anyone to go up to the top camp, get to within a few hundred feet of the South Summit Gully and then come back down and so I had decided to combine the task of running out the route and making the first summit bid, even though this meant a hard day's work and an extra night at 27300 feet, before the most exacting day of all.

I only just managed to make all my plans before the four o'clock call. I was uncomfortably aware that I had not had time to work out any subsequent bids, even though the climbers resting at Camp 2 would undoubtedly be getting anxious about their chances for the summit. Our progress had been so fast that I now had a surfeit of reserve climbers all justifiably anxious to take their part in the final drama. All I could do was to promise them that I would work out the logistics of subsequent ascents the following afternoon.

I then settled down for the night. We had just discovered we had only four oxygen sleeping sets and I therefore decided I would have to do without oxygen that night, since I had a tent to myself; I took the occasional breath from my climbing mask, but it did not do much to help me. To gain the maximum benefit from a demand system you have to breathe hard. Even so I dropped off into a light sleep and dozed through the night.

12 Through the Rock Band

(20 September)

The oxygen cylinder that Tut Braithwaite and Nick Estcourt were using for sleeping, ran out at about two a.m. They lay half awake for a time, just willing each other to start making a brew, and finally Nick won the contest; Tut was thirstier and got his arm out of the sleeping bag to light the stove. Getting ready in the morning is a slow process. It took them three hours to have a couple of brews, nibble some chocolate and get dressed, setting out from camp just after half past five. Mick Burke and I could afford to be more leisured in our approach, for once again we were short of rope and were going to have to await the arrival of two Sherpas setting out early from Camp 4 with enough rope, we hoped, to reach the top of the Rock Band. As a result the sun was already on the slope when we set out.

I felt bad from the very start that day. I suspect it was partially the result of spending a night without any sleeping oxygen, but also of general fatigue, for this was my fourth day at Camp 5, and I had been on the go without a day's rest for six days. I felt as if I hadn't slept at all. Mick Burke, who had a heavy load of film gear in addition to a couple of ropes, was going just a little slower than I. The sun hammered down as we slogged up the endless slope, but at least we had well-trodden steps. The tracks we had made the previous day had filled in during the night but Nick and Tut had rebroken the trail and by this time had reached our high point of the previous day. It was like the first climb of the day on any crag in Britain; the ritual to decide who should lead the first pitch. Tut had hidden a small piece of rock in the palm of one hand, had held out his clenched fists and told Nick to guess which hand. Nick had guessed wrong. Tut led.

By the time I caught up with them Tut was out of sight

round the corner. There was a hammering of a piton, scuffling in the snow, but no movement at all. I was tired and petulant and asked Tut what the hell he was doing. We'd never get up the Rock Band if he couldn't even get into the foot of the gully. Tut ignored me; probably didn't even hear. The climbing was the most difficult we had yet encountered, with insubstantial snow lying over steep smooth rock. There were hardly any piton cracks and insufficient snow for a deadman anchor. It would have been awkward at any altitude, but at nearly 27000 feet, encased in high-altitude clothing with an oxygen mask clamped over the face, it was desperate.

Cramponed boots slithered on the sloping rock holds, there was nothing for his glove-encased hands. He stuck his axe into the snow, but it just tore through the loosely coagu-lated powder. He managed to hammer a long ice piton a couple of inches into a crack, clipped into it, and then, taking rope tension from Nick, leant across from one small spur to the next, his balance thrown out by the weight of his rucksack holding oxygen cylinder and spare rope. He reached a haven of balance, panting hard into the set, paused for breath, and then continued the delicate traverse, using three more pitons for protection and aid. This was real climbing; fatigue and altitude, the grinding plods up lines of fixed rope were all forgotten in the riveted concentration of negotiating those few feet. The angle began to ease, the snow deepened, he was in the flared-out funnel leading to the dark gash of the Left-Hand Gully. He buried a snow anchor, fastened the rope and called Nick up to join him. I followed.

Nick led out the next pitch into the mouth of the gully. It was about twelve feet wide, with sheer inescapable rock walls towering on either side. The floor of the gully was covered in deep compact snow, sweeping smoothly at an angle of about fifty degrees to a snowclad overhanging bulge which probably covered a rock jammed between the gully walls. Above this first barrier, it stretched up to a point where the gully curved slightly and seemed to open out, for the upper part was lit by sunlight. A small spindrift avalanche curled down the right-hand retaining wall. It wasn't big enough to be danger-ous, but it made me feel very vulnerable. We were in a trap;

there was no shelter from any big avalanche that might pour down that gully.

In the bottom of the gully we were in deep shade. Nick had run out of oxygen, taken off his mask and abandoned the bottle, but was determined to keep going. It was now Tut's turn to lead and he kicked up the even slope leading to the jammed rock about fifty feet above. He describes what happened next.

On the right there appeared to be a ledge with a possible belay but there were no cracks for pitons and the ledge turned out to be little more than a sloping shelf. I'd run out of rope but managed to pull a spare one out of my sack, tied on and then threw the tangle down to Nick fifty feet below, with the idea that he could sort out the tangle while I negotiated the overhang.

By this time Chris had caught up with us and had started to untangle the rope, muttering abuse about inefficiency and how stupid it had been to just throw the rope down, without first untangling it. He didn't realize that this was an arrangement that Nick and I had already worked out to save time. Chris insisted that I shouldn't move till he'd sorted out the mess. An understanding glance from Nick, but we both kept quiet until he had it sorted out some dozen curses later.

I placed an angle piton on the right and wriggled up the groove between the rock and the wall behind, my oxygen bottle catching on every protrusion, boots kicking in thin air. At last, panting hard, I was above it. The gully narrowed and steepened; excellent snow conditions made the next section almost enjoyable. Above me were huge overhangs, with powder snow streaming down over them, from either side of the gully. How the hell were we going to get out?

I managed to find a good piton belay, and Nick, moving slowly but with great determination, followed up the rope. I set out again and soon the gully widened. I had to see what there was round the corner, but had now run out of rope. I tied onto my last rope, dropped the slack to Nick and carried on for another sixty feet; then at last I could see out to the right. There seemed to be a gangway leading up to some snow ledges. Too tired even to tell the others I just kept going until a small rocky step stopped me. It looked easier on the right and I edged my way over, stepped carefully up sloping little rock ledges, nothing much for the hands. I was excited at the prospects offered by the gangway, and totally involved in the climbing. Suddenly my oxygen ran out. I don't think I shall ever forget the feeling of suffocation as I ripped the mask away from my face. I was on the brink of falling, beginning to panic, felt a warm trickle run down my leg. God, what's happening? Scrabbled up the rock arête until at last I reached some firm snow. I collapsed, exhausted. I had no runners out and was over a hundred feet above Nick; I'd have had it if I'd fallen. I just dug my axe into the snow and hung on to it till I got my breath back; got a grip of myself. I then got my rucksack off, took the oxygen bottle out, shoved that in the snow and belayed on to it.

Tut had reached a spot where the gully widened out into a small amphitheatre. The main arm of the gully continued to the left, but a ramp forked out to the right, beneath an impending wall of yellow rock. This seemed to lead out above the Rock Band. Nick, ever courageous, followed up the rope to join Tut. He had almost become accustomed to going without oxygen, and said later that he had felt like a hundred-and-five-year-old war veteran and had paced himself accordingly.

Tut had stopped about twenty feet below the bottom of the ramp. Nick led on through to the beginning of the rocks, brought Tut up to him, but then was determined to have his full fair share of leading even though it meant tackling what was obviously going to be a difficult piece of climbing, without oxygen. At least he wasn't going to be blinkered by the mask and encumbered by the rucksack containing the bottle. The first few feet were quite straightforward; the ramp sloped off gently and had a reasonable covering of snow; but after twenty feet it tapered into nothing, forcing Nick into the impending wall, which, in turn, forced him out of balance. The snow was thin and insubstantial over steep, hideously loose rock. There was nothing for his feet, no holds for his hands. The snow was too soft to use his ice axe. His entire weight was now resting on his left arm which he had jammed behind a boss of snow that had formed between the impending wall above and what was left of the ramp.

Somehow he had to get in a piton. He tried to clear the snow away with his other hand, but the rock was either smooth and compact or, on the ramp itself, little more than rubble, cemented together by snow.

I was getting desperate; goggles all misted up, panting helplessly. I somehow managed to clear some of the snow behind the boss, using my fingers, while my arm still held weight. I was losing strength fast. I think the others thought I was about to fall off, but whatever happened I wasn't going to give up. If I had, and let Tut do it, I'd have kicked myself for years.

Anyway, I found a crack that was about an inch wide, fumbled for a piton that was the right size. It was hanging on my harness behind my back, couldn't see it, didn't have any sense of feel with my gloves. Somehow got an angle peg that was the right size, eased it behind the boss and shoved it into the crack. I then had to get out my hammer, had a desperate struggle to pull it out of my holster. It had jammed somehow, but I couldn't see how. I got it out at last and managed to tap in the piton.

It was obviously useless, but if you pulled it, in just one direction, it was safe. I managed to lean out on it a little bit, walked my feet up, jammed my other arm behind the boss, reached up, dug into the snow and found something, I'm not sure what, and just kept going. It was still hard and there was nothing secure to hold on to or stand on. It was a question of just keeping going.

I now came out into the sun, and the snow was even softer, no longer holding the rocks together. I just had to keep going. I couldn't possibly have got back even if I'd wanted to. Another twenty feet, and I found a decent crack, got a good peg in and brought Tut up. Given the conditions it was the hardest pitch I've ever led.

In leading it, Nick had solved the problem of the Rock Band and had led the most difficult pitch on the South West Face of Everest. We had been waiting, cold and anxious, down below. Tut followed Nick up, jumaring up the rope, while Mick Burke and I started back down the fixed ropes. That day the pair in front pushed on another forty feet, on to a snow spur that seemed to lead up onto the Upper Snow Field. We dropped down tired but jubilant. Nick and Tut had cracked the Rock Band.

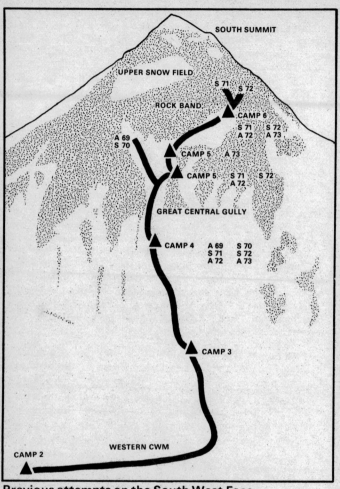

SOUTH SUMMIT

UPPER SNOW FIELD

S 71   S 72

ROCK BAND

CAMP 6
S 71   S 72
A 72   A 73

A 69
S 70

CAMP 5   A 73

CAMP 5   S 71   S 72
A 72

GREAT CENTRAL GULLY

CAMP 4   A 69   S 70
S 71   S 72
A 72   A 73

CAMP 3

WESTERN CWM

CAMP 2

Previous attempts on the South West Face

A 69 Japanese reconnaissance expedition in autumn 1969
S 70 Japanese expedition in spring 1970
S 71 International expedition in spring 1971
A 72 Bonington's 13-man British expedition in autumn 1972
A 73 Japanese expedition in autumn 1973
Note—the autumn 1972 and autumn 1973 expeditions both reached the
    height of Camp 6 at 27,300 ft, but did not establish camp there.

photo Keichi Yamada

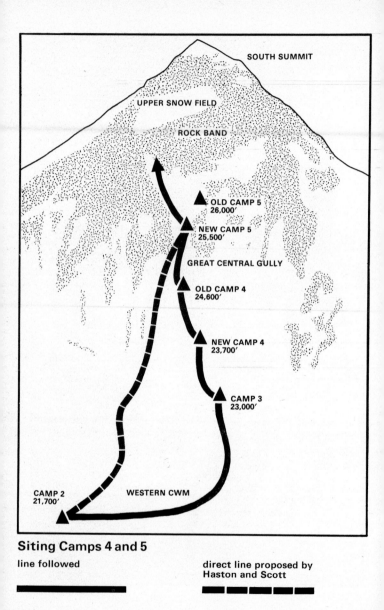

Siting Camps 4 and 5

line followed

direct line proposed by
Haston and Scott

photo Keichi Yamada

Overleaf An aerial view of the South West face
looking North East into Tibet

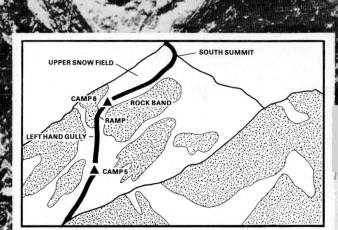

Aerial view of the South West Face which clearly shows the route through the Left-Hand Gully and up the ramp. We only saw this photograph by Keichi Yamada after our successful ascent. If we had seen it before we should have known there was an almost one hundred per cent certainty of climbing the Rock Band by this route.

photo Keichi Yamada

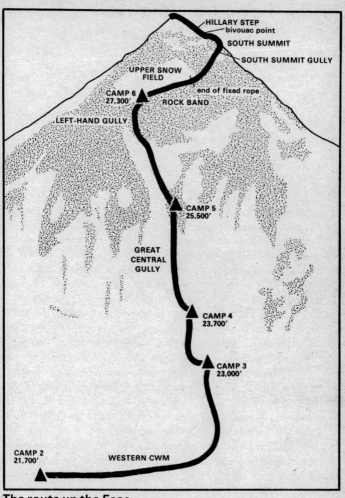

The route up the Face

13   Poised for the top

(21 September–22 September)

The return to Camp 5 seemed even further, even more arduous, than the way up. I stopped for a rest every few feet, slid down the ropes on my backside wherever possible and had to force myself to take each step on the last traverse back to the camp. It was five o'clock, time for the evening call, but I was too tired to think, let alone talk, and asked Doug Scott to take it. With a bit of luck I would come round in an hour's time, and asked him to arrange a later call. It was all I could do to dump my pack frame, pull off my boots and collapse into my sleeping bag. The others were just as tired.

Ang Phurba had moved up to Camp 5 that day and was sleeping in my tent. He brewed up endless mugfuls of tea through the evening to slake my thirst. Between gulps of hot tea, I dozed and from time to time tried to force my addled brain to come to grips with the problem, not only of ensuring we had everything we needed for the summit bid but also for subsequent ascents.

Six o'clock came all too fast, however, and I hadn't managed to plan out anything further than our requirements for the following day. Dougal Haston, Mike Thompson, Pertemba and Tenzing were to move up to Camp 5 next morning. Dave Clarke was going to take over the running of Camp 4 from Mike and had already moved up so that Mike could put him in the picture. Pete Boardman seemed an obvious potential candidate for one of the summit bids after that of Doug and Dougal. So I asked him also to go up to Camp 4, not fully appreciating how the others at Camp 2 would interpret my action. At the end of the call, Martin came up on the radio and asked if I had any plans for him; all I could do was ask him to wait patiently till the next day, the 21st, when I hoped to plan the subsequent ascents in detail.

I spent much of the night trying to balance out different permutations of climbers. I had originally planned on just one subsequent ascent; back in England even this seemed optimistic, but our progress had been so fast that for some days it had seemed we might be able to have a series of ascents as long as the weather lasted. The obvious choices for the second ascent were Tut Braithwaite and Nick Estcourt. They were here at Camp 5, had shown that they were fully capable of making a fast safe summit bid and had opened the way for Doug and Dougal. We had discussed the second summit bid and I had told them that they would be making it, but now I began to worry about the wider implications of what I had said. I was all too aware of how frustrated the lead climbers sitting it out at Camp 2 must be. If I allowed Nick and Tut to stay up at Camp 5 for the second summit bid, I should be excluding the rest of the team from all further involvement in the climb as they waited their turns in the queue for the summit. I therefore reluctantly decided I should have to break the news to Nick and Tut that I wanted them to return to Camp 2, to go to the back of the queue, and let some of the others have their turn.

I then began to think of the ascents themselves. I definitely wanted to include at least one Sherpa in the subsequent ascents. Quite apart from having promised Pertemba that I would try to get a Sherpa up, they had done so much to help us, entered so much into the spirit of the expedition that I felt it only fair that they shared in the summit experience. But that meant one less place for the climbers.

It then occurred to me that we might be able to support a party of four at Camp 6. This would mean that we could avoid a long-drawn-out series of summit bids and, in two further bids, get another eight to the top. Quite apart from the extra tent, this meant at least ten bottles of oxygen, five loads to be carried up to 6 for each four-man summit bid. I began to work on it in the early hours of the morning. We had to get all that oxygen and a bit of food up to Camp 5, then on to Camp 6. We had to do this with the Sherpas and climbers we had available, allowing them sufficient rest days and the necessary changeovers at both Camps 4 and 5. How many carries would anyone be able to make from Camp 5 to 6? This carry was obviously going to be long and arduous. But by breakfast I had worked out that it was logistically feasible. It was now a matter of fitting names to the eight places for the two subsequent bids. Tut and Nick were going to be in the third summit bid, and I climbed up to their tent to break the news. They took it marvellously well, even though it must have been infuriating to have to give up all that height, in dropping back to Camp 2, only to come back up again in six days' time.

I then started to work out the other possible places. A couple of days earlier, Hamish had told me over the radio that he was going to drop back down to Camp 1, whose Ice Island seemed on the point of sliding down the Ice Fall. Hamish was going to see if we needed to resite the camp. I knew that he was still suffering from the after-effects of the powder-snow avalanche and assumed that he would not be sufficiently fit to make a summit bid. Allen Fyffe also seemed out of the running. He had acclimatized very slowly and had not yet managed to get above Camp 4. Of the lead climbers, this left Mick Burke with me at Camp 5, Pete Boardman, who was now at Camp 4, Martin Boysen and Ronnie Richards at Camp 2. Mick had been moving slightly more slowly than I on the fixed ropes, but he was cheerful and seemed able to pace himself well. In addition he had consistently been carrying heavy loads, determined not only to fulfil his filming commitment as the BBC high-altitude cameraman, but also to contribute to the climbing of the mountain as a climber. I very much wanted it to be a good film and to give Mick as much scope as possible. I therefore decided to put him into the second summit party. Martin and Pete were two other obvious candidates, so I included them and brought it up to four with the inclusion of a Sherpa. On this score I consulted Pertemba, telling him that I would like to put a Sherpa into both the second and third summit bids. He nominated himself for the second ascent and Ang Phurba for the third team. That left just one place on the third ascent, with three possible candidates, Mike Thompson, Ronnie Richards and myself.

The lure of the summit; I couldn't resist it, but would I be fit enough? The third summit team wouldn't move up to Camp 6 until 27 September. It was now the 21st and I had already been up for a week. But I felt fine, rationalized that this was the best place for me to stay until everyone was ready to come down from the mountain. But what about Mike or Ronnie? Would they want to go for the summit? I rationalized once again that my experience was greater than theirs. In those final days of the expedition I think we were all in a state of euphoria, were rather like a group of men suddenly offered the chance of a limitless fortune, were looking at each other assessing each other's share.

I announced the results of my logistic planning at the two o'clock radio call. Martin Boysen recollects the impact at Camp 2.

We waited tensed with expectation and ambition. Hamish took the call and Chris came over loud and clear in the warm air of the afternoon.

'I've decided after a lot of thought . . .' Wait for it, I listened only for the names not the justifications . . . 'Mick, Martin, Pete and Pertemba . . .' Thank God for that. 'Tut, Nick, Ang Phurba . . .' I had no further interest in listening; I had been given my chance and now I looked at the others. Poor Allen, his face hardened with disappointment as the names poured out, but not his own. The radio stopped and everyone departed quietly with their own hopes, ambitions and disappointments.

Back at Camp 5, we were absorbed in our preparations for the morrow, sorting out the loads, ensuring that Doug and Dougal would have everything they needed to push the route out above the Rock Band. The four o'clock call came with more logistic details, last-minute demands of gear to be brought up to the camp the following morning. I discovered there was a critical lack of oxygen bottles for our summit attempts and had to arrange for a midnight carry from Base Camp, for it to get up the mountain in time. Pertemba then had to deploy his Sherpas and spent half an hour on the radio talking to Camp 4, Camp 2 and Base. As the wireless closed down he told me that Charlie wanted to talk to me privately at seven o'clock that night. I waited, intrigued, slightly worried to hear what he had to tell me.

Seven o'clock came. Nobody else would be listening out on any of the radios littered up and down the mountain. Charlie's voice came over the air from Camp 2. He asked me to reconsider my decision to stay on at Camp 5 and take part in the third summit bid, pointed out the length of time that I had been living above 25000 feet, the fact that my voice was often slurred over the radio, that my calls that day had sometimes been muddled. He also made the point that I was getting out of contact with the situation on the rest of the mountain, my eyes focused on establishing the top camp and making the summit.

He also told me that he had come to this conclusion without consulting any of the others and was approaching me in his capacity as expedition doctor. It certainly made sense, even brought out some of the doubts that had lurked in the back of my mind. I agreed to think it over, and then Charlie told me that Hamish would also like to talk to me. There was a pause, and then Hamish's clipped Scots voice crackled through the speaker. 'I've decided to go home, Chris.' I was staggered, but he went on to tell me that he was still feeling the after-effects of his experience in the avalanche and was worried about the state of his lungs. I could understand how he felt and accepted his decision. We were all sorry to see Hamish forced to leave when a successful outcome seemed to close. He had done so much to help achieve it, in designing the face boxes and the assault box in which Dougal and Doug were comfortably ensconced two thousand feet above me, in building our bridges in the Ice Fall and Western Cwm and in setting up Camp 4; most of all though for his quiet sense of humour and canny judgement that had helped us along throughout the expedition.

Once the wireless was switched off, I began to consider my course of action. I had undoubtedly become divorced from the rest of the team down below; I didn't feel, however, that I was suffering from anoxia, or had been muddled in my thinking. I doubt if I could have worked out our plan for the next week any quicker or better had I been down at Camp 2;

in fact it would have been much more difficult there, for it was only by moving up to Camp 5 that I had been able to get a full understanding of the problems involved and what we were all capable of in terms of load carrying and lengths of stay at the various camps. At the same time, though, I had undoubtedly become obsessive in my drive for the summit, an obsession which I suspect was necessary to build the essential urgency for the summit bid. Combined with this obsessiveness, however, I had just, and only just, managed to make logistic sense. We had the supplies we needed at Camp 5 and the ability to sustain the subsequent summit bids. Charlie Clarke had brought home to me that I was being unwise in putting myself into that third summit team, for by then, if I stayed at Camp 5, I should have been there for nearly a fortnight, much too long a stay at that altitude under any circumstances, let alone prior to trying to reach the summit of Everest. I decided therefore to hand over to Ronnie Richards, who would be better rested than I and certainly deserved the chance. Mike Thompson had decided to go down for a rest after making a tiring carry. I flirted with the thought that perhaps Allen Fyffe, Dave Clarke, Mike Thompson and I could make a fourth summit bid, and with these thoughts dropped off to sleep.

The following morning, 22 September, eight of us set out for Camp 6. Dougal and Doug left first, for they were going to have to complete the route from the top of the ramp on to the Upper Ice Field where they hoped to find a suitable camp site. Ang Phurba, probably the strongest and most talented of all the Sherpas, followed close on their heels, dressed in ski pants and sweater, his oxygen set and mask looking incongruous with such attire. Pertemba and Tenzing went at a slightly more leisured rate, while Mike Thompson, Mick Burke and I brought up the rear.

The chapter that follows belongs to Dougal Haston and Doug Scott, and I leave them to tell their story between them.

14 The summit

(23 September—25 September)

DOUG SCOTT: I caught Dougal up at the bottom of the Rock Band and carried on up into the foot of the gully. I cleared the rope of ice as I jumared up, conscious of the struggle that Tut must have had, firstly traversing into the gully and then clambering over a giant snow-covered chock stone half-way up. I noted the new perspective with interest, for the ropes led through a huge gash – a veritable Devil's Kitchen of a chasm 300 feet deep into the rocks, whereas the rest of Everest had been wide slopes and broad open valleys. At the top of the gully I followed Nick's rope out and up steeply right. I clipped onto the rope, using it as a safety rail, rather than pulling on it directly with my jumars, for he had warned me that the rope was anchored to pegs of dubious quality. It was awkward climbing with a framed rucksack, especially as the straps kept slipping on crucial hard sections. Nick had done a first-class job leading it without oxygen. I was glad to get to his high point and hammer in extra pegs.

Ang Phurba came up the rope next, for Dougal had stopped lower down to adjust his crampons which kept falling off his sponge overboots and also to disentangle the remains of Nick's rope. Ang Phurba belayed me with all the confidence of a regular Alpine climber. I think he is the most natural climber I have ever met amongst the Sherpas. After only thirty feet of difficult climbing I tied off the rope and Ang Phurba came up to me. I stood there exhausted from having climbed a vertical ten-foot block with too much clothing and too heavy a sack. From there I led out 250 feet of rope to a site for Camp 6. Ang Phurba came up and we both kicked out a small notch in a ridge of snow which could be enlarged to take our summit box tent. Dougal came up with his crampons swinging from his waist.

DOUGAL HASTON: I hauled on to the proposed site of Camp 6. Straight away my energy and upward urges came rushing back – there ahead in reality was the way we'd been hypothetically tracing for so long with fingers on photographs and making us forget everything else was the fact it looked feasible. There was a steepish-looking rock pitch just ahead, but after it seemed like unbroken snow slopes to the couloir. It looked as if progress was inevitable as long as the others were successful in their carry. Ang Phurba kept muttering about a camp site further up under some rocks, but this looked like wasted effort to us, as the traverse line started logically from where we were at the moment. Diplomatically we told him that we were staying there, it being mainly Doug's and my concern, as we were going to have to occupy the camp, and he started off down leaving his valuable load. We began digging in spells, without oxygen, but using some to regain strength during the rests.

Mick, Chris and Mick arrived one after the other looking tired, as well they should be. Carrying heavy loads at over 27 000 feet is no easy occupation.

DOUG SCOTT: Theirs had been a magnificent carry, especially Chris who had now been at Camp 5 and above for eight days and also Mick who was carrying a dead weight of cine equipment. He had been at Camp 5 for five days, and Pertemba had worked hard practically every day of the expedition carrying heavy loads and encouraging his Sherpas. While Mike Thompson, who had never been above 23 000 feet before, had arrived carrying a heavy sack with apparent ease at 27 300 feet. We sat there talking confidently in the late afternoon sun. There was a strong bond of companionship as there had been all the way up the Face. One by one they departed for Camp 5 and they left us with the bare essentials to make this last step to the top of our route and perhaps the summit itself. I yelled our thanks down to Mike as they were sliding back down the rope. He must have known his chances of making a summit bid were slim yet he replied, 'Just you get up, that's all the reward I need.' And that's how it had been from start to finish with all members of the team. It had taken the combined effort of forty Sherpas and sixteen climbers, together with Chris's planning, to get the two of us into this position. We knew how lucky we were being the representatives of such a team and to be given the chance to put the finishing touches to all our efforts. Finally Mick left, having run all the film he had through the cameras. Dougal and I were left alone to dig out a more substantial platform and to erect the two-man summit tent. We were working without oxygen and took frequent rests to recover, but also to look across the Upper Snow Field leading up to the South Summit couloir. After the tent was up Dougal got inside to prepare the evening meal, while I pottered about outside stowing away equipment in a little ice cave and tying empty oxygen bottles around the tent to weight it down. They hung in festoons on either side of the snow arête. Finally I bundled rope and oxygen bottles into our sacks for the following morning and dived into the tent to join Dougal.

DOUGAL HASTON: Inside, we worked on plans for the next day. We had 500 metres of rope for fixing along the traverse and hoped to do that, then come back to 6 and make our big push the day after.

I was higher on Everest than I'd ever been before, yet thoughts of the summit were still far away in the thinking and hoping process. It had all seemed so near before in 1971 and 1972: euphoric nights at Camps 5 and 6 when progress had seemed good and one tended to skip the difficult parts with visions of oneself standing at the top of the South West Face, then really shattering the dreams in progressive phases as realization of certain failure burst the bubble. There had been an inevitability about both previous failures, but still carrying a lot of disappointment. Failure you must accept but that does not make it any easier, especially on a project like the South West Face where so much thinking, willpower and straight physical effort are necessary to get to the higher points. This time it seemed better. We were above the Rock Band and the ground ahead looked climbable, but I kept a rigid limit on my thoughts, contemplating possible progress along the traverse to the exit couloir, nothing more. If that proved possible then I would allow for further up-type thinking.

Our physical situation felt comfortable. Maybe that is a reflection of the degree of progress that we have made in our adaptation to altitude. Many the story we had read or been told about assault camps on the world's highest peak. No one ever seemed to spend a comfortable night at Camp 6 on the South Col route. Their nights seemed to be compounded of sleeplessness, discomfort and thirst. Here there was none of that. The situation was very bearable. We weren't stretched personally, didn't even feel tired or uncomfortable, despite a long day. The stove brewed the hours away – tea, lemon drinks and even a full-scale meal with meat and mashed potatoes. Each was deep into his own thoughts with only one slightly urgent communal reaction as a change of oxygen cylinder went wrong and the gas stove roared into white heat. Order was restored before an explosion, with Doug fixing the leak at the same time as I turned off the stove. Emergency over, we laughed, conjuring visions of the reaction at Camp 2 as Camp 6 exploded like a successfully attacked missile target. It would have been a new reason for failure!

Thereafter sleep claimed its way and I moved gently into another world of tangled dreams, eased by a gentle flow of oxygen. The night was only disturbed by a light wind rocking our box and a changing of sleeping cylinders. One would need to be a good or very exhausted sleeper to sleep through a cylinder running out. From a gentle warm comfort one suddenly feels cold, uneasy and very awake. Just after midnight and the changeover, we gave up sleeping and started the long task of preparing for the morning's work.

Shortly after first light I moved out into blue and white dawn to continue the upward way, leaving Doug wrapped in all the down in the tent mouth, cameras and belays set up for action. There was a rock step lurking ahead that had seemed reasonably close in the setting afternoon sun of the previous day. Now in the clear first light a truer perspective was established, as I kept on thrusting into the deep powdered fifty-degree slope, sliding sideways like a crab out of its element reaching for an object that didn't seem to come any closer. 100 metres of this progress it was, before I could finally fix a piton and eye the rock step. It wasn't long, seven or eight metres, but looked difficult enough. Downward sloping, steep slabs with a layer of powder. Interesting work. Grade 5 at this height. Much concentration and three more pitons saw a delicate rightwards exit and back, temporarily thankful, into deep snow to finish the rope length and finally give Doug the signal to move.

DOUG SCOTT: I traversed on his rope and up the difficult rocks to his stance. I led out another 400 feet over much easier ground, parallel with the top of the Rock Band. We gradually warmed to the task and began to enjoy our position. After all the months of dreaming, here we were cutting across that Upper Snow Field. Dougal led out the next reel of rope.

DOUGAL HASTON: The conditions and climbing difficulty began to change again. Kicking through with crampons there was now no ice beneath. Rock slabs only which have never been renowned for their adherence to front points. A few tentative movements up, down, sideways proved it existed all around. It seemed the time for a tension traverse. But on what? The rock was shattered loose and worse – no cracks. Scraping away a large area a small moveable flake appeared. It would have to do. Tapping in the beginnings of an angle, which seemed to be OK to pull on it not for a fall, I started tensioning across to an inviting looking snow lump. Thoughts flashed through my mind of a similar traverse nine years before, near the top of the Eiger Direct. There it would have been all over with a slip and suddenly, working it out, things didn't look too good here, if you cared to think in those directions. Not only didn't I care to, I also didn't dare to think of full consequences and chasing the dangerous thoughts away concentrated on tiptoeing progress. Slowly the limit of tension was reached and feet were on some vaguely adhering snow. It would have to do for the present, were my thoughts as I let go the rope and looked around. A couple of probes with the axe brought nothing but a sense of commitment.

'No man is an island', it is said. I felt very close to a realization of the contrary of this, standing on that semi-secure snow step in the midst of a sea of insecurity. But there was no racing adrenalin only the cold clinical thought of years of experience. About five metres away the snow appeared to deepen. It would have to be another tension traverse. Long periods of excavation found no cracks. Tugs on the rope and impatient shouting from Doug. Communication at altitude is bad in awkward situations. One has to take off the oxygen mask to shout. Then when one tries to do this the throat is so dry and painful that nothing comes out. Hoping that Doug would keep his cool I carried on looking for a piton placement. A reasonable-looking crack came to light and two pitons linked up meant the game could go on. This time I felt I could put more bearing weight on the anchor. Just as well. Twice the tension limit failed and there was the skidding movement backwards on the scraping slabs. But a third try and a long reach saw me in deep good snow, sucking oxygen violently. The way ahead relented, looking reasonable. My voice gained enough momentum to shout to Doug and soon he was on his way. Following is usually monotone – sliding along on jumars. This one was not so. I could almost see the gleam in Doug's eyes shining through his layers of glasses as he pulled out the first tension piton with his fingers.

'Nasty stuff, youth.'

I had to agree as he passed on through.

DOUG SCOTT: I continued across further, using up one of our two climbing ropes, before dropping down slightly to belay. We had probably come too high, for there was easier snow below the rocks that led right up towards the South Summit couloir. However, avalanches were still cascading down the mountain, so we climbed up to the rocks in an effort to find good peg anchors for the fixed ropes. We didn't want to return the next day to find them hanging over the Rock Band. Dougal led a short section on easy snow, then all the rope was run out and we turned back for camp.

I sat in the snow to take photographs and watched the sun go down over Gaurishankar. What a place to be! I could look straight down and see Camp 2 6000 feet down. There were people moving about between tents, obviously preparing to camp for the night. Mounds of equipment were being covered with tarpaulins, one or two wandered out to the crevasse toilet, others stood about in small groups before diving into their tents for the night. A line of shadow crept up the face to Camp 4 by the time I was back to our tent. I again sorted out loads and pushed in oxygen bottles for the night, whilst Dougal melted down snow for the evening meal.

We discovered over the radio that only Lhakpa Dorje had made the carry to Camp 6 that day. He had managed to bring up vital supplies of oxygen but, unfortunately, the food, cine camera and still film we needed had not arrived. Anyway they were not essential, so we could still make our bid for the summit next day. There was also no more rope in camp, but I think we were both secretly relieved about this. Chris had always insisted that whoever made the first summit bid should lay down as much fixed rope as possible so that if that first attempt failed the effort would not be wasted. This made good sense, but it did take a lot of effort up there and we all longed for the time when we could cut loose from the fixed ropes. It was a perfect evening with no wind at all as we sat looking out of the tent doorways supping mugs of tea. Finally the sun was gone from our tent and lit up only the upper snows, golden turning red, before all the mountain was in shadow. We zipped up the tent door and built up quite a fug of warm air heating up water for corned-beef hash.

DOUGAL HASTON: 500 metres of committing ground was a good day's work on any point of the mountain. The fact that it was all above 27000 feet made our performance-level high and, more to the point, we hadn't exhausted ourselves in doing it. This was crucial because deterioration is rapid at such altitudes. Over tea we discussed what to take next day. I still reckoned deep down on the possibility of a bivouac. Doug seemed reluctant to admit to the straight fact, but didn't disagree when I mentioned packing a tent sac and stove. The packs weren't going to be light. Two oxygen cylinders each would be needed for the undoubtedly long day, plus three

50-metre ropes, also various pitons and karabiners. Even if a bivouac was contemplated we couldn't pack a sleeping bag. This would have been pushing weight too much. The bivouac idea was only for an emergency and we would have hastened that emergency by slowing ourselves down through too much weight – so we tried to avoid the possibility by going as lightly as possible. The only extra I allowed myself was a pair of down socks, reckoning they could be invaluable for warming very cold or even frostbitten feet and hands. There was no sense of drama that evening. Not even any unusual conversation. We radioed down and told those at Camp 2 what we were doing, ate the rest of our food and fell asleep.

DOUG SCOTT: About one in the morning we awoke to a rising wind. It was buffeting the tent, shaking it about and pelting it with spindrift, snow and ice chips. I lay there wondering what the morning would bring, for if the wind increased in violence we should surely not be able to move. At about 2.30 we began slowly to wind ourselves up for the climb. We put a brew on and heated up the remains of the corned-beef hash for breakfast. The wind speed was decreasing slightly as we put on our frozen boots and zipped up our suits. Dougal chose his duvet suit, whilst I took only my windproofs, hoping to move faster and easier without the restriction of tightly packed feathers around my legs. I had never got round to sorting out a duvet suit that fitted me properly.

Because of the intense cold it was essential to put on crampons, harnesses, even the rucksack and oxygen system in the warmth of the tent. Just after 3.30 we emerged to get straight on to the ropes and away to the end. It was a blustery morning, difficult in the dark and miserable in the cold. It was one of those mornings when you keep going because he does and he, no doubt, because you do. By the time we had passed the end of the fixed ropes the sun popped up from behind the South Summit and we awoke to the new day. It was exhilarating to part company with our safety line, for that is after all what fixed ropes are. They facilitate troop movements, but at the same time they do detract from the adventure of the climb. Now at last we were committed and it felt good to be out on our own.

DOUGAL HASTON: There's something surrealistic about being alone high on Everest at this hour. No end to the strange beauty of the experience. Alone, enclosed in a mask with the harsh rattle of your breathing echoing in your ears. Already far in the west behind Cho Oyu a few pale strands of the day and ahead and all around a deep midnight blue with the South Summit sharply, whitely, defined in my line of vision and the always predawn wind picking up stray runnels of spindrift and swirling them gently, but not malignantly, around me. Movement was relaxed and easy. Passing by yesterday's tension points only a brief flash of them came into memory. They were stored for future remembrances, but the today mind was geared for more to come. Not geared with any sense of nervousness or foreboding just happily relaxed, waiting – anticipating. Signs of life on the rope behind indicated that Doug was following apace and I waited at yesterday's abandoned oxygen cylinders as he came up with the sun, almost haloed in silhouette, uncountable peaks as his background. But no saint this.

'All right, youth?' in a flat Nottingham accent.

'Yeah, yourself?'

A nod and the appearance of a camera for sunrise pictures answered this question, so I tied on the rope and started breaking new ground. The entrance to the couloir wasn't particularly good, but there again it was not outstandingly bad by Himalayan standards, merely knee-deep powder snow with the occasional make-you-think hard patch where there was no snow base on the rock. On the last part before entering the couloir proper there was a longish section of this where we just climbed together relying on each other's ability, rope trailing in between, there being no belays to speak of.

The rope length before the rock step changed into beautiful hard front pointing snow ice but the pleasure suddenly seemed to diminish. Leading, my progress started to get slower. By now the signs were well known. I knew it wasn't me. One just doesn't degenerate so quickly. Oxygen again. It seemed early for a cylinder to run out. Forcing it, I reached a stance beneath the rock step. Rucksack off. Check cylinder gauge first. Still plenty left. That's got to be bad. It must be the system. Doug comes up. We both start investigating. Over an hour we played with it. No avail. Strangely enough I felt quite calm and resigned about everything. I say strangely, because if the system had proved irreparable then our summit chance would have been ruined. There was only a quiet cloud of disappointment creeping over our heads. Doug decided to try extreme unction. 'Let's take it apart piece by piece, kid. There's nothing to lose.' I merely nodded as he started prising apart the jubilee clip which held the tube on to the mouthpiece. At last something positive – a lump of ice was securely blocked in the junction. Carving it out with a knife, we tentatively stuck the two points together again, then shut off the flow so we could register oxygen being used. A couple of hard sucks on the mask – that was it. I could breathe freely again.

Doug started out on the rock step, leaving me contemplating the escape we'd just had. I was still thinking very calmly about it, but could just about start to imagine what my feelings of disgust would have been like down below if we'd been turned back by mechanical failure. Self-failure you have to accept, bitter though it can be. Defeat by bad weather also, but to be turned back by failure of a humanly constructed system would have left a mental scar. But now it was upward thinking again. Idly, but carefully, I watched Doug. He was climbing well. Slowly, relaxed, putting in the odd piton for protection. Only his strangely masked and hump-backed appearance gave any indication that he was climbing hard rock at 28 000 feet.

DOUG SCOTT: At first I worked my way across from Dougal's stance easily in deep soft snow, but then it steepened and thinned out until it was all a veneer covering the yellow amorphous rock underneath. I went up quite steeply for thirty feet, hoping the front points of my crampons were dug well into the sandy rock underneath the snow. I managed to get in three pegs in a cluster, hoping that one of them might hold, should I fall off. However, the next thirty feet were less steep and the snow lay thicker, which was fortunate seeing as I had run out of oxygen. I reached a stance about a hundred feet above Dougal and with heaving lungs I started to anchor off the rope. I pounded in the last of our rock pegs and yelled down to Dougal to come up. Whilst he was prussiking up the rope I took photographs and changed over to my remaining full bottle of oxygen. I left the empty bottle tied on the pegs.

We were now into the South Summit couloir and a way seemed clear to the top of the South West Face. We led another rope length each and stopped for a chat about the route. Dougal's sporting instincts came to the fore – he fancied a direct gully straight up to the Hillary step. I wasn't keen on account of the soft snow, so he shrugged his shoulders and continued off towards the South Summit. I don't know whether the direct way would have been any less strenuous, but from now on the route to the South Summit became increasingly difficult.

DOUGAL HASTON: The South West Face wasn't going to relax its opposition one little bit. That became very evident as I ploughed into the first rope length above the rock step. I had met many bad types of snow conditions in eighteen years of climbing. Chris and I had once been shoulder deep retreating from a winter attempt on a new line on the North Face of the Grandes Jorasses. The snow in the couloir wasn't that deep, but it seemed much worse to handle. In the Alps we had been retreating, now we were trying to make progress. Progress? The word seemed almost laughable as I moved more and more slowly. A first step and in up to the waist. Attempts to move upward only resulted in a deeper sinking motion. Time for new techniques: steps up, sink in, then start clearing away the slope in front like some breast-stroking snow plough and eventually you pack enough together to be able to move a little further and sink in only to your knees. Two work-loaded rope lengths like this brought us to the choice of going leftwards on the more direct line I had suggested to

Doug in an earlier moment of somewhat undisciplined thinking. By now my head was in control again and I scarcely gave it a glance, thinking that at the current rate of progress we'd be lucky to make even the South Summit.

It seemed that conditions would have to improve but they didn't. The slope steepened to sixty degrees and I swung rightwards, heading for a rock step in an attempt to get out of this treadmill of nature. No relief for us. The snow stayed the same, but not only was it steeper, we were now on open wind-blown slopes and there was a hard breakable crust. Classic wind slab avalanche conditions. In some kind of maniacal cold anger I ploughed on. There was no point in stopping for belays. There weren't any possibilities. I had a rhythm, so kept the evil stroking upwards with Doug tight on my heels. Two feet in a hole, I'd bang the slope to shatter the crust, push away the debris, move up, sink in. Thigh. Sweep away. Knees. Gain a metre. Then repeat the process. It was useful having Doug right behind, as sometimes, when it was particularly difficult to make progress, he was able to stick two hands in my back to stop me sliding backwards. Hours were flashing like minutes, but it was still upward gain.

DOUG SCOTT: I took over the awful work just as it was beginning to ease off. I clambered over some rocks poking out of the snow and noticed that there was a cave between the rocks and the névé ice ; a good bivvy for later perhaps. Just before the South Summit I rested whilst Dougal came up. I continued round the South Summit rock whilst Dougal got his breath. I was crawling on all fours with the wind blowing up spindrift snow all around. I collapsed into a belay position just below the frontier ridge and took in the rope as Dougal came up my tracks. After a few minutes' rest we both stood up and climbed onto the ridge and there before us was Tibet.

After all those months spent in the Western Cwm over this and two other expeditions now at last we could look out of the Cwm to the world beyond – the rolling brown lands of Tibet in the north and north-east, to Kangchenjunga and just below us Makalu and Chomo Lonzo. Neither of us said much, we just stood there absorbed in the scene.

DOUGAL HASTON: The wind was going round the South Summit like a mad maypole. The Face was finished, successfully climbed, but there was no calm to give much thought to rejoicing. It should have been a moment for elation but wasn't. Certainly we'd climbed the Face but neither of us wanted to stop there. The summit was beckoning.

Often in the Alps it seems fine to complete one's route and not go to the summit, but in the Himalayas it's somewhat different. An expedition is not regarded as being totally successful unless the top is reached. Everything was known to us about the way ahead. This was the South East ridge, the original Hillary/Tenzing route of 1953. It was reckoned to be mainly snow, without too much technical difficulty. But snow on the ridge similar to the snow in the couloir would provide a greater obstacle to progress than any technical difficulties. There were dilemmas hanging around and question marks on all plans.

My head was considering sitting in the tent sac until sunset or later, then climbing the ridge when it would be, theoretically, frozen hard. Doug saw the logic of this thinking but obviously wasn't too happy about it. No other suggestions were forthcoming from his direction, however, so I got into the tent sac, got the stove going to give our thinking power a boost with some hot water. Doug began scooping a shallow snow cave in the side of the cornice, showing that he hadn't totally rejected the idea. The hot water passing over our raw, damaged throat linings brought our slide into lethargic pessimism to a sharp halt.

Swinging his pack onto his back Doug croaked, 'Look after the rope. I'm going to at least try a rope length to sample conditions. If it's too bad we'll bivouac. If not we carry on as far as possible.'

I couldn't find any fault with this reasoning, so grabbed the rope as he disappeared back into Nepal. The way it was going quickly through my hands augured well. Reaching the end Doug gave a 'come on' signal. Following quickly I realized that there were now summit possibilities in the wind. Conditions were by no means excellent, but relative to those in the couloir they merited the title reasonable. There was no need to say anything as I reached Doug. He just stepped aside, changed the rope around and I continued. Savage, wonderful country. On the left the South West Face dropped away steeply, to the right wild curving cornices pointed the way to Tibet. Much care was needed but there was a certain elation in our movements. The Hillary Step appeared, unlike any photograph we had seen. No rock step this year, just a break in the continuity of the snow ridge. Seventy degrees of steepness and eighty feet of length. It was my turn to explore again. Conditions reverted to bad, but by now I'd become so inured to the technique that even the extra ten degrees didn't present too much problem.

DOUG SCOTT: As I belayed Dougal up the Hillary Step it gradually dawned upon me that we were going to reach the summit of Big E. I took another photograph of Dougal and wound on the film to find that it was finished. I didn't think I had any more film in my rucksack, for I had left film and spare gloves with the bivvy sheet and stove at the South Summit. I took off my oxygen mask and rucksack and put them on the ridge in front of me. I was sat astride it, one leg in Nepal the other in Tibet. I hoped Dougal's steps would hold, for I could think of no other place to put his rope than between my teeth as I rummaged around in my sack. I found a cassette of colour film that had somehow got left behind several days before. The cold was intense and the brittle film kept breaking off. The wind was strong and blew the snow Dougal was sending down the Nepalese side right back into the air and over into Tibet. I fitted the film into the camera and followed him up. This was the place where Ed Hillary had chimneyed his way up the crevass between the rock and the ice. Now with all the monsoon snow on the mountain it was well banked up, but with snow the consistency of sugar it looked decidedly difficult.

A wide whaleback ridge ran up the last 300 yards. It was just a matter of trail breaking. Sometimes the crust would hold for a few steps and then suddenly we would be stumbling around as it broke through to our knees. All the way along we were fully aware of the enormous monsoon cornices, overhanging the 10000-foot East Face of Everest. We therefore kept well to the left.

It was whilst trail breaking on this last section that I noticed my mind seemed to be operating in two parts, one external to my head. In my head I referred to the external part somewhere over my left shoulder. I rationalized the situation with it making reference to it about not going too far right in the area of the cornice, and it would urge me to keep well to the left. Whenever I stumbled through the crust it suggested that I slowed down and picked my way through more carefully. In general it seemed to give me confidence and seemed such a natural phenomenon that I hardly gave it a second thought at the time. Dougal took over the trail breaking and headed up the final slope to the top – and a red flag flying there. The snow improved and he slackened his pace to let me come alongside. We then walked up side by side the last few paces to the top, arriving there together.

All the world lay before us. That summit was everything and more that a summit should be. My usually reticent partner became expansive, his face broke out into a broad happy smile and we stood there hugging each other and thumping each other's backs. The implications of reaching the highest mountain in the world surely had some bearings on our feelings, I'm sure they did on mine, but I can't say that it was that strong. I can't say either that I felt any relief that the struggle was over. In fact, in some ways it seemed a shame that it was, for we had been fully programmed and now we had to switch off and go back into reverse. But not yet, for the view was so staggering, the disappearing sun so full of colour that the setting held us in awe. I was absorbed by the brown hills of Tibet. They only looked like hills from our lofty summit. They were really high mountains, some of them 24000 feet high, but with hardly any snow to indicate their importance. I could see silver threads of rivers meandering down between them, flowing north and west to bigger rivers which might have included the Tsangpo. Towards the east

Kangchenjunga caught the setting sun, although around to the south clouds boiled down in the Nepalese valleys and far down behind a vast front of black cloud was advancing towards us from the plains of India. It flickered lightning ominously. There was no rush though, for it would be a long time coming over Everest – time to pick out the north side route – the Rongphu Glacier, the East Rongphu Glacier and Changtse in between. There was the North Col, and the place Odell was standing when he last saw Mallory and Irvine climbing up towards him. Wonder if they made it? Their route was hidden by the convex slope – no sign of them, edge out a bit further – no nothing. Not with all that monsoon snow, my external mind pointed out.

The only sign of anyone was the flag, it was some time before I got round to looking at it. It was an unwelcome intrusion and there had been more to do that look at man-made objects. Still, you couldn't help but look at it, seeing as how it was a tripod and a pole nearly five feet high with a rosary of red ribbons attached to the top. Take a photograph. Ah, yes! Dougal ought to get some of me. He hadn't taken a single photograph on the whole trip. 'Here you are, youth. Take a snap for my mother.' I passed him my camera. 'Better take another one, your glove's in front of the lens. Now a black and white one.' He's never been keen on photography, but he obliged.

DOUGAL HASTON: We were sampling a unique moment in our lives. Down and over into the brown plains of Tibet a purple shadow of Everest was projected for what must have been something like 200 miles. On these north and east sides there was a sense of wildness and remoteness, almost untouchability. Miraculous events seemed to be taking place in the region of the sun. One moment it seemed to dip behind a cloud layer lying a little above the horizon. End Game – thought we. But then the cloud dropped faster than the sun and out it came again. Three times in all. I began to feel like Saul on the road to Tarsus. More materially, right in front of me was an aluminium survey pole with a strip of red canvas attached. The Japanese ladies in the spring hadn't mentioned leaving or seeing anything. Puzzlement for a moment. Then the only answer. There had been a Chinese ascent of the North East Ridge claimed, just after the Japanese ascent. Some doubt, however, had been cast on the validity of this, due to the summit pictures lacking the detail associated with previous summit shots. It was good to have the ultimate proof in front of us. Having to play the doubt game in climbing is never a pleasant experience.

Slowly creeping into the euphoria came one very insistent thought as the sun finally won its race with the clouds and slid over the edge. The thought? Well, we were after all on the top of the world but it was still a long way back to Camp 6 and it was going to be dark very soon and then what would we do? We knew we could get back to the South Summit in the half light. On the previous nights there had been a very bright moon and it seemed reasonable to assume we could retrace our steps down the Face if this came out. If it didn't, as a last resort we could bivouac. That after all was the reason for bringing the tent sac. I'd always reckoned a bivouac possible at such altitude, but that doesn't mean to say I looked upon the project with a great degree of enthusiasm. We finally turned our back to the summit and set off down.

Our tracks were already freezing up, making the going reasonable. An abseil got rid of the Hillary Step with the rope left in place. Moving together we were soon back at our little cave. Much cloud activity didn't bode well for the appearance of a moon. The oxygen cylinders dribbled out their last drops of usefulness and became mere burdens. Standing vaguely waiting for some light to happen, it was good to take off the tanks and mask. Lighter feeling but not lighter headed. Slowly, as it clouded over, the choices were gradually cut down. We decided to have a look at the possibility of a descent in the dark, knowing the up-trail to be deep and maybe now frozen, but a tentative fifty-foot grope on the South West Face side of the ridge into the strong night wind with finger and toes going solid finally slammed all the alternative choices to a bivouac out of mind. Dropping back to the sheltered side I told Doug the news. There was nothing really to say. He started enlarging the hole.

DOUG SCOTT: Dougal melted snow on the stove once again whilst I continued digging into the hillside. After we had had a few sips of warm water, Dougal joined me and we quickly enlarged the snow cave, digging away with our ice axes, pushing the loose snow out through the entrance. By nine o'clock it was big enough to lie down in, we pushed out more snow against the entrance and reduced it to a narrow slit. We were now out of the wind, which was fortunate, as already our oxygen bottles were empty, or our sets had refused to function. The little stove, too, was soon used up. So there we lay on top of our rucksacks and the bivvy sheet, wishing perhaps we had given more thought to the possibility of bivouacking, for we had no food and no sleeping bags. I was wearing only the clothes that I had climbed up in, a silk vest, a wool jumper, a nylon pile suite and my wind suit. I don't think we were ever worried about surviving for we had read of other climbers who had spent the night out on Everest without much gear, although lower down. However, they had all subsequently had some fingers and toes cut off. What worried us was the quality of survival and we brought all the strength of our dulled listless minds to bear upon that. I shivered uncontrollably and took off my gloves, boots and socks to rub life back into my extremities for hours at a time. We were so wrapped up in our own personal miseries that we hardly noticed each other, though at one point Dougal unzipped the front of his duvet suit and kindly allowed me to put my bare left foot under his right armpit and my other at his crutch which seemed to help. Without oxygen there didn't seem to be any internal heat being created, so I mostly sat and rubbed and rubbed my fingers and toes. This was no time for sleep. It needed the utmost vigilance to concentrate on survival, keeping my boots upright out of the snow, keeping the snow off my bare hands and feet, warming my socks against my stomach, keeping my head from brushing snow off the roof of the cave. The temperature was probably $-30°$ Centigrade. It was so cold that at first when I left a sock on my rucksack the foot of the sock went as stiff as a board. Most of the night I dug away at the cave just to keep warm, hacking away at the back with the ice axe into the hard snow and pushing it out through the doorway. By the dawn it was to be big enough to sleep five people lying down!

Our minds started to wander with the stress and the lack of sleep and oxygen. Dougal quite clearly spoke out to Dave Clarke. He had quite a long and involved conversation with him. I found myself talking to my feet. I personalized them to such an extent that they were two separate beings needing help. The left one was very slow to warm up and, after conversations with the right one, we decided I had better concentrate on rubbing it hard. And all the time my external mind was putting its spoke in as well.

DOUGAL HASTON: I was locked in suffering silence except for the occasional quiet conversation with Dave Clarke. Hallucination or dream? It seemed comforting and occasionally directed my mind away from the cold. That stopped and then it was a retreat so far into silence that I seemed to be going to sleep. Shaking awake I decided to stay this way. We'd heard too many tales of people in survival situations falling asleep and not waking up. It seemed as if we'd both come to this conclusion and Doug's incoherent speech served to keep both awake. There was no escaping the cold. Every position was tried. Holding together, feet in each other's armpits, rubbing, moving around the hole constantly exercising arms. Just no way to catch a vestige of warmth. But during all this the hours were passing. I don't think anything we did or said that night was very rational or planned. Suffering from lack of oxygen, cold, tiredness but with a terrible will to get through the night all our survival instincts came right up front. These and our wills saw the night to a successful end.

First light came and we were able to start the process of preparing for downward movement. Checks showed an ability to stand up and move. Extremities had slight numbness, but no frostbite. Kidney pains were locking us in an almost bent-in-two position. Boots were difficult to get on. I gave up my frozen inner boots and used duvet boots as a replacement. The sun came up, but with no hope of getting any warmth to our bodies. Movement was the only way and soon we were across the cornice, saying adieu to Tibet and starting off back down the Face. The warmth of movement was almost orgasmic in its intensity as the blood started recirculating. Aware of the possibilities of lack of oxygen hallunications and their potentially dire effects we kept a wary eye on each other as we belayed down the first few pitches.

DOUG SCOTT: We had not slept or eaten for nearly thirty hours, we had actually spent the night out in China, and we had done it at 28 700 feet without oxygen. Eventually we made the fixed rope and at nine a.m. fell into our sleeping bags at Camp 6. I put the stove on and looked around for something to eat and came across the radio. We had been so absorbed in surviving the night and the descent that at times it had all seemed so much like a dream, just the two of us and no one else in the world to share the cold swirling snow. The radio brought us back to reality, it crackled into life. Answering voices – Chris concerned, relieved – happy with the success. Put on a good voice I thought, don't want to sound slurred, although I felt it. 'No, I don't think we are frostbitten,' I said, for by then our fingers and toes were tingling.

The quality of survival had been good.

15   Success and tragedy

(25 September–26 September)

Back at Camp 2, we had followed the progress of Doug and Dougal through our binoculars and the 600 mm lens of the camera. They were tiny black dots, whose spidery arms and legs were just visible in the eye piece. On the 24th we first picked them out near the end of their traverse across the line of rope they had fixed the previous day. They were making good progress, for it was only nine o'clock in the morning and they were already at the foot of the gully leading up to the South Summit. They vanished into it and the hours through the day began to drag out with someone every few minutes taking a look through the binoculars at the head of the gully. Surely we must have somehow missed them as they came out of the gully. Perhaps they had gone onto the other side of the Ridge.

It was four o'clock. Nick Estcourt was gazing through the 600 mm lens. He let out a shout. He had seen someone at the top of the gully; we crowded around, impatiently waiting our turn to look. Surely they're on their way down. They must be. And then the realization came that they were on their way up, they should make the summit, but at that time of day a night bivouac was going to be inevitable. I don't think any of us slept well that night or really relaxed until the following morning we saw the two tiny figures crawl back across the long traverse to Camp 6. Then there was the joyous call that they were home, that they'd made the summit, and had no more than frost nip as their payment for the highest bivouac that has ever been undertaken and one of the boldest bids that has ever been made on the summit of Everest. There was a feeling throughout the expedition of undiluted joy; I couldn't help crying as I ended my wireless conversation with Doug. Dougal could hardly talk; his throat was so parched and sore.

They were on their way down, but the second party was already on its way up. Martin Boysen, Pete Boardman, Mick Burke and Pertemba, had set out from Camp 5 that morning, prepared either for a summit bid or a semi-rescue operation if Dougal and Doug were in a bad way. The momentary euphoria soon wore off; I was going to have to sit through two more summit bids, powerless to do anything but wait and hope that nothing went wrong. I knew all too well that the next few days, until all eight climbers returned safely, were going to be hell. I sat at Camp 2, tensed and anxious, waiting for the two o'clock call, when I should learn that my second summit party were ensconsed at Camp 6. They had with them two Sherpas, Lhakpa Dorje and Mingma, who were going to carry up the vital bottles of oxygen for their bid.

It was Martin who came on to the air. He told me that Mick had not yet arrived and that Lhakpa Dorje had also failed to make it. Only Mingma had reached them. As a result they had only enough oxygen for Pete, Pertemba and Martin, for their summit bid the following day. They were therefore going to have to tell Mick that he would have to stand down, particularly as he seemed the slowest of the four; they had been at the site of Camp 6 for over two hours and there was still no sign of him.

I think I had been quietly worrying about Mick, in the very back of my mind. When I had decided to drop out of the third summit bid and return to Camp 2, I put it to Mick that he also had been up at Camp 5 for some time. (He had arrived with Doug on the 18th and so by the morning of the 23rd, when I dropped back, he had been there for six nights compared to my eight. By the 25th, however, on his way up to Camp 6 he had been up there for eight nights as well). He had replied that he felt he was still going well and that he would be able to get a good rest in the next few days. I knew how determined he was, how savagely disappointed he would be, if having told him he could take part in the second summit bid, I changed the decision, and so I had let him stay.

But now my anxiety, triggered by Martin's, burst out with all the violence of suppressed tension. I told him very strongly that under no circumstances did I want Mick to go for the summit next day. I wanted him to come back down. Martin was shaken by the violence of my reaction and after he went off the air I realized I was perhaps ordering the impossible. Once climbers have got to the top camp on Everest they are very much on their own. Up to that point, they are members of a team, dependent on each other and the over-all control of a leader, but the summit bid was different. This was a climbing situation that you might get on a smaller expedition or in the Alps. It was their lives, in their own hands, and only they could decide upon their course of action. We kept the radio open and I had told Martin that Mick was to call me as soon as he reached camp.

It was an unenviable message that Martin, as spokesman of the trio at Camp 6, had to give Mick. Lhakpa Dorje was the first to arrive and gave him a confused story that he had been delayed because of oxygen failure. Mick reached the camp a short time later. Martin heard the fixed rope stretch and rattle and had gone out to help Mick up the last few feet, grabbed his rucksack and was immediately impressed by how heavy it was. Mick was his old chirpy self, explained that he had sorted out some of the fixed ropes below the Rock Band, something that I had asked him to do; he had then overtaken Lhakpa Dorje, to find that his oxygen set had failed. He had stopped him going back, had waited for Mingma to return from carrying his load up to Camp 6 and had then exchanged Mingma's good set for Lhakpa's unserviceable one so that Lhakpa could complete the carry to Camp 6. All this had taken time.

Confronted with Mick's explanation, the decision they had taken to leave him behind no longer seemed tenable, especially since they had subsequently discovered a further two bottles of oxygen buried in the snow. When told that I wanted to talk to him on the radio to tell him to come back down, he commented, 'Chris can get stuffed.'

I was sitting in my tent, the walkie-talkie radio turned on, trying to write a letter, when Mick's voice called me from Camp 6. He sounded guarded, potentially aggressive as he said he believed I wanted a word with him. I explained that I was worried about his slowness and the fact that he had been high on the mountain for such a long time. He countered this with the explanation of why he had taken so long. There was no point in having a confrontation by radio, so I asked him to put me on to Martin. It was up to them to decide whether they wanted to take Mick on the summit bid. Martin, obviously embarrassed and worried, said that Mick seemed to be going sufficiently strongly and that they didn't see how they could leave him out from the summit push. All I could do was exhort them to stick together and that if anyone did retreat, that they should all return.

In retrospect, even this exhortation was fairly meaningless in the reality of the situation. A line of fixed rope, followed by tracks, stretched towards the summit of Everest just fifteen hundred feet above. I was asking too much. They talked it over that night and agreed that if anyone was going so slowly that he might jeopardize their chances of reaching the summit, he should turn back, before reaching the end of the fixed rope.

Meanwhile, my third summit party also were moving into position. Ronnie Richards was already at Camp 5 with the two Sherpas, Lhakpa Dorje and Mingma; Tut Braithwaite and Nick Estcourt were at Camp 4 and Ang Phurba was still down at Camp 2, intending to move straight up into Camp 5 that day, a height gain of 4000 feet, to show us, I suspect, how much fitter at altitude he was than any of us. Our supply line was still stretched to the limit. It was essential that day, to deliver four bottles of oxygen up to Camp 6, ready for the exhausted summit bidders on their return, and also to build up a stockpile for the third summit bid on the 28th. There were only three bottles, however, in Camp 5, and Nick Estcourt therefore volunteered to leave Camp 4 in the early hours of the morning to arrive at Camp 5 in time to deliver an oxygen bottle, so that it could be carried on, that same day, up to Camp 6. In doing this he had a strange experience; Nick Estcourt tells the story.

I set off on my own at about 3.30 in the morning, pulling up the fixed ropes leading up to Camp 5. It was a moonlit night and the shapes of the rocks were etched clearly against the brightness of the snow. I was about two hundred feet above the camp when I turned round. I can't remember why, but perhaps I had a feeling that someone was following me. Anyway, I turned round and saw this figure behind me. He looked like an ordinary climber, far enough behind, so that I could not feel him moving up the fixed rope, but not all that far below. I could see his arms and legs and assumed that it was someone trying to catch me up.

I stopped and waited for him. He then seemed to stop or to be moving very, very slowly, he made no effort to signal or wave. I shouted down, but got no reply, and so in the end I thought, 'Sod it, I might as well press on.' I wondered if perhaps it was Ang Phurba coming through from Camp 2, hoping to surprise us all by being at Camp 5 when we arrived that morning.

I carried on and turned round three or four times between then and the old site of Camp 4 [the one used by the previous expeditions, about six hundred feet above the present site in the middle of the Great Central Gully] and this figure was still behind me. It was definitely a human figure with arms and legs and at one stage I can remember seeing him behind a slight undulation in the slope, from the waist upwards as you would expect, with the lower part of his body hidden in the slight dip.

I turned round again as I reached the old site of Camp 4 and there was no one there at all. It seemed very eerie. I wasn't sure if anyone had fallen off or what. He couldn't possibly have had time to have turned back and drop down the ropes out of sight, since I could see almost all the way back to Camp 4. The whole thing seemed very peculiar.

Nick Estcourt told Ronnie Richards of his experience when he arrived at Camp 5 at around six o'clock that morning. Tut Braithwaite and the rest of the Sherpas came up from Camp 4 later on in the day, arriving at around eleven o'clock. Nick immediately asked Tut if anyone had left the Camp shortly after he had set out but was told that no one had set out before eight o'clock. The figure that Nick had seen could not possibly have been a member of the team.

There could be several explanations. Climbers have had hallucinations caused by lack of acclimatization to altitude. Perhaps the most famous story is that of Frank Smythe who made a solitary bid for the summit of Everest in 1933, after his companion had been forced to turn back. He was not using oxygen and at a height of around 27000 feet was convinced that he was linked to a second man on a rope. This was undoubtedly a hallucination. Nick Estcourt, however,

14

15

16

21

22

13. Ronnie Richards uncoiling a rope, while running the route out towards the Rock Band beyond Camp 5.

14. A spindrift avalanche coming down the Left-Hand Gully, our route through the Rock Band. Nick Estcourt in the lead.

15. Tut Braithwaite, belayed by Nick Estcourt, climbing a snow-covered boulder jammed across the gully.

16. Looking down the Left-Hand Gully at Mick Burke carrying a load of rope in support on the first ascent.

17. Nick Estcourt leading the crucial ramp pitch which provided the key to the ascent of the Rock Band.

18. Dougal Haston climbing the fixed rope on the ramp on the way to the top for the summit assault.

19. Mick Burke helping to establish Camp 6 on the 22nd September.

20. Haston following Scott in making the route across the Upper Snow Field.

21. Haston on the Col between the South Summit and Main Summit at the spot where he and Scott made their bivouac snow hole.

22. Haston leading through towards the final slope of the summit the Chinese emblem just visible.

was at a very much lower height, between 23 900 feet and 24 500 feet, was well acclimatized to the altitude, and is a very matter-of-fact individual with the analytical mind of the mathematician. I suspect that he saw some kind of psychic phenomenon linked perhaps with what was to happen later on that day, or to a tragedy of the past. It was only a short way below this point that Jangbo, a Sherpa who had worked very closely with Nick in the Autumn of 1972, had perished in an avalanche in the Autumn of 1973 whilst climbing with the Japanese.

Meanwhile, at Camp 6, Boysen, Burke, Boardman and Pertemba were getting ready for their summit bid. They were ready to start at 4.30 a.m. It was an ominous dawn. Although there was no wind, a thin high haze covered the western horizon and a tide of cloud was fast lapping up the valley bottoms, filling the Western Cwm below them and creeping up the Face itself. The weather seemed on the point of change and they all realized that they were going to have to move fast to avoid a bivouac.

Martin Boysen, ever impatient, was away first, Pete Boardman was next, closely followed by Pertemba, and Mick Burke brought up the rear. It is almost impossible to stay together while climbing a fixed rope, for each person is individually clipped into it, travelling at his own speed, and high on Everest is cocooned behind mask and goggles.

Martin suffered an early and bitter setback when his oxygen set packed up and he lost a crampon, this misfortune effectively putting him out of the summit bid; the others overtook him and despairingly he retreated to the tent.

I crawled inside and howled with anguish, frustration and self-pity. Later the sun crept round, but a strong breeze sprang up. I poked my head out and scanned the gully. Two tiny specks were visible, one just below the summit ridge. I wondered where Mick was and eventually spied him at the bottom of the gully as the two figures above reached the crest. It was only 11 a.m. – they were doing well. I closed the door. I could hardly bear to watch.

Pete Boardman and Pertemba had made good progress, climbing unroped beyond the end of the fixed ropes along the

G

track leading to the foot of the South Summit Gully and then on up to its top. Although some of the tracks had been filled in by wind-driven spindrift, the snow was much better consolidated than it had been two days before. Pete had glanced back once or twice, had seen a distant figure on the traverse across the Upper Snow Field but had assumed that this was Martin or Mick watching them and that they both would return to camp.

On reaching the South Summit, Pertemba had trouble with his oxygen, when his set jammed. The problem was similar to the one that had beset Dougal and they spent an hour fiddling with it before they managed to clear two inches of ice blocking the airflow. Even so, they were still making excellent time, changed their oxygen bottles and forged on towards the summit roped up, but climbing together.

The cloud had now crept up the Face, engulfing them in a thin mist. The wind was rising steadily, but visibility was still quite reasonable. They could see the line of tracks snaking up the South East Ridge in front of them and felt comfortably in control of the situation.

They reached the top at about ten past one, a very fast time indeed, even allowing for the tracks left by the first summit pair. They were not rewarded by the magnificent view that Doug and Dougal had enjoyed, for they were still enclosed in fine wind-driven mist, the Chinese maypole, the only sign that they were standing on the highest point on earth. Pete was wearing a specially decorated T-shirt presented to him by the Mynydd Mountaineering Club in honour of the occasion. It was like a medieval knight's surcoat worn over his down suit of armour. Pertemba took out a Nepalese flag, which they attached to the Chinese emblem. They took photographs of each other and Pete addressed the world on miniature tape recorder: 'Hello, here is the first bit of recorded sound from the summit of Mount Everest. Would you like to say a word to the viewers, Pertemba?' A muffled sound followed, due to Pertemba still being encased in his oxygen mask, but when asked if he was tired, there came a very firm 'No'. Pete then went on to outline briefly the details of their ascent and the weather conditions and signed off with the cheerful comment,

'Well, I can't see a Barclays Bank branch anywhere.' In this totally relaxed mood they ate some chocolate and mint cake, and then set off down. They still had plenty of time: it was barely 1.40.

They had not gone more than a few hundred yards when to their utter amazement a figure began to take shape through the mist. Pete Boardman tells what happened next:

Mick was sitting on the snow only a few hundred yards down an easy angled snow slope from the summit. He congratulated us and said he wanted to film us on a bump on the ridge and pretend it was the summit, but I told him about the Chinese maypole. Then he asked us to go back to the summit with him. I agreed reluctantly and he, sensing my reluctance, changed his mind and said he'd go up and film it and then come straight down after us. He borrowed Pertemba's camera to take some stills on the top and we walked back fifty feet and then walked past him whilst he filmed us. I took a couple of pictures of him. He had the 'Blue Peter' flag and an auto-load camera with him. He asked us to wait for him by the big rock on the South Summit where Pertamba and I had dumped our first oxygen cylinders and some rope and film on the way up. I told him that Pertemba was wanting to move roped with me – so he should catch us up fairly quickly. I said, 'See you soon,' and we moved back down the ridge to the South Summit.

After they parted company the weather began to deteriorate fast. Pete and Pertemba continued down to wait with increasing apprehension.

All the winds of Asia seemed to be trying to blow us from the ridge. A decision was needed. It was four in the afternoon and the skies were already darkening around the South Summit of Everest. I threw my iced and useless snow goggles away into the whiteness and tried, clumsily mitted, to clear the ice from my eyelashes. I bowed my head into the spindrift and tried to peer along the ridge. Mick should have met us at least threequarters of an hour before. We had been waiting for nearly one and a half hours. There was no sign of Doug and Dougal's bivouac site. The sky and cornices and whirling snow merged together, visibility was reduced to ten feet and all tracks were obliterated. Pertemba and I huddled next to the rock of the South Summit where Mick had asked us to wait for him. Pertemba said he could not feel his toes or fingers and mine, too, were nailed with cold. I thought of Mick wearing his glasses and blinded by spindrift, negotiating the short length of fixed rope on the Hillary Step, the fragile one-foot windslab on the Nepal side and the cornices on the Tibetan side of the ridge. I thought of our own predicament, with the 800 feet of the South Summit Gully – guarded by a sixty-foot rock step halfway – to descend, and then half of the two-thousand-foot great traverse above the Rock Band to cross before reaching the end of the fixed ropes that extended across from Camp 6. It had taken Doug and Dougal three hours in the dawn sunshine after their bivouac to reach Camp 6 – but now we had only an hour of light left. At 28 700 feet the boundary between a controlled and an uncontrolled situation is narrow and we had crossed that boundary within minutes – a strong wind and sun shining through clouds had turned into a violent blizzard of driving snow.

A decision was needed. I pointed at my watch and said, 'We'll wait ten more minutes.' Pertemba agreed. That helped us – it shifted some responsibility to the watch. I fumbled in my sack and pulled out our stove to leave behind. The time was up. At first we went the wrong way, too far towards the South Col. About a hundred and fifty feet down we traversed back until we found what we thought was the South Summit Gully. There was a momentary lessening in the blizzard, and I looked up to see the rock of the South Summit. There was still no sign of Mick and it was now about half past four. The decision had been made and now we had to fight for our own lives and think downwards. The early afternoon had drifted into approaching night and our success was turning into tragedy.

Pertemba is not a technical climber, not used to moving away from fixed ropes or in bad conditions. At first he was slow. For three pitches I kicked down furiously, placed a deadman and virtually pulled him down in the sliding, blowing powder snow. But Pertemba is strong and adaptable. He began to move faster and soon we were able to move together. Were we in the gully? I felt panic surge inside. Then I saw twin rocks in the snow that I recognized from the morning. We descended diagonally from there and in the dusk saw Doug's oxygen cylinder that marked the top of the fixed rope over the rock step. We abseiled down to the end of the rope and tied a spare rope we had to the end and descended the other hundred and fifty feet. From there we descended down and across for one thousand feet towards the end of the fixed ropes. As soon as we started the traverse we were covered by a powder-snow avalanche from the summit slopes. Fortunately our oxygen cylinders were still functioning and we could breathe. We threaded our way blindly across the thin runnels of ice and snow that covered the sloping rocks. I felt a brush of snow on my head and looked up to see another big avalanche coming, channelled, straight at me. I looked across Pertemba was crouched to hold my fall, and was whipping in the rope between us tight to my waist. I smashed my axe into the ice and hung on. The surging snow buffeted over and around me for minutes. Then it stopped. Pertemba had held; the axe had stayed in the ice. We moved on. It was a miracle that we found the end of the fixed ropes in the dark marked by two oxygen cylinders sticking out of the snow. On the fixed rope Pertemba slowed down and I pulled him mercilessly until he shouted that one of his crampons had fallen off. The rope between us snagged and, in flicking it free, I tumbled over a fifteen-foot rock step to be held on the fixed rope. At one point a section of the rope had been swept away. At half past seven we stumbled into the summit boxes at Camp 6. Martin was there and I burst into tears.

16   Clearing the mountain

(27 September–30 September)

Back at Camp 2 we had waited, helpless, through the day. In the early morning we had glimpsed two figures, probably Pete and Pertemba, near the foot of the South Summit Gully and were filled with hope for a fast, safe ascent, but then the cloud had rolled over us and all we could see through the occasional break were banners of spindrift being blown from the top of the Rock Band and the South East Ridge.

After two o'clock we kept the radio permanently open, could detect the growing anxiety in Martin's voice whenever he called us, as the wind hammering his little tent rose through the afternoon. It became dark and there was still no sign of them. We were all sitting, tensed and silent round the piled boxes of the mess tent at Camp 2; the only sounds, the wind howling across the Face above us and the crackle and buzz of the radio. A severe storm had broken and a bivouac would be an even more serious business than it had been for Doug and Dougal.

And then at seven o'clock Martin's voice came through. There was a momentary glimmer of relief; they were back. But our hopes were quickly dashed by the agony in his voice as he told us that only Pete and Pertemba had returned and that Pete would tell me what had happened.

None of us could believe that Mick was dead; he'd stagger back along the ropes in an hour or so's time; he'd bivouac, and return to Camp 6 the following morning; the same irrepressible, cocky Mick whom we'd known for so many years on so many climbs. But as the night dragged out, the fury of the storm increased; it raged throughout the following day, and as the hours crept by our hopes began to vanish, to be replaced with anxiety not only for Mick but for the safety of the three now pinned down, tired and exhausted at the end of the Upper Snow Field, with only a limited quantity of food and oxygen, exposed to the full force of the powder-snow avalanches that were pouring down from the summit rocks. Pete had arrived back first at the tent, and Pertemba, still tied to Pete, took over half an hour just to crawl the last hundred feet and also tumble into the small tent occupied by Martin. He took off their crampons and forced a brew down them, before shifting them to the other tent, since he had organized his own as the camp kitchen. Pete's feet were numb and he was afraid they were frostbitten, while Pertemba just lay in his sleeping bag suffering from snow blindness and in the last stages of exhaustion. Pete had got him back only just in time.

Martin will never forget the next thirty-six hours.

The night and following day is a permanent scar on my memory, a tender wound, painfully healed but all too easily broken open again. Two nights and a day are not, in themselves a long period of time, yet every hour of waiting seemed stretched to infinity. At first I could hardly accept Mick's death; I clung to slender hope, but with each passing hour all hope disappeared, torn and blown away by the raging winds and blizzard.

I had hoped to go back up the ropes with a working oxygen set, to look for Mick, perhaps to go to the top, but the next morning crushed any such plan. The wind still gusted and tore at the boxes, the air was full of eye-stinging spindrift and I emerged outside but briefly to dig furiously at the torrent of snow that was engulfing the tents intent on squeezing us out like pips from a lemon. Pete and Pertemba's box was already badly deformed, a low white hump out of which an arm occasionally stretched to accept tea, soup and porridge.

Conversation was impossible in the shrieking wind and muffled tents; even if it hadn't been, there was nothing to say. I sat in my box and brewed up. The stove would no longer work without some more air, but if I opened the door more than a chink the spindrift came flooding in.

A wave of panic, claustrophobia overcomes me. I'm incarcerated in an airless little tent; I can't even sit it out here without oxygen. What the hell do we do when it runs out? 'Martin, could you possibly find us another bottle of oxygen?' It's Pete. I cook for them, dig for them, find oxygen for them; I'm their bloody nurse maid.

Still it's time to dig snow off their tents again and have a look outside. I can only stand a few moments at a time as the spindrift blasts my face. I dig frantically until exhausted and then throw myself into the little green grotto, rest a few moments, and out again. Metal hits metal; at last an oxygen bottle emerges from under the accumulated snows. Back in my tent and try to warm up. Snow gradually drifting in, hands and feet icy cold. Every time outside chills me deeper and it takes longer to warm up back in my sleeping bag. Another brew and take full stock. A couple of oxygen cylinders, 2 tea bags, 2 gas cartridges and a packet of soup; that's all. We can manage for a few days, but what if the storm continues? Oh Christ, please let's get out.

Time for a radio call – Thank God. We never appreciated the wretched thing before. Chris comes on the air, calm, soothing: 'Just hold out for a little; Nick, Tut and Ronnie are in support at Camp 5 . . . try to conserve fuel . . . the storm can't last much longer . . . there's no need to worry.'

Worry – I'm beyond worry. Mick's dead . . . Poor Beth and little Sarah. Oh God, emptiness, loss. If only my oxygen had worked; not even the consolation of the summit; self-pity, anger . . . I'm getting out of this hole somehow.

'Want a brew, Pete?'

'Thanks, mate.'

'Well, it's the last, there's bugger all else.'

Darkness came and with it, another night of doubt. Would the storm just carry on, tents collapse, the fuel and oxygen run out?

I woke up; an unnatural calm prevailed. The wind had died; we were saved. A sudden wave of emotion overwhelmed me; I cried bitterly, for Mick, for myself, for everything.

It was the morning of 28 September. In the last twenty-four hours we had been shown how puny and fragile were our carefully laid plains, logistic build-up and human strength against the power of wind and snow. Mick was dead and every camp was threatened. We had been forced to evacuate Camp 1 on the afternoon of the 26th; its occupants had felt the ice island shift beneath their feet, in its inexorable slide down into the Ice Fall. This, in effect, cut our line of supply with Base Camp, but we reckoned that we had enough supplies at Camp 2 for the last few days of the expedition.

As the storm raged through the day of the 27th, we also abandoned all hope of Mick's survival. Dougal and Doug, who had seen how badly corniced and how narrow was the ridge leading down from the foot of the Hillary Step, felt that it would have been all too easy for him to have walked over the edge in the white-out conditions that must have beset him on his descent. If he had stopped for the night, hoping to get back down to the end of the fixed rope the following morning of the 27th, he could not possibly have moved that day, and there was no way he could have survived two nights at that altitude without food, shelter or oxygen, even if he had dug a snow-hole.

I was getting increasingly worried about the safety of the rest of the team. Nick, Ronnie, Ang Phurba and Tut, at Camp 5, seemed safe enough, tucked away in the small gully that was guarded by a rock buttress above, but they reported huge powder-snow avalanches pouring in a constant torrent down the Great Central Gully. There was no question of movement either up or down, until these ceased.

Camp 4, however, was in a more exposed situation, only partially protected by the slender snow arête above it. I was frightened of the huge build-up of snow that was probably forming on the snow fields above the camp. Even though they had now spread tarpaulin sheets over all the boxes, the memory of the avalanche that had damaged one of them when the camp was established made me wonder what might happen if the whole slope slid away.

At five o'clock, therefore, on the afternoon of the 27th I told Adrian Gordon, who was in charge of Camp 4, to abandon the camp and bring down the six Sherpas who were manning it. Very shortly we were involved in another crisis. The Sherpas raced down the fixed ropes and got back to Camp 2 just before dark. Adrian had delayed a little, ensuring that the camp was left secure, and moved more slowly because he was less experienced; this was the first time he had been on the Face. As a result, he was caught in the dark. His head torch failed; he couldn't see where he was going, took a wrong turn following some old rope that had been left by the Japanese, and eventually decided he had better stay where he was. By this time it was nine o'clock at night and the storm was raging unabated. We sent some Sherpas back to see what had happened to him, but they had gone up without any jumar clamps. Very courageously Ang Phu had climbed a full rope length hand over hand, but could see no sign of him and was forced to return. Increasingly worried, I set out from Camp 2 with Dave Clarke, Mike Rhodes, Arthur Chesterman, Mike Thompson and another group of Sherpas armed with survival gear. It was past ten o'clock that night when eventually Mike Rhodes and I reached Adrian half-way up the fixed ropes to the site of Camp 3. He was characteristically calm, in fact had just decided to feel his way back up the rope to the site of Camp 3 and dig himself a snow hole for the night. At the same time, though, he was desperately tired. It is quite possible that if we hadn't reached him, he could have collapsed and died from exposure. It took him a long time to walk back to Camp 2, but he steadfastly refused to take any help, courageously stumbled fifty paces or so, paused for a few minutes, and then stumbled on once again. Our tracks had been covered in the short time between walking out and returning and, without the marker flags placed every hundred feet or so, we should have been lost in the maze of crevasses that barred the way back to the camp. We only saw the light of the camp when we got within fifty paces of the first tent, the wind-driven snow was so dense.

It was midnight before we all got to bed. I dropped off into a deep sleep, only to wake dimly to the sound of someone shouting my name. It was Charlie Clarke, who describes what happened in his diary:

Shortly before four a.m. there was a deafening roar and in the moment of wakening I felt myself turning, lifted and pitched for a few seconds. It was immediately obvious that we had been hit by a large avalanche and I thought to myself 'Yes, I'm alive and I can breathe.' The tent zip was very near to my hand and I was out into the still icy night in seconds. Chris Ralling's tent was completely flattened, while the BBC super box which stood beside ours was no longer there. Eventually I realized that the twisted mass of metal and canvas was both our tent and theirs – containing in all, Doug and Dougal, Ned and Ian, Arthur and myself. Sherpas peeped from the remains, grinning, still warm in their sleeping bags. I walked round. No one was hurt or missing. Several tents had remained unscathed among them Chris Bonington's face box.

I wandered over to it and woke him up, told him the rest of the camp was flat. 'Anyone dead?' he asked. I replied that all was well and he crashed back into drugged sleep. We wandered about, re-orientating ourselves. 'Looters will be shot,' shouted someone, We all seemed in a jovial mood, wholly unfrightened by the episode which had seemed so sudden yet so short lived.

Within minutes the kitchen was re-erected and the good Kanchha was making tea – always so necessary in accidents. The remarkable thing was how coolly we took it all. None of the sick, shaky feeling or even relief that it was all over. It seemed as if it was just another chapter in the struggle to get off the mountain safely.

It dawned into a brilliant clear still morning. There was no question of mounting a search for Mick or another summit bid. He couldn't possibly be alive. I wanted to clear the mountain, which had a dangerous quantity of snow on it, as quickly as possible. I told the party at Camp 5 to wait for the arrival of Pete, Pertemba and Martin and then to accompany them back to Camp 2. I had decided to abandon everything that they couldn't carry down with them. I was not prepared to take any further risks just to rescue pieces of equipment, however valuable.

That morning of 28 September, they had crawled out of the two battered little tents at Camp 6, and crammed their frozen sleeping bags into their rucksacks. Pete Boardman almost dreaded the return.

I felt isolated from my friends lower down the mountain by a decision and experience I could not share. We looked across the traverse and up the gully to the South Summit, but there was no sign of Mick. We turned and began the long repetitive ritual of clipping and unclipping the piton brake and safety loop and abseiling rope length after rope length, 6000 feet down to the Western Cwm.

As we emerged from the foot of the gully through the Rock Band we could see tiny figures outside the three boxes of Camp 5, a thousand feet below us. It took a long time to reach them for many of the anchors on the fixed rope had been swept away. Ronnie, Nick, Tut and Ang Phurba were waiting for us and helped us down into the living air and warmth of the Western Cwm and the reassuring faces of Camp 2.

'Everest is not a private affair; it belongs to many men.' That afternoon I was in front of a camera, explaining what had happened. But now friends were all around me. Dougal, usually so distant and undemonstrative, had walked out in the midday heat of the Western Cwm to meet me. Doug had tenderly taken off my boots, Chris had reassured me. It was good to hear about other people's experiences, and all the individual traits I had noticed in others in the last few months seemed refreshingly evident – Tut, strutting about like a starved turkey, Ronnie hoovering the table, Doug his hair still at half-mast, Charlie dressed in his red underwear.

The following morning we turned our backs on the South West Face of Everest and headed down the Western Cwm, in a long straggly line of climbers and Sherpas, bowed under monstrous loads of up to eighty pounds. We were trying to clear the Cwm in just two carries. Adrian Gordon and Allen Fyffe had volunteered to stay behind just one more day and the bulk of our Sherpas returned to Camp 2 after carrying their loads down to the head of the Ice Fall, while most of the climbers and the Sherpas who had been working in the upper camps, continued down to Base. Adrian, Allen and the remaining Sherpas were able to clear the Western Cwm the following day and that high valley once more was left empty of life, except for a few goraks (huge, crow-like birds) who were scavenging the last of the food left in our rubbish dump, before it was covered for evermore by the snows.

I didn't relax until the last man came down the Ice Fall on 30 September. That night the Sherpas had a party to celebrate the successful outcome of the expedition and the safe return of all their numbers. They lit a huge bonfire and danced round it, late into the night, arms linked, chanting out their songs, swaying in and out, to the brink of the flames and out into the dark, throwing great shadows onto the tents and snow behind us. Plastic jerry cans of chang were passed round; we were offered mugfuls of throat-searing rakshi, tried our hand at dancing and contributed a few noisy and very tuneless chorus songs. There was plenty of laughter and shouting, but there were moments of reflection as well.

I know that I and, I suspect, most of the other members of the team, would have followed the same course as Mick, in similar circumstances. In pressing on alone he took a climber's

calculated risk, in principle similar to the ones one often takes
on British hills, the Alps or other mountains of the Himalaya.
He balanced in his mind the risks of going on by himself in the
face of deteriorating weather, with the knowledge that there
were fixed ropes on all the awkward sections and a line of
tracks stretching away before him. Although he was travelling
more slowly than Pertemba and Pete Boardman, he was still
making good progress and always had plenty of time before
dark to return to Camp 6. Had the weather not deteriorated
into white-out conditions so quickly, I am convinced he
would have caught up with Pete Boardman and Pertemba on
the South Summit. Sadly, his calculations didn't work out.

We were rather like the mourners after the funeral; glad to
be alive, getting on with our own lives, the memory of Mick
held with sadness and regret, yet accepted as an act that had
happened; one of the risks of our climbing game.

Is there a self-centred selfishness in this attitude? For those
of us who are happily married and have children, there must
be or we should not have carried on our life of climbing aware,
as we are, of the risks involved. In our own single-minded
drive and love for the mountains, we hope that the fatal
accident will never happen to us, are frightened to contem-
plate the cruel long-lasting sorrow suffered by the widows,
parents and children – an endless tunnel that for them must
never seem to end.

Our doubts and sorrow were mixed with a feeling of
satisfaction at having taken part in a successful, demanding,
yet very happy expedition. Inevitably there had been moments of tension and misunderstanding within the team, but
these had been very few and had been quickly dispelled with
frank words. Our friendship and respect for each other had
been heightened rather than weakened.

In our race to beat the winter winds and cold, we had
climbed the mountain in thirty-three exacting, exhilarating
days after arriving at Base Camp. Everyone had stretched
himself to his limit. Each of us had known moments of
immense personal fulfilment, of self-revelation or just simple
wonder at the beauty and scale of the mountain itself and, the
ever-expanding view to be gained from it.

The South West Face of Everest was a major landmark in all our climbing lives, one that had taken up so much of our mental and physical energy in the months of preparation, planning and finally of climbing, but already we were beginning to talk of future objectives in the Karakoram, Garhwal, Nepal, in Alaska or Patagonia. There are so many mountains in the world, many of them still unclimbed, all with unclimbed facets, ridges or faces.

There is no question of anticlimax in tackling smaller peaks than Everest, for simply by reducing the size of the team one can maintain the level of challenge that is the essence of climbing. Each problem, whether it be a granite spire in the Karakoram, a great unclimbed snow face in the Nepal Himalaya or a complex ridge in the Garhwal, has its own special mystery and appeal.

One of the joys of mountaineering in this fast shrinking world, is that mountaineers for many generations to come will still be able to discover untrodden corners in the greater mountain ranges of the earth. We, however, shall always feel fortunate and privileged to have been able to unravel the complex problems that were presented by the world's highest and steepest mountain face.

Appendix 1

Members of the expedition and a diary of events

THE TEAM

Chris Bonington Leader
Aged 41. Married with two children; writer and photographer, living in Lake District. 1st ascent Annapurna II (26041 feet) in Nepal, 1960. 1st ascent Nuptse (25850 feet), third peak of Everest, 1961 1st ascent Central Pillar of Freney, Mont Blanc, 1961. 1st British ascent of North Wall of Eiger, 1962. 1st ascent Central Tower of Paine, Patagonia, 1963. 1st ascent Old Man of Hoy, 1966. Leader Annapurna South Face Expedition, 1970. Leader British Everest Expedition, 1972. 1st ascent Brammah (21036 feet) in Kashmir, 1973. 1st ascent Changabang in Garhwal Himalaya, 1974. Fellow of Royal Geographical Society.

Hamish MacInnes Deputy Leader
Aged 44. Equipment designer, writer and photographer living in Glencoe. Has climbed extensively in Scotland, the European Alps, New Zealand, Caucasus and the Himalayas with many new routes to his credit. Member of the spring 1972 European Everest Expedition and autumn 1972 British Everest Expedition. 1st ascent of the Prow of Roraima in Guyana, 1973. World authority in mountain rescue. Secretary Scottish Mountain Rescue Committee.

Peter Boardman
Aged 24. National Officer British Mountaineering Council. North Face of Matterhorn and 5 First British ascents in the Western Alps including the North Face Direct of the Olan and the North Faces of the Nesthorn and the Lauterbrunnen Breithorn. 1st ascents of North Faces of Koh-i-Mondi and

Koh-i-Khaaik in the Central Hindu Kush, 1972. 1st ascent of the South Face of Mount Dan Beard in the Central Alaska Range, 1974. Expedition to Caucasus, 1975.

Martin Boysen Assistant Food
Aged 32. Married with one child – School teacher living in Manchester. 2nd ascent South Face of the Fou, one of the most difficult rock routes in the Alps. 1st ascent of the West Face of the Pic Sans Nom, near Mont Blanc, 1967. Member of the 1967 Cerro Torre Expedition; 1970 Annapurna South Face Expedition. 1st ascent Point Innominata in Patagonia, 1974. 1st ascent Changabang, 1974.

Paul Braithwaite Assistant Equipment
Aged 28. Decorator living in Oldham. 1st British ascent of Croz Spur on the Grandes Jorasses, Couzy Pillar of the Droites, Grand Pilier d'Angle on Mont Blanc, expedition to Caucasus. 1st ascent E. Pillar Asgard in Baffin Island, 1972. Expedition to Baffin Island, 1973. 1st ascent Point Innominata, in Patagonia, 1974. 1st ascent S E Spur of Pik Lenin in the Pamirs, 1974.

Mick Burke Mountain Camerman
Aged 32. Film cameraman living in London. Married with one child. Cerro Torre Expedition. North Face of Matterhorn in winter. 1st British ascent of the Nose of El Capitan in Yosemite, 1968. Member of Annapurna South Face Expedition, 1970 and of British Everest Expedition in 1972. President Alpine Climbing Group.

Mike Cheney Base Camp Manager
Aged 46. Director of Mountain Travel, Kathmandu. Extensive trekking experience in Nepal.

Charles Clarke Expedition Doctor
Aged 31. Married with one child. Registrar in Neurology, Middlesex Hospital, London. Six Himalayan expeditions, including 1st ascent Swargarohini in Garhwal Himalaya, 1974.

Dave Clarke Equipment Organizer
Aged 37. Married with two children. Proprietor of Centresport, a climbing shop in Leeds. Expedition to Paine area of South Patagonia, 1961.

Jim Duff 2nd Expedition Doctor
Aged 28. Qualified physiologist with medical experience in Nepal. 14 years' climbing experience including the Great Troll Wall in Norway.

Nick Estcourt Treasurer and Insurance
Aged 31. Married with three children. Systems analyst from Manchester. 2nd ascent South Face of the Fou. 1st ascent of the West Face of the Pic Sans Nom, 1967. Member of the Annapurna South Face Expedition, 1970 and British Everest Expedition, 1972. 1st ascent Brammah in Kashmir, 1973.

Allen Fyffe
Aged 28. Climbing instructor at Glenmore Lodge in Cairngorms. 1st British ascent of North Face Direct of Les Droites. 1st winter ascent of Central Spur of North Face of Les Courtes. North Face of Eiger. Member of the British Dhaulagiri Expedition, 1973. Over 40 first ascents in Scotland, summer and winter.

Adrian Gordon Advanced Base Manager
Aged 28. Administrative officer in British Gurkha Ex-Servicemen's Re-integration Training Scheme in Nepal. A fluent Nepali speaker with extensive trekking experience.

Dougal Haston
Aged 32. Married. Director of International School of Mountaineering in Leysin. 1st ascent Eiger Direct, one of the most difficult climbs in Alps, 1966. Winter ascent of North Face of Matterhorn. Cerro Torre Expedition. Member of Annapurna South Face Expedition, reaching its summit. Member of International Everest Expedition, 1971 and British Everest Expedition, 1972. 1st ascent Changabang, 1974.

Mike Rhodes
Aged 27. Married with three children. Clerk with Barclays Bank International in Bradford. Member of Barclays Bank Climbing Club with extensive climbing experience in Britain, the Alps and the Dolomites.

Ronnie Richards Transport and Communications
Aged 29. Chemist living in the Lake District. Extensive Alpine experience. West ridge of Pik Lenin, Pamirs, 1974.

Doug Scott Assistant Equipment
Aged 33. Married with two children. Teacher, writer and photographer living in Nottingham. Atlas mountains, 1962, Tibesti Mountains in Sahara, 1965, Cilo Dag Mountains in Turkey, 1966, Hindu Kush with 1st ascent of South Face Koh-i-Bandaka (22500 feet), 1967. 1st British ascent Salathe Wall in Yosemite, 1970. European Everest Expedition, spring 1972. 1st ascent of E. Pillar of Mount Asgard, Baffin, summer 1972, British Everest Expedition, autumn 1972. 1st ascent Changabang, 1974, 1st ascent S E Spur Pik Lenin, 1974. Member training committee of B M C, F R G S.

Mike Thompson Food Organizer
Aged 37. Married with two children. Anthropologist living in London. Expedition to Indrasan in Kangra Himalaya. Member of Annapurna South Face Expedition, 1970, and of Roraima Expedition, 1973.

Lt Mohan Pratap Gurung, of the Royal Nepalese Army, Liaison Officer.

Gurkha Signallers

L/C Jai Kumar Rai.
Cpl Prembahadur Thapa.

BBC team

Arthur Chesterman Sound Recordist
Aged 33. Married with one child. Sound recordist with the

BBC. Very experienced technician in mountain environment. Was sound recordist on International Everest Expedition, 1971.

Ned Kelly Film Producer
Aged 40. Married and living in Bristol. BBC film producer of natural history and mountaineering films. Very experienced in mountain photography with four previous vists to Nepal, including filming of International Everest Expedition, 1971. Producer of award-winning Alplamayo film, 1966.

Chris Ralling Film Producer
Aged 46. Married with one child. Producer of television documentary films. Also experienced climber and ski mountaineer.

Ian Stuart Film Cameraman
Aged 43. Married with three children. BBC film cameraman with considerable experience of mountain and expedition photography, including International Everest Expedition, 1971.

Sunday Times correspondent

Keith Richardson
Aged 38. Married with three children. Journalist of considerable experience. Also mountaineer who has taken part in climbs in the Alps, and an expedition to Arctic Norway.

Transport

Bob Stoodley Overland Transport Organizer
Aged 51. Married with five children. Chairman and Managing Director of Manchester Garages Limited. British Everest Expedition, 1972.

Allen Evans Driver
Aged 23. Married and living in Manchester.

John O'Neill Driver
Aged 28. Single and living in Manchester.

Alan Riley Driver
Aged 27. Born in Kenya, but living in Worcestershire. Not married.

Committee of Management

Chairman: The Rt Hon. the Lord Hunt, CBE, DSO, DCL, LlD.
              Sir Jack Longland
              Ian McNaught Davis
              Alan Tritton
              Lt-Col Charles Wylie
              Chris Bonington, CBE
              Doug Scott

Louise Wilson Expedition Secretary

High-altitude porters

NAME	AGE	VILLAGE	HIGHEST CAMP CARRIED TO
Pertemba Sherpa (Head Sirdar)	27	Khumjung	Camp 6
Ang Phu Sherpa (2nd Sirdar)	26	Khumjung	
Ang Phurba 'I' Sherpa	29	Khumjung	Camp 6
Lhakpa Dorje Sherpa	22	Khumjung (4 times)	Camp 6
Mingma Sherpa	23	Khumjung	Camp 6
'Young' Tenzing Sherpa	24	Namche Bazar	Camp 6
Pasang Tenzing Sherpa	40	Khumde	Camp 6
Phutsering Sherpa	32	Khumjung	Camp 5
Ang Nuru Sherpa	30	Phortse	Camp 5
'Long' Tenzing Sherpa	36	Namche Bazar	Camp 5
Lhakpa Gyalu Sherpa	26	Phortse	
Nawang Tenzing Sherpa	26	Namche Bazar	Camp 5
Sundhare Sherpa*	22	Pangpoche	Camp 5
Pasang Gyalzen Sherpa*	20	Phortse	Camp 4
Mingma Gyalzen Sherpa	24	Phortse	Camp 5

NAME	AGE	VILLAGE	HIGHEST CAMP CARRIED TO
'Smali' Tenzing Sherpa	25	Namche Bazar	
Urken Dorje Sherpa	34	Ghat	Camp 5
Sonam Jangbo Sherpa	35	Pangpoche	Camp 5
Lhakpa Gyalzen Sherpa	28	Pangpoche	Camp 5
Pasang Wangchup Sherpa*	21	Namche Bazar	Camp 4
Dorje Sherpa	21	Drokkharka	Camp 5
Ang Phurba 'II' Sherpa	35	Chermading	Camp 5
Ang Lhakpa Sherpa	35	Khumjung	
Dawa Gyalzen Sherpa*	23	Khamche	Camp 5
Mingma Nuru Sherpa*	24	Thame	Camp 4
Pasang Namgyal Sherpa	38	Namche Bazar	Camp 5
Ang Nima Sherpa	37	Namche Bazar	
Nima Kanchha Sherpa	28	Jarok	Camp 5
Dawa Norbu Sherpa	39	Thame	
Pema Tham Jen Sherpa	28	Thame	
Nima Tsering Sherpa	42	Rolwaling	
Phurtenzing Sherpa	38	Thame	Camp 5
Nimachiri Lhawa Sherpa	39	Khumjung	

BBC team's high-altitude porters

Jagatman Tamang (BBC Sirdar)	33	Temal	
Pemba Lama	26	Junbesi	Camp 4
Pasang Tema Sherpa	36	Khumjung	Camp 4
Chowang Rinzi Sherpa	27	Namche Bazar	Camp 4
Sona Sherpa	36	Khumde	Camp 4
Gyalzen Sherpa	33	Phortse	Camp 2
Pema Tsering*	30	Darjeeling	Camp 2
Saila Tamang*	40	Temal	Camp 2

Ice Fall porters

NAME	AGE	VILLAGE
Phurkipa Sherpa (Ice Fall Sirdar)	54	Namche Bazar
Ang Tenzing Sherpa	38	Thomde
Changpa Sherpa*	31	Namche Bazar
Gyane Sherpa	29	Namche Bazar
Temba Sherpa*	28	Khumjung
Sangke Sherpa	20	Namche Bazar
Nimanuru Sherpa*	20	Khumjung

*Indicates a man on his first expedition.

NAME	AGE	VILLAGE
Ang Dali Sherpa*	23	Khumde
Ang Pasang Sherpa*	22	Phortse
Mingma Dorje Sherpa*	34	Namche Bazar
Phuri Sherpa*	28	Solu
Pasang Sherpa*	27	Solu
Dawa Sherpa	20	Namche Bazar
Ang Pemba Sherpa*	28	Thomde
Nima Dorje Sherpa*	21	Phakding
Ang Nima Sherpa	27	Khumde
Sonam Gyalzen Sherpa	28	Phortse
Pasang Kipa Sherpa	38	Rolwaling
Gyalzen Sherpa	25	Chhulemd
Sontemba Sherpa	32	Phulungtokpa
Ang Dorje Sherpa	29	Rolwaling
Thawa Gyalzen Sherpa	30	Pangboche
Nawang Yonden Sherpa*	31	Surke
Phutharke Sherpa	29	Yulajung
Nuru Jangbo Sherpa	29	Lomjo
Tsering Phenjo Sherpa	25	Namche Bazar

Base Camp staff/Cook staff

NAME	POSITION	AGE	VILLAGE
Lhakpa Thondup Sherpa	Base Camp Sirdar	25	Khumjung
Purna Sherpa	Base Camp Head Cook	32	Darjeeling & Kathmandu
Pasang Tendi Sherpa	Base Camp 2nd Cook	33	Khumjung
Kanchha Sherpa	Camp 2 Cook	29	Chhabel
Wangchu Gyalu Sherpa	Base Camp Sherpa Cook	48	Khumde
Sona Sherpa	Kitchen boy	42	Namche Bazar
Changpa Sherpa	Kitchen boy	21	Temal
Dome Sherpa	Kitchen boy	22	Namche Bazar
Ang Dawa Sherpa	Mail-runner	48	Namche Bazar
Tashi Sherpa	Mail-runner	26	Namche Bazar
Tendi Sherpa	Mail-runner	19	Khumde
Athutup Sherpa	Mail-runner	46	Khumjung
Damai Singh	Mail-runner	24	Temal
Pema Sherpa	Mail-runner	18	Chawa Khorye

*Indicates a man on his first expedition.

A diary of events

May 1974   Permission for Everest was granted to Bonington.

18 December   Barclays announced their support for the expedition. Without it the expedition could not have taken place.

9 April 1975   The expedition gear is sent overland in two Ford D 1614 standard box vans, loaned by Godfrey Davis, carrying 24 tons of food and equipment. The lorries were driven by Bob Stoodley, our Transport Organizer, and three professional drivers. They were accompanied by Ronnie Richards, a member of the climbing team.

3 May   The Lorries reached Kathmandu.

9 May to 10 June   Gear was air-freighted from Kathmandu to the air strip at Luglha and then carried by porters to Khumde where it was stored.

29 July   The team left Britain by an Air India 747 en route for Kathmandu.

2 August   The first party left Kathmandu as planned, travelling by Land Rover to Lamosangu and then starting the walk. The weather was surprisingly good for monsoon conditions with fine sunny mornings and afternoon rain.

The journey was completed in thirteen days and the party arrived in Khumde on 14 August.

4 August   The second party left Kathmandu, reaching Khumde on 16 August.

17 August   Nick Estcourt and Dougal Haston with four Sherpas set out from Khumde as an advanced party to site Base Camp.

18 August   The first main party set out from Khumde with 200 porters for Base Camp, followed by a second party on the 19th.

The remainder of the expedition gear was ferried up over the succeeding ten days.

21 August Nick Estcourt and Dougal Haston reached and sited Base Camp at a height of 17800 feet, accompanied by the Ice Fall Sirdar, Phurkipa and four Sherpas.

22 August Base Camp was reached by Chris Bonington, Mick Burke, Charles Clarke, Arthur Chesterman, Allen Fyffe and Ronnie Richards. This party included sixteen high-altitude Sherpas and thirteen Ice Fall Sherpas with 300 loads carried by porters and yaks. Base Camp could be considered established on this date.

Nick Estcourt and Dougal Haston made a recce of the Ice Fall reaching a height of approximately 19000 feet.

23 August Bonington, Fyffe, Burke, Chesterman and Richards with twelve Sherpas consolidated the route made by Estcourt and Haston and pushed on for a further few hundred feet up the Ice Fall. The middle section of the route through the Ice Fall seemed more complex than it was in 1972, with a series of lateral crevasses.

The second party arrived at Base Camp, consisting of Peter Boardman, Mike Cheney, Hamish MacInnes, Dave Clarke, Mike Thompson, Chris Ralling and Ian Stuart with fourteen high-altitude and twelve Ice Fall Sherpas.

25 August A strong party continued to make progress in the Ice Fall. Martin Boysen reached Base Camp after his delayed arrival at Kathmandu.

26 August Haston and Scott reached the site of Camp 1 and time was spent in improving the Ice Fall route with ladders and fixed rope.

28 August Camp 1 was established when MacInnes, Haston, Scott and Fyffe as lead climbers moved into the camp. Accompanying them were Mike Rhodes as Camp Manager, Mick Burke and Arthur Chesterman, filming, and ten Sherpas.

2 September Camp 2 was established at a height of 21700 feet. The Western Cwm was forced by the four lead climbers supported by six Sherpas.

6 September The South West Face was first stood on by

Scott, Burke, Fyffe and Richards who reached the site of Camp 3, fixing ropes along the route.

7 September   Braithwaite and Estcourt move into Camp 3 and push route out towards Great Central Gully.

8 September   Bonington decided to drop the proposed site of Camp 4 to about 800 feet above Camp 3. This was the last point giving real protection from avalanches or stone fall from above.

11 September   MacInnes, Boysen and Boardman moved up to Camp 4.

By this time the expedition was well ahead of schedule.

17 September   Bonington and Richards established Camp 5 at 25 500 feet.

18 September   Scott and Buke move up to Camp 5.

19 September   Scott, Bonington and Richards run rope out to foot of Rock Band.

20 September   Estcourt and Braithwaite, supported by Burke and Bonington, solved the problem of scaling the 1000-foot high Rock Band, the major obstacle on the South West Face. They found a ramp that led out of the deep-cut Left-Hand Gully towards the top of the Band.

22 September   Haston and Scott completed the ascent of the Rock Band and moved into Camp 6, loads being carried by three Sherpas, Bonington, Burke and Thompson.

23 September   Haston and Scott prepared for the first assault of the summit, running 1500 feet of fixed rope across the Upper Snow Field towards the South Summit Gully. There was one difficult rock pitch that required five pitons to surmount.

24 September   Doug Scott and Dougal Haston set out from Camp 6 at 3.00 a.m. They made good progress to the foot of the gully leading to the South Summit, which they reached at 1.00 p.m. Doug Scott led a difficult rock step of about 60 feet which was thinly covered in snow. This was time-consuming and then the gully itself proved very laborious, being filled with deep soft snow.

It was already 3.00 p.m. when they reached the South Summit. They had a brew here and dug a small snow hollow for a bivouac before setting out for the Summit, which they reached at 6.00 p.m. They found there the Chinese flag with some red bunting on a four-foot pole, clear proof of the Chinese ascent pre-monsoon 1975. It was a magnificent sunset and Doug took some magnificent photographs.

They then returned to the site of their bivouac and had what Doug described as the coldest bivouac of his life. They did have a bivvy stove with them. As this bivouac was actually on the South Summit it must be the highest in history. They only suffered frost-nipped toes and fingers.

25 September They left the bivouac at 6.00 a.m. and were, back at Camp 6, at a height of approximately 27300 feet, at 9.00 a.m. The second assault party were already on their way up and, of course, would have acted as a back-up team had Dougal and Doug needed help. There was ample oxygen in the top camp.

26 September A second attempt to reach the summit was made by Boysen, Burke, Boardman and Sherpa Pertemba. The party set out at 4.30 in the morning from Camp 6. Boysen was forced to turn back at about 5.30 after his oxygen failed and a crampon fell off. At this point Boardman and Pertemba were ahead and continued to the summit of Everest which they reached at approximately 1.10 p.m. On their way down, a short distance from the top, they were surprised to meet Burke. He was in good spirits and continued to the summit, whilst Boardman and Pertemba made their way down towards the South Summit where they had agreed to wait for Burke. They waited for over an hour during which time the weather deteriorated seriously into white-out conditions and a violent gale. Their own position was now critical. Boardman therefore took the agonizing decision to continue down. They only just managed to get back to their camp, an hour after dark. The storm raged throughout the next day making any kind of movement impossible. There was therefore no question of further search for Mick Burke and on 28 September, in the interest of safety, the mountain was cleared.

30 September All expedition back in Base Camp.

11 October All expedition back in Kathmandu to prepare for the journey back to Britain.

17 October Expedition fly into London.

Appendix 2

Logistics

by Chris Bonington

Logistics and planning may seem the very antithesis of the romantic adventure that mountaineering undoubtedly is. Without careful planning, however, even the smallest two-man trip may fail through lack of food or equipment at the right place at the right time and the romance will quickly turn sour. Personally I have found the planning of an expedition, particularly one as complex as Everest, an intriguing intellectual exercise. These notes are designed to show the course of my thinking in planning our attempt on the South West Face of Everest, but they would be relevant to the planning of any siege-style mountaineering expedition, where a series of camps, linked by fixed rope, are set up.

First step

The way I set about it was to start with the summit bid, and then to work back down to determine the number of camps, amount of fixed rope, tentage and other supplies I was going to need. This also indicated the ideal size of team for the climb in hand. At this stage it is also possible to make an initial assessment of the consumption of food and oxygen in the higher camps, but as one gets further down the mountain this becomes too complex and one needs a separate set of calculations.

I have listed in Annexe A the quantities I assessed we needed from Camp 6 back down to Camp 1. This provided the foundation of my planning for our rate of progress up the mountain and my deployment of the climbers and Sherpas at my disposal. Annexe A also sets out the basic approach to the climb.

Deployment on mountain

I had now worked out the weight and quantity of non-consumable supplies (items such as tents, cooking stoves, rope and medical kits, that would stay at each camp or in place on the mountain once they had been carried there). I also calculated the reserves of consumable items such as food/fuel and oxygen to be held at each camp. All this weighed 8785 lb. (251 35-lb. loads) and had to be carried from Base Camp to the appropriate camp on the mountain. The simplest way would have been to shift the lot from one camp to the next using all our carrying power to do it, only moving up as each stage was completed. This course, however, would have been slow and cumbersome, since this would have involved moving all our gear up to our highest point before moving on up to the next camp. This in effect would mean that the speed of our advance would be determined by the build-up of supplies and not by the pace set by our lead climbers.

The solution was to move no more supplies into each camp than was necessary to sustain the advance; this made it possible to ensure that the lead climbers were never held back for lack of supplies. To achieve this ideal however, was not easy, for it meant calculating exactly what supplies would be needed at each camp at any time and then ensuring that we had sufficient carrying power, and that it was correctly deployed.

The rate at which we could carry gear up the mountain, assuming a given number of carriers, depended on four factors:

1. The number of rest days required.
2. The effective payload that could be carried by climbers and Sherpas at different heights.
3. An estimate of failures to make carries because of sickness, misunderstandings, etc.
4. The weather – this was something that one couldn't predict. I therefore worked out the best possible rate of progress and ensured we had sufficient reserves at each camp so that we could sit out periods of bad weather.

The estimates I worked out are shown below.

Planning factors – reproduced from the original planning document before the expedition

1 REST RATES

a Sherpas

Base to 3	1 day in 4.
2 to 4	1 day in 2.
4 to 5	Last time we only managed to keep the Sherpas at 4 for 2 days, during which they made two carries, then returning to 2. To keep 6 Sherpas at 4 this would mean one would need 18 altogether, the other 12 resting or moving.
	This time, with a better Camp 4, I hope to keep the Sherpas up for 4 days, one of which would be resting. They would then return to 2 and have three days' rest before returning. This would mean we should only need 12 Sherpas for the 2 to 4 carry.
5 to 6	Probably not more than 2 carries in succession without a rest – we will have to play by ear. They would use oxygen.

b Climbers

Base to 3	Allow every other day.
2 to 4	It is unlikely that the climbers would manage this carry – we might be able to use carries for a 3 to 4 carry once again on an every-other-day principle.
4 to 5	Every other day. Last time several members of the team made this carry without oxygen – a definite plus.
5 to 6	Same as Sherpas. At this height the climbers probably have the edge on the Sherpas.

2 LOADS

a Sherpas

Base to 3	35 lb. (Camp 2 food boxes 38 lb., which they should manage)
2 to 4	30 lb.
4 to 5	30 lb.
5 to 6	20 lb.

b Climbers
Base to 3   24 lb. (·66 load)
3 to 4   20 lb.
4 to 5   20 lb.   } using oxygen to bring it to 32 lb.
5 to 6   20 lb.

These weights are based on what happened last time. If climbers can manage more without smashing themselves this will obviously be a good plus. All climbers carry their personal gear from camp to camp which almost certainly will be more than the above.

3 FAILURE TO MAKE CARRIES

This is very difficult to assess, since it can depend on sickness, lack of morale or alternative use of people. In any day's carry I have reckoned on the following percentage of loads not being taken to their destination –
Base to 3   10%   2 to 4   20%   4 to 5   40%

Formula for movement up mountain

Using the above information I now had to work out the most effective way of deploying our carrying power, in the first instance to place in the appropriate camp all the non-consumable items and then to ensure that the expedition's daily consumption was met. There were two major consumable items – food/fuel – which could be considered together, and above Camp 4 oxygen for both climbing and sleeping.

I therefore calculated the weights involved of both durable and consumable items as shown in Annexe B.

Having done this I was ready to calculate our rate of progress and deployment on the climb. In the early stages the vital factor was the problem of clearing firstly Base Camp and then Camp 1 of all the non-consumable items and reserves of food/fuel and oxygen, sufficiently quickly so that I could move the bulk of my thirty-four high-altitude porters up to Camp 2, to start relaying our gear up the Face. With fifty-seven Sherpas and climbers at Camp 2 and above, I had calculated I needed a minimum of twelve carries a day to Camp 2 just to keep them supplied with food/fuel and oxygen (to keep my oxygen reserve at 2 at the desired level as bottles were taken out of it, up the Face). My calculations are shown as follows:

Day 0: At Base – 17 climbers, 60 Sherpas, 2 cook staff – independent 12 BBC team 251/35 lb. loads to go to 1 and above plus daily consumption.

Day 1: 'A' team plus four Sherpas move to 1.

Day 1 to Day 3:

Available Manpower

Climbers/ Sherpas	× Rest Days	× Sherpa Loads	No. of days available to carry		Effective Loads
15 (Cl.)	·50	·66	3	15	
54 (Sh.)	·75		3	121	

$$136 \text{ less } 10\%^* = 123 \text{ loads}$$
$$- \quad 4 \text{ loads (consumed)}$$
$$\overline{ \quad 119}$$
$$- \quad 48 \text{ loads stay at } 1$$
$$\overline{ \quad 71 \text{ loads to go on}}$$

Calculation of food/fuel consumed at
1 and above for Day 4 on: 45 people × 5 lb.=   7 loads per day

Time taken to clear base with 30
Sherpas at Base: 251–119   = 132 loads to be shifted from Base =

30 (Sh.)   ·75   = 23 loads per day
                                              less 10%* == 20 loads
                                                        − 7 loads consumed at 1
                                                        ___
                                              13 loads per day with stockpile to go on

Therefore it will take 11 days to clear Base Camp of all non-consumable items and consumable remains.

Climbers/ Sherpas	× Rest Days	× Sherpa Loads	× Loads	No. of days available to carry	
Day 5 to 7 from 1:					10
					63
10 (Cl.)	·50	·66	3		
28 (Sh.)	·75		3		$\overline{73}$ less 10%* = 66 loads
					− 2 loads consumed at 2
					___
					64 loads to go on

H

Effective Loads

Available Manpower			No. of days available to carry	Effective Loads
Climbers/Sherpas	× Rest Days	× Sherpa Loads		
Day 8 to 12 from 1:				
5 (Cl.)	·66			
from Day 9 on				
5 (Cl.)	·50		5	8
24 (Sh.)	·75		5	90

95 less 10%* = 88 loads
−11 loads consumed at 2

77 loads to go on
141 loads accumulated at 2

*Inefficiency factor

Daily consumption at 1 and above, including
BBC team − 71 people

= 11 loads food/fuel
1 load film stock

Available Manpower

Climbers/ × Rest × Sherpa × Loads
Sherpas   Days   Days

No. of days
available
to carry

Daily consumption at 2 and above, including
BBC team – 41 people

= 6 loads food/fuel
1 load film stock
—
7 loads per day

Day 13 to 15 from 1 to 2:
Holding consumption rate plus a bit more taken up with
the many things I can't have accounted for, from Mick's
false teeth to a forgotten pair of boots.

Day 16 to 22 from 1:
Time taken to shift 66 loads to Camp 2 to clear 1:
204 – 138 = 66 loads. After consumption at 1, 10 loads
per day

7 days to shift

Effective Loads

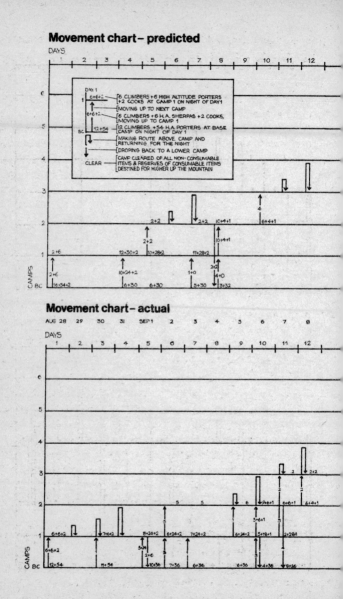

Movement chart – predicted

DAYS

DAY 1

- **6+6+2** — 6 CLIMBERS +6 HIGH ALTITUDE PORTERS +2 COOKS AT CAMP 1 ON NIGHT OF DAY 1
- MOVING UP TO NEXT CAMP
- **6+6+2** — 6 CLIMBERS +6 H.A. SHERPAS +2 COOKS, MOVING UP TO CAMP 1
- **12+54** — 12 CLIMBERS +54 H.A. PORTERS AT BASE CAMP ON NIGHT OF DAY 1
- MAKING ROUTE ABOVE CAMP AND RETURNING FOR THE NIGHT
- DROPPING BACK TO A LOWER CAMP
- CLEAR — CAMP CLEARED OF ALL NON-CONSUMABLE ITEMS & RESERVES OF CONSUMABLE ITEMS DESTINED FOR HIGHER UP THE MOUNTAIN

Movement chart – actual

AUG 28 29 30 31 SEP 1 2 3 4 5 6 7 8

DAYS

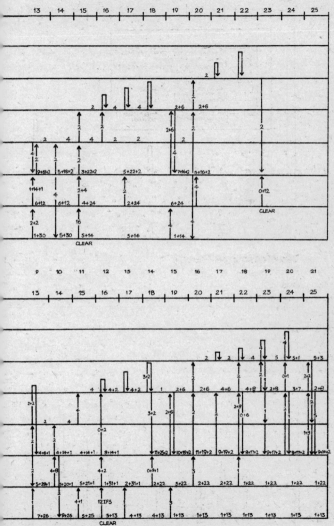

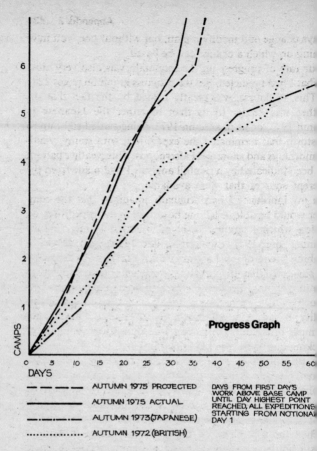

Progress Graph

— — — — AUTUMN 1975 PROJECTED	DAYS FROM FIRST DAY'S WORK ABOVE BASE CAMP UNTIL DAY HIGHEST POINT REACHED, ALL EXPEDITIONS STARTING FROM NOTIONAL DAY 1
———— AUTUMN 1975 ACTUAL	
—·—·—·— AUTUMN 1973 (JAPANESE)	
················· AUTUMN 1972 (BRITISH)	

These calculations gave me the most effective initial strateg
for shifting all the gear we needed from Base to Camp
We followed it very closely on the mountain as comparison
of the predicted and the actual movement charts, below, w
show.

Above Camp 2 we altered our plans a great deal, changin
the sites of Camps 4 and 5, introducing the concept of two ten
at Camp 6 for the second and third summit bid, allowin
four men to take part in each bid. I was able to cope with the
changes even in the rarefied atmosphere of Camp 5, becau
of the depth of planning and thinking earlier on. You ca

ays change and modify a plan, but without one, you have
thing on which a change can be based.

our rate of progress up the mountain was also very close
that I had predicted. See the progress graph on pages 228–
This, of course, was greatly helped by the fact that the
ther was kinder to us than to either the Japanese in
umn 1973, or us in autumn 1972, being settled right up to
storm that terminated the expedition, with sunny, wind-
mornings and snow most afternoons. This weather pattern
been indicated by a rainfall analysis I had made from the
rent sources that were available.

n my innocence I had originally imagined that the com-
er would be able to tell me how to plan the expedition, an
sion which I suspect is shared by most laymen. Whilst
nning our 1972 expedition, Ian McNaught Davis, a
bing friend of mine and managing director of Comshare,
suggested that we might like to use one of his computers to
in planning. Because the expedition had been organized
uch a rush, we had been unable to make full use of this
lity; it had, however, shown me its value as a means, not
much of finding the perfect logistic answer, but one of
cking out one's own planning thinking.

the spring of 1975 Ian McNaught Davis once again
red his help making available one of his programmers,
hen Taylor, and through the spring and early summer we
ed out a series of computer games, simulating the move-
nt of men and supplies up the mountain. We never actually
hed the top, since we always seemed to get stuck in a
stic bottleneck about the time that Camp 4 was established,
reason being that I was moving my men and supplies by
ition rather than by logic based on a clear-cut formula. I
created the formula described above after three abortive
mpts. Stephen Taylor now describes his approach to the
puting problem.

ting and working the programme
Stephen Taylor

ially, the problem seemed quite daunting, and far removed

from my usual fare of business and OR models. C[
inspection revealed the critical similarity: despite the fact
the problem involved climbers and Sherpas, and tents
whatever else, I could consider the whole thing as a pro[
in stock control. I had seven camps on the mountain,
men and equipment to put in them, plus some rules gover[
how I might move them around. All my model had to do[
to accept instructions regarding the movements, check
the rules weren't being broken, and keep track of w[
everybody and everything went, including the food, w[
disappeared.

We managed to break the equipment into four catego[
tentage; food and gas cartridges; oxygen cylinders;
climbing gear.

These four categories had to be treated differently. Ten[
determined how many people could sleep in a camp. The [
and gas cartridges were consumed at a reasonably predict[
rate, which depended upon altitude. The same went for
oxygen cylinders except that the rate was different, and
didn't start to be used until Camp 5. The climbing gear
mostly hammered into the mountain, but without an adeq[
supply in the highest established camp, the lead clim[
would have been stranded. Every member of the exped[
was allowed a limited allowance of personal baggage, w[
was kept with him wherever he went, but we didn't hav[
account for this in the model: every time someone m[
camp, he didn't carry anything other than his bedroll.
expected that only European climbers would need to
oxygen at Camp 4. All these rules had to be built into
model.

The model was constructed around five system arr[
These were:

1. MOVE – this array held the current day's orders,
   the proposed movements of men and materials bot[
   and down the mountain.
2. POSITION – this array held details of the number[
   men and weights of equipment of different categories[
   each of the seven camps.

3. NPOSITION – a 'working' array which held the results of performing the moves held on MOVE in the situation described in POSITION. The programme validated this position and checked back with the user before saving the old POSITION and overwriting it with NPOSITION.

4. HISTORY – this was a 3-D matrix which consisted of successive POSITIONs laminated together to form a 'history' of the stock positions on the mountain.

5. STRATEGY – similar to HISTORY, this matrix consisted of successive layers of the MOVE arrays.

At the end of a 'run' we were able to have the HISTORY and STRATEGY arrays printed out, and these constituted a plan for the assault.

In accordance with the current dogma of system design and programming, I took as structured an approach to implementing the model as the limitations of APL would permit. The main features of the model were the seven APL functions START, CONTINUE, ORDERS, PROJECT, CHANGE, SAVE and DISPLAY; and I arranged them like this:

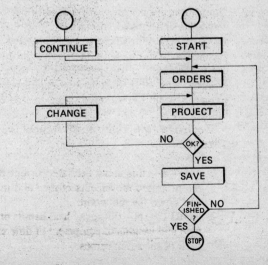

Briefly, the effect of each function was as follows:

1. START – initializes the system variables for the beginning of the expedition, putting correct supplies in Base Camp (Camp 0). After initialization, it called ORDERS.

2. CONTINUE – similar to START, but continued work on previously defined HISTORY and STRATEGY arrays, allowing the user to take up a plan where he had left it.

3. ORDERS – this function handled and prompted for instructions from the user, and built them up into the MOVE matrix, displaying the final MOVE array, and calling CHANGE if the user was dissatisfied with what he had asked for.

4. CHANGE – an editing function which handled changes to be made to the MOVE array.

5. PROJECT – this function calculated the results of making the moves described in MOVE on the position as described by POSITION. I stored the result in NPOSITION, and checked for mistakes, issuing warnings, and invoked CHANGE if errors were found, or if the user was dissatisfied with the results of his instruction. This was an iterative function to the extent that the use could continue to modify and 'project' the results of his orders until he reached the position that he wanted.

6. SAVE – a simple function that laminated MOVE and POSITION onto STRATEGY and HISTORY respectively, overwrote POSITION with NPOSITION, and reset MOVE and NPOSITION at zero.

7. DISPLAY – a utility function to print the system matrices. Having been passed a matrix as its argument, it determines from the size of the matrix whether it is MOVE, STRATEGY, HISTORY, or POSITION/NPOSITION, and prints the array using an appropriate format. Although all the supplies were stored in the system as weights, DISPLAY, by reference to a number of tables within the workspace, was able to show weight of oxygen as so many bottles, weight of

food as so many man/days (it varied with height . . .) and so on. It was an enormous help during development of the model to be able to print out (intelligibly!) any of the system arrays with a single command, as for instance 'DISPLAY POSITION'.

Running the model

Ideally, I should have disappeared into a hole in the ground sometime in the spring of 1975, and emerged after a suitably short period with a fully documented and tested model to hand over to Chris, who would then be freely and easily able to play with it until he had evolved his Master Strategy.

Often as we were working on the model, I was debugging and reprogramming as we went along; something that is only really feasible to my knowledge in APL. There were many times that the entire programme seemed to be held together with string and recycled chewing-gum; but the overall soundness of the structured approach held up and allowed me to extricate myself from some very messy situations. An immeasurable help was the compactness of the APL code – the seven main functions comprised no more than 150 lines of code – and the amenability of the APL interpreter to my amending the programme in the middle of its execution.

I had originally visited Chris Bonington in March to discuss the model, and I returned with a trial version in April for three days. On this occasion, I took with me a portable computer terminal, which I was able to use via the telephone. Time was getting short and subsequent sessions were held by telephone, late at night, with me sitting at a terminal in the basement of Comshare's London office, and Chris doing all the hard work up in Cumbria.

I'd like to emphasize the last point. Once the model had been written, the hard work really became his department. I would be sitting at the terminal 'driving', with a book on my lap, and Chris would telephone me with his proposals for the next moves. I'd type them in, and read back to him the results. I could then go back to my book, while Chris struggled with the next set of moves. As a model, the programme in no way

solved his problem – it served as a tool for discussing it, handling the very tedious and involved calculations concerning
weight allowances, food reserves, and gear and food
consumption.

And so the work went on, usually late into the night and
small hours, exploring Chris's ideas and strategies, and trying
to identify critical points, phases in the climb which were
very sensitive to variation. It was during this period when I
was acting as a 'chauffeur' that I carried out the second part of
the study.

By the green glow of a terminal screen, about midnight on
a May night, I shuffled the seventy-eight cards of the Waite
Tarot deck, and spread them out in the Grand Cross reading
to see what could be read of the expedition's future. The
prognosis was excellent, with strong indications of success
based on the united efforts of a balanced team, and fame at
the end. For the interested, some of the details were:

Significator	The Fool
Beneath him	Two of Swords
Crowning	Three of Pentacles
Covering	Ace of Swords
Tenth card	The Sun
Ninth card	Ace of Pentacles

The final plan, as used on Everest, was never tested on the
computer model before the expedition left; and I think that
this gives a clue to the real benefits of the study. Chris handed
me a copy of the Final Solution just before he left, announcing
blithely that he'd reconsidered his plans and had come up
with a new one. Momentarily, I was appalled. Was he going
to reject the results of all the work that we had done?

In fact not. The Final Solution was very much, I think, the
child of the work that Chris had put into the study. The
process of exploring and testing his ideas on the logistical
problems had yielded the insights into the problem that we
had originally been aiming for, and as a result of this he was
able to construct the strategy that was so successfully employed, confident in his ability to modify it in action. My

biggest thrill of the expedition was a card from the mountain reporting that Camp 4 had been established at the same time that Base Camp was cleared – a point which had been established as critical. My personal satisfaction at the end came from the realization that Chris had been able to use his resources so that the climbing problems were not unnecessarily complicated by logistical ones; and in doing so had managed to take the biggest expedition by the hardest route in the shortest time – to the top of Everest.

Annexe A: Outline plan of the mountain (*prepared August 1974*)

1 *Team strength to go to Camp 2 and above*
    14 climbers (European)
     2 climbers (European) based on Camp 2
     2 climbers (European) based on Base Camp
    26 Sherpas shared between Camp 1 and Base
    34 Sherpas available for Camp 2 and above

2 *Forcing the Ice Fall* It is impossible to determine when we can start climbing the Ice Fall. This depends on the pattern of weather during the monsoon. We should be in a position, however, to start work on the Ice Fall from 25 August. It should not take longer than 5 days.

3 *Making route to Rock Band, once Ice Fall has been climbed*
We shall have 3 parties of 4 climbers each who will take turns in making the route up to Camp 5.
    Party A makes the route from Camp 1–3
    Party B makes the route from Camp 3–4
    Party C makes the route from Camp 4–5
We push the route out as quickly as we can – avoiding any delays.

4 *Build-up of supplies to Rock Band* This build-up is made as fast as possible by Sherpas and climbers not involved in lead climbing. Sherpas and climbers moving up to high camps in such a way as to enable the forward momentum to be kept up – in other words, Advance Base is built up at the same time as supplies are shifted from it up the Face.

5 *Carrying policy on Face* Camp 3 is used solely as a staging post. Sherpas prefer to carry straight through to 4 from 2 and have a rest day in between. In autumn 1972 very few Sherpas did more than two carries from 2 to 5 without coming down for a rest at 2. We shall make 4 a much more comfortable place in the hope of getting at least three carries from Sherpas. We should try to maintain 2 climbers and 6 Sherpas at Camp 4 while building up Camp 5 and 6. There will be space for 4 climbers at Camp 5.

6 *Forcing Rock Band* It is impossible to tell how long this will take. We want to start work on the Rock Band as quickly as possible. In the first instance, therefore, a pair will go up – then a foursome – to work on it.

7 *Fixed-roping above 6* This will be carried out by 4 climbers operating from 5, once the Rock Band has been fixed-roped, using 1000 feet of 7 mm rope, which should reach most of the way across the traverse.

8 *Establishing Camp 6* Camp 6 will be established by climbers and Sherpas making one carry on the following day the summiters supported by 2 moving into the camp.

9 *Resting* Climbers can rest at either Base or 2. If there is to be a prolonged rest it is best for climbers to return to Base.

10 *Oxygen policy* Sherpas do not use oxygen till Camp 5 and above. Climbers do not use oxygen until Camp 4 and above. It is not necessary to use oxygen at Camp 4 for sleeping, but there is enough there for anyone in a bad way to use it.

11. Tentage Plan

Camp 6	1 assault box	Sleeps 2
Camp 5	2 face boxes with platforms and reinforced nylon covers	Sleeps 4
Camp 4	4 face boxes with platforms and covers	Sleeps 8
Camp 3	2 boxes (for staging)	Sleeps 4
Camp 2	4 super boxes	Stores, mess kitchen, but can be used for sleeping in emergency
	4 face boxes	Sleeps 8
	8 Vango tents	Sleeps 24
	4 tunnel tents	Sleeps 8
		—
		40
Camp 1	2 super boxes	Sleeps 16
	2 Vango tents	Sleeps 4
		—
		20
Base	2 super boxes	
	3 big bell tents	
	3 cook shelters	
	10 Vango tents	

	Weight/ lb.	Oxygen	Gas	Food
ABOVE CAMP 6				
1 assault 4 bottles oxygen	48	4		
120 m 7 mm climbing rope	8			
Karabiners and pegs/stakes	5			
Pack	3			
Oxgen system	3			
Bivvy sack	1			
Movie camera and magazine	5			
Still camera	3			
2 × 38-lb. loads	76	4	—	—
2nd assault Same as above				
2 × 38-lb. loads	76	4	—	—
TO CAMP 6				
For 1st assault Assault box	30			
Camp kit, inc. stove, etc.	5			
2 man-days food	5			2
4 carts. gas	3		4	
1 bottle oxygen	12	1		
2 men's personal gear	30			
Radio and batteries	3			

For 2nd assault				
2 man-days food	88	1	4	2
4 carts. gas	5			2
	3		4	
2 men's personal gear	30			
1 bottle oxygen	12	1		
TOTALS TO CAMP 6:	50	1	4	2
	290	10	8	4

Payload for 1st assault, allowing 20 lb. per man:
    8 loads

Payload for 2nd assault, allowing 21 lb. per man:
    6 loads

    TOTAL LOADS TO CAMP 6
    = 14 loads

CAMP 5–6

Fixing 6+ from 5		
3 × 120 metres 7 mm rope (972 ft)	24	
10 snow stakes	10	
16 karabiners	3	
4 deadmen	4	
4 bottles oxygen	48	4
	89	4

		Weight/ lb.	Oxygen	Gas	Food
Fixing 5 to 6	4 men carrying 22 lb. each	78			
	3 × 200 metre 8 mm ropes	20			
	600 ft 9 mm climbing rope	20			
	Assorted ironware	240			
	5 × 4 man-days 20 btls. oxygen		20		
	8 man-days carry for 1st assault				
	8 bottles oxygen	96	8		
	4 man-days carry 2nd assault				
	4 bottles oxygen	48	4		
		502	32		

AT CAMP 5
4 men

			Oxygen	Gas	Food
8 × 4 man-days work	2 face boxes with platforms	200			
	2 camp kits plus foams	40			
4 × 4 man-days reserve	48 man-days food 3 lb.	144			48
	96 carts. gas	60		96	
48 man-days	Sleeping oxygen and spare – 24	288	24		
	Radio and batteries	12			
	Medical kit	6			
	Film stock and cameras	60			

		1685	70	104	52
Less personal gear – 20 lb. each					
RUNNING TOTAL TO 5		1685	70	104	52
CAMP 4–5	*Payload of 30 lb. – 56 loads*				
	4 × 200 metre 8 mm ropes	104			
	Ironware	20			
	32 climber trips with oxygen – 32 bottles	384	32		
AT CAMP 4	4 face boxes with platforms	508	32		
	4 tent kits	400			
		20			
6 Sherpas	140 man-days food	420			
2 climbers	280 carts. gas	175		280	
60 man-day carry	Radio and batteries	16			
	Medical kit	10			
80 man-day rest	Spare oxygen (16)	192	16		
	Film cameras and stock	90			140
	RUNNING TOTALS TO 4	1323	16	280	140
		3516	118	384	192

	Weight/ lb.	Oxygen	Gas	Food
CAMP 3–4 *Payload of 30 lb. – 118 loads*				
8 × 200 metre 8mm	208			
Assorted ironware	20			
	228			
AT CAMP 3				
Used as staging post – 2 boxes	120			
Sherpas carry from 2 — 2 camp kits	40			
Radio and batteries	10			
Medical kit	6			
40 man-days food	120			40
80 carts. fuel	50		80	
	346			
RUNNING TOTAL THROUGH 3	4090	118	464	232
CAMP 2–3 *Payload of 30 lb. – 137 loads*				
2 × 200 metres 8 mm rope	52			
Assorted ironware	15			
	67			

With bad weather there could be greater delays, demanding more food and fuel.

AT CAMP 2

4 super boxes	480			
8 Vango tents	240			
4 face boxes	240			
4 tunnel tents	80			
4 lightweight tarps.	40			
Medical kit	80			
Kitchen kit	80			
Lighting	20			
Radios and batteries	50			
Office	40			
Tool kit	40			
Extras	300			
Spare oxygen (25)	300	25		
560 man-days reserve				
Camp 2 food (4 lb.)	2240			
560 man-days reserve				
kerosene	600			
80 man-days reserve				
mountain rations	240		160	
160 reserve carts.	100		160	80
	5170	25	160	80
Allow 40 lb. per man personal gear going to 2 –	2000			
50 men				
RUNNING TOTALS TO 2	11327	143	624	312

	Weight/lb.	Oxygen	Gas	Food

Payload of 35 lb. – 324 loads

(I have not allowed for day-to-day servicing of food and fuel – allow an average population of 42 consuming 5 lb. per day of food and fuel=210 lb. per day – 6 loads)

CAMP 1-2

	Weight/lb.
Marker poles (200)	200
8 ladders	160
3 × 200 metres 8 mm rope	78
Assorted ironware	20
	458

AT CAMP 1

	Weight/lb.
2 super boxes	240
2 Vango tents	60
Kitchen kit	40
70 man-days reserve fuel/food	350
Radio and batteries	20
360 man-days food/fuel to feed men carrying to 2 – 5 lb.	1800
	2510
RUNNING TOTAL TO 1	14295

Payload of 35 lb. – 409 loads

Annexe B: Weight distribution

1. NON CONSUMABLE

1. Ropes and fixings

To camp	Net weight to camp	Accumulative
Camp 6	32	32
Camp 5	159	191
Camp 4	124	315
Camp 3	228	543
Camp 2	67	610
Camp 1	458	1068

2. Tentage and camp gear

Camp 6	48	48
Camp 5	318	366
Camp 4	506	872
Camp 3	176	1048
Camp 2	1690	2738
Camp 1	360	3090

2. RESERVES – Consumable items at camps when fully established.

1. Oxygen

Camp 6	10 bottles	120	120
Camp 5	12 bottles	144	264
Camp 4	16 bottles	192	456
Camp 2	32 bottles	384	840
Camp 1	4 bottles	48	888

Oxygen used in initial run out from 4 to 5 and then in movement of climbers from 4 to 5, can be drawn from reserve, which will automatically be topped up allowance for basic consumption.

2. Food/fuel

For Camps 1 and 2 this represents 4 lb. food plus 1 lb. kerosene. For Camps 3 to 6 this represents 3 lb. food plus 1 lb. Camping Gaz.

Camp 6	2 m/d	8	8
Camp 5	20 m/d	80	88
Camp 4	42 m/d	168	256
Camp 3	7 m/d	28	284
Camp 2	530 m/d	2650	2934*
Camp 1	160 m/d	800	3734

*To be divided into a third mountain and two thirds Camp 2 rations.

265 man/days mountain ration and 318 man/days Camp 2 ration
because of different weights there is a discrepancy in no. of man/day
at 2.

C. TOTAL WEIGHTS AT CAMPS

		Lb.	Loads/
Camp 6	208	208	11/20
Camp 5	701	909	31/30
Camp 4	990	1899	64/30
Camp 3	432	2331	67/35
Camp 2	4791	7122	204/35
Camp 1	1666	8788	215/35

Acknowledgement to suppliers

We were able to organize the expedition with the help of
very small administrative staff, thanks to the hard work of th
secretaries of the organizers, many of whom carried out th
work in addition to their normal jobs without any extra pa
and also to a high level of automation in my own small offic

IBM loaned us two typewriters, the 82 Selectric and
memory typewriter. I used the latter machine to draft th
book. Everything you type goes into a computer-type memor
which can then be recalled. This makes it neat and easy
correct the text alterations, but with the memory typewrit
I could make my alterations, switch it on to automatic an
have a page of typescript hammered out for me as I sippe
my coffee.

Rank Xerox very kindly loaned us a 660 Copier/Duplicato
which proved invaluable for duplicating newsletters, lists ar
letters. Sinclair gave us their Cambridge Calculators. The
proved invaluable throughout the expedition, being used
our treasurer Nick Estcourt to calculate VAT and add
endless invoices, by myself and my secretary to make over
thousand currency conversions into Indian and Nepale
rupees for our import documents, and on the mountain itself
calculate Sherpa wages and expedition logistics.

CONSUMPTION RATE WHEN CAMP 5 IS FULLY OCCUPIED

Daily Consumption

Camp	Cl.	Sh.	Cks.	BBC+ HA Sh.	Total	Items	Wt per unit	Wt each Camp	Loads at each Camp	Acc. Wt.	Acc. Loads
5	4	—	—	—	4	6 btls. oxygen	12	72			
						4 man-days ff	4	16			
						Film bats		10			
								98	3 × 30	98	3 × 30
4	2	6	—	—	8	1 btl oxygen	12	12			
						8 man-days ff*	4	32			
								44	—	142	8 × 30
2	7	28	2	8	45	45 day ff	5	225			
						1 load film		35			
								260	8 × 35	402	12 × 23
1	2	12	2	2	16	16 man-day ff	5	80	2+ × 35	482	14 × 35
Base	4+2	14	10	2	32						

*BBC team responsible for getting film up to Camp 4 from 2 with their 4 HA Sherpas.

Appendix 3

Organization in Nepal

by Mike Cheney

In organizing the expedition arrangements in Nepal I was helped by Lt-Col Jimmy Roberts, owner of our trekking and mountaineering agency, Mountain Travel, and also by my own very experienced staff at Mountain Travel, Mr Dawa Norbu Sherpa of the Sherpa Co-operative Trekking (P) Ltd and Sirdar Pertemba Sherpa.

My five main tasks were to obtain import licences for the expedition equipment and stores, and liaise with the various Nepalese government departments; to meet the expedition's two trucks on arrival at the border and clear them through Customs; to have all the stores and equipment flown to Luglha and stored safely in Khumde before the monsoon; to recruit the Sherpa team of eight high-altitude and Ice Fall porters; and to make all the arrangements for the approach march.

As well as the import licences, special government permits had to be obtained to operate wireless sets from Base Camp to Namche Bazar, as well on the mountain. The expedition was the first to make full use of the Nepal Meteorological Service for weather forecasts, instead of getting forecasts from India. Weather reports were received daily at five p.m. for the following twenty-four hours together with the outlook for the day after. The weather reports were sent by wireless from Kathmandu to the Syangboche Meteorological Station, from Syangboche the reports were relayed to Base Camp on the expedition's own radio, installed at the Namche Bazar Police Post. To assist the Meteorological Department reports on the weather at Base Camp were sent to Kathmandu by wireless twice a day at eight a.m. and twelve noon.

Recruitment of Sherpa Team

As early as July 1974 Chris Bonington was anxious to have

Pertemba as Sirdar for the expedition: Pertemba was not so sure he wanted the job at that point, but agreed in principle.

In December 1974 selection of the Sherpa team started in all seriousness. Colonel Roberts and I selected a hard core from Mountain Travel staff Sherpas. Ang Phu as assistant to Pertemba, Lhakpa Thondup as Base Camp Sirdar, Purna Sherpa, my personal cook-bearer for sixteen years, as Base Camp cook, together with some twelve regular Mountain Travel employees as high-altitude porters, Ice Fall porters and Base Camp/Camp 2 staff. Phurkipa was selected for Ice Fall Sirdar, an older man with more experience of the Ice Fall than any other Sherpa or climber.

Between December 1974 and July 1975 the lists for thirty-four high-altitude porters and twenty-six Ice Fall porters were completed from the many volunteers. There were many young Sherpas from villages outside Khumbu anxious to join the expedition, also Tamangs, usually employed as low-altitude porters, who were anxious to prove that they were as good as Sherpas as high-altitude porters. The final selection of the high-altitude porter team rested with Pertemba and Ang Phu. The final team selected reflected the combination of experience, strength of character and youthfulness of Sirdar Pertemba who used his authority in the matter of selection to very good effect. His team was a good mix of experienced men from previous South West Face expeditions, experienced young Ice Fall porters, nearly all in their twenties, being given a chance to go high for the first time, and a few keen young men on their first expedition. Similarly the Ice Fall team consisted of approximately half old hands, some selected on arrival in Khumbu in August, and half keen young men who had failed to make the high-altitude team.

The Base Camp staff, cooks and kitchen boys who would remain at Base Camp or Camp 2, were selected by Purna and Lhakpa Thondup. The mail-runners, also, were a combination of youth and keenness and past experience. The express mail team were two youngsters, one Sherpa, Tendi, and one Tamang, Damai Singh Lama. Their best time was eighteen days from Base Camp to Kathmandu and back to Base Camp

– sixteen days actually on the move for the approximately 240-mile round journey.

After the expedition Sherpa team had been largely completed the BBC film team came up in May 1975 with a requirement of their own. They wanted a Sherpa team of eight, two of whom were to be high-altitude porters to go above Camp 2, and during the approach march they wished to be semi-independent, able to camp separately, if necessary. Jagatman Lama, a Tamang, was selected as their Sirdar and another Tamang, Saila, was a camera porter. Saila had worked with Ned Kelly as a camera porter on previous filming projects in Nepal.

The total Sherpa team of eighty-two was completed by the inclusion of two Gurkha serving soldiers as signalmen to operate the main Squadcal radios between Base Camp and Namche Bazar. The two men selected by HQ Brigade of Gurkhas for service with the expedition were Cpl Prembahadur Thapa 6GR and L/C Jaikumar Rai 7GR. L/C Jaikumar had served with the Army Nuptse Expedition in the spring of 1975 and both men were to go with the Army Everest Expedition in the spring of 1976.

We had hoped to employ more Tamangs in the team, but this went against the grain with the Sherpas, on the grounds that Tamangs were unproven as high-altitude and Ice Fall porters and there were plenty of Sherpas available, especially as the expedition was the only one in the Khumbu area at the time. Four Tamangs were, in fact, employed by the expedition and worked in perfect harmony with the Sherpas.

In accordance with Nepalese regulations, our Sherpas and Liaison Officer were insured. Cover was obtained in the UK. In addition, due to the very large sum (£6000) to be paid in compensation on the death of any Sherpa killed during the expedition, I introduced for the first time a Form of Will to be completed by all Sherpas employed by the expedition so that the compensation payable on their death should go to relatives of their own choice. The Will Form was prepared by Messrs Robson and Morrow, Auditors to Mountain Travel and was accepted as an authorized legal document by the Solicitor General of the Government of Nepal.

Appendix 4

Transport

by Ronnie Richards and Bob Stoodley

When it became evident in November 1974 that the expedition gear was going to need to be transported overland to Kathmandu, the Transport Section was soon immersed in what was almost an expedition of its own. Bob Stoodley, who is chairman of Manchester Garages, was able to enlist the assistance of Diana Lister in dealing with many hundreds of letters and documents required. It is comparatively straightforward to obtain a cheap lorry or van and just set out with fairly minimal preparations, as is done by many small expeditions. To transport over 20 tons introduces complications, however.

Bob had first of all to identify and obtain suitable vehicles. A camel train of small trucks seemed extravagant where two elephantine ones would suffice, but these would then require drivers of professional standard. One truck would come straight back empty, while the other would stay in Kathmandu and bring back gear at the end of the expedition. We were fortunate that Cecil Redfern, chairman of Godfrey Davis, agreed to make two 16-ton Ford D 1614 lorries available on very generous terms for hire somewhat outside their customary area. The lorries each had a separate 1700 cu. ft van container capable of carrying ten tons and were adapted for the journey by Manchester Garages. A sleeper cab, complete with cupboards, light and signal to the driver below was built on top of each driving cab so that we could sleep while on the move and drive fairly continuously. Side lockers were constructed below the container chassis to store food, spares, tools and anything needed for the journey. Extra fuel tanks, a tow bar and other refinements were also added. Total cargo volume was about 2200 cu. ft per lorry.

Three experienced and qualified HGV drivers were then contacted who were willing and able to tackle this sort of journey. Allen Evans and John O'Neill were lorry drivers for a subsidiary of Manchester Garages, had been in the Army together and had travelled overseas. Alan Riley originally came from Kenya, knew Mike Cheney and was contemplating starting an overland trucking service to Nepal. Our trip would be a useful reconnaissance. (On seeing the problems facing a commercial operation further east, particularly crossing India, the idea was shelved.) Ronnie Richards was also part of the overland team as navigator and occasional driver, since he had done the journey before and would then help with the further transport of gear in Nepal. Bob Stoodley's experience in maintaining as well as driving large vehicles filled the crucial role of mechanic.

The other main problem was documentation to cover both vehicles and their contents. We would be carrying a large quantity and high value of goods and all the tedious paper work would have to be in order for each of the 22 Customs posts crossed and up to the strict commercial requirements. Expeditions carrying a fraction of our cargo have been known to experience delays or difficulties at some frontier through inadequate documentation. On our scale we seemed unlikely to get through by the usual ploy of waving an expedition leaflet and making impromptu explanations.

In addition to standard considerations of insurance and visas, countries en route require assurance that vehicles and valuable goods in transit are not going to be sold or offloaded and this is given in the form of Bank Guarantees or deposits. Vehicle Carnets are a familiar requirement for many countries and easily obtainable from the AA. For the journey out we decided to follow the example of most international lorry traffic and registered as a haulage company with the Freight Haulage Association so that we could used the TIR system. Basically this is an arrangement where a company can lodge a single guarantee with a central organization in Geneva who issue via local agents certificates of approval for vehicles and a contents carnet which must be completed and then endorsed by Customs. The one set of documents is valid across Europe, Turkey and Iran. For the return journey we would only have a small cargo of little value and could bumble back in a less professional expedition fashion.

As we were operating to a tight time schedule, we also contacted foreign embassies in London and British embassies abroad in countries where border delays were probable or uncertainties prevailed. Letters of introduction were often valuable and some borders had even been given advance notice which accelerated our clearance considerably. A few days at least were probably saved by these efforts, since there were the inevitable officials who otherwise made difficulties over minor regulations or discrepancies. Our dead-line departure date of 9 April put pressure on Dave Clarke getting equipment together in time, but it was the latest we could delay in order to reach Kathmandu by early May and then secure enough flights to the Khumbu so that everything could be stored in Khumde before the monsoon came.

Weeks of work were compressed into a few intense days in Leeds before departure. All the oxygen and equipment had to be packed into hundreds of boxes and comprehensively listed; lorries had to be carefully loaded and detailed manifests compiled with dozens of copies. A final task, classifying and coding each of our hundreds of items for Government export statistics was waived at the last moment, although we did register items which might be re-imported.

In addition to those already mentioned in the text, we also gratefully acknowledge help from the following: the Barclays Representative in Tehran, Mr Grand, and his wife, Captain and Mrs Robbins in New Delhi, HM Customs Dover and Leeds, Ford Motor Co. (Spare Parts), Total Oil Ltd, Townsend Thorensen Ferries, Willcox Chains and many Embassy Officials in London and abroad who gave us assistance.

Journey data

MILEAGE		FRONTIERS AND SOME MAIN TOWNS	NIGHT STOPS
CUMULATIVE	STAGE	EN ROUTE	
		LONDON	Dep. 9 April
	73	UK – Belgium	
		Zeebrugge	
	158	Belgium/Germany	
	405	Munich (via Brussels, Nuremberg)	10/11 April
	79	Germany/Austria	
	191	Graz (via Radstadt)	
	31	Austria/Yugoslavia	
	324	Belgrade	
	212	Yugoslavia/Bulgaria	
	38	Sofia	
	201	Bulgaria/Turkey	
	159	Istanbul	
2153	282	Ankara	14/15 April
	278	Sivas	
	285	Erzurum	
	201	Turkey/Iran	
	189	Tabriz	
	408	Tehran	18/20 April
3514	626	Mashhad (via Sari)	21/22 April
	150	Iran/Afghanistan	

23

24

25

26

29

30

31

23. Doug Scott beside the Chinese emblem.

24. Looking south west across the West Ridge of Nuptse towards Taboche and the Rolwaling Himal.

25. The summit view slightly south of east, with the shadow of Everest, Haston and Makalu behind right.

26. Looking slightly north of east, Chomo Lonzo on the right, Kangchenjunga in the background left.

27. Pertemba, climbing solo, reaching the top of the south Summit Gully on the second summit bid.

28. Pete Boardman on the summit.

29. The South East Ridge, with the South Summit behind Haston, Lhotse in the background.

30. Pertemba following up the South East Ridge, taken from the same viewpoint as the photograph above, which shows how seriously the weather has deteriorated.

31. The last time anyone saw Mick Burke, when Pete Boardman and Pertemba met him just below the summit.

	83	Herat	22/23 April
	350	Kandahar	
5041	318	Kabul	24/25 April
	155	Afghanistan/Pakistan	
	139	Rawalpindi	
	171	Lahore	
	17	Pakistan/India	
5820	297	Delhi	27/28 April
	304	Kanpur (via Agra)	
	197	Benares	
	390	Raxaul (India)/Birganj (Nepal)	1/2 May
6835	124	KATHMANDU	Arr. 3 May

Notes:

The lorries covered a total of 6996 miles due to various detours.

Three of the indicated night stops were scheduled, the other five were incurred at frontiers. About fifty hours were actually spent waiting for Customs formalities to be settled.

On the return journey, the shorter and easier route via Gorakhpur (208 m. to Kanpur) was taken and this now links up with both main Nepalese entry points. The road via Nautanwa/Bhairawa and Pokhara (Gorakhpur–Kathmandu 292 m.) was less difficult but Import clearance and collection of deposits had to be done at Birganj (Gorakhpur–Kathmandu over new Gandak bridge 261 m.).

The empty lorry returning in May took only 19 days to cover the 6624 miles. In November the partially filled lorry took 27 days, due to border delays.

Our 6·2 litre lorries each averaged 9·5 m.p.g. and a fuel cost of 3p/mile. Diesel fuel costs ranged from 70p/gallon in Germany to 6p/gallon in Iran!

Appendix 5

Equipment

by Dave Clarke

The reader who has reached this point in the book should already know the story of how and why we attempted to climb Everest the Hard Way. This appendix is therefore directed firstly to those who would like to know just what equipment is necessary to climb the highest mountain in the world and secondly to those who would like to benefit from my involvement in order to organize equipment for their own expeditions in the future. For readers in the first category I hope the following few pages of tables and notes will give you all the information you require, and for the second category I should start off by advising you, very firmly, not to say yes if you should ever be asked to organize equipment for an Everest expedition! But for those who, like me, find the lure irresistible, let me add that you will need a very sympathetic set of friends, family and firm to help you through the months of preparation and winding up as well as the actual climb. I was lucky to have all three and would like to thank them for making my involvement possible.

I was also very grateful to have from the beginning, the list of gear prepared by Graham Tiso who was responsible for the equipment on the 1972 trip. There were also in the 1975 team six climbers who had been on Everest before and they were only too willing to pass on to me their experience and advice. Everest is no place to try out new ideas and equipment, development rather than innovation is the only way to secure maximum performance which can be relied on. Despite the formidable financial backing Chris had organized with Barclays Bank, we still needed a great deal of support from manufacturers and suppliers both in cash forms and also in design time. Most important from my point of view was to secure help from those firms who were prepared to spend time in producing equipment to our design specifications. The trade did respond very generously to the challenge and I can only hope that materials and techniques developed during the manufacture of our equipment will benefit the general climber in much the same way that rally testing results in safer motoring for the general public. We spent almost four months developing our equipment and two months manufacturing the finished results before delivering to our packing centre in Leeds. The accumulated twenty-four tons of equipment and food were listed and packed into well over a thousand boxes before loading into the two sixteen-ton trucks which were to take them overland to Kathmandu.

Chris had gambled that by going earlier in the year we would enjoy better weather than on his previous expedition and that by using a larger team our build-up time would also be improved. His forecast was right, with the result that equipment designed for the worst conditions was never subjected to really extreme weather. Put simply, this meant that in the event we were over-equipped but this proved to be a big physical and psychological advantage. It meant that at all times climbers could choose a clothing combination best suited to their own temperament or temperature needs and the resulting comfort meant maximum performance.

It must be obvious that our climbing success was due, not only to our own efforts but also the accumulated experience of all previous climbs on the mountain and in the same way the successful performance of our equipment would not have been possible without the knowledge gained on those attempts. One can only hope therefore that, by recording the details of our own equipment and experiences, these will in turn serve future expeditions to climb more safely and efficiently in the high mountains of the world.

Scale of issue

It might seem, to the non-climber, that all members of an expedition should be issued with the same clothing and equipment but there are two main reasons why this is not so. One purely physical and the other largely political.

When the expedition is fully deployed on the mountain, porters and climbers operate all the way from the relatively sheltered small town that is Base Camp up to the unbelievably exposed and vulnerable Camp 6 and the equipment they require is correspondingly varied. The political reason for varying the equipment is due to the fact that over the years the clothing issue to porters has become a very real part of the bargain struck when they agree to join the team. When the issue is first made it is quite a tense time as they inspect clothing, first to assess its resale value at the end of the trip and only secondly, I suspect, to see whether it is capable of keeping them warm on the mountain. So one has to establish an accurate social pecking order and here, as I was such a novice in Sherpa affairs, we were fortunate to have as our Base Camp organizer Mike Cheney who lives and works in Nepal. He was able to point out the subtle differences between say a mail-runner employed by the BBC team and runners working for the expedition proper. Altogether we had fourteen different classifications and the following table shows our eventual distribution. The issue was made in Khumde, four days' march from Base Camp and it needed four days to complete. So near their own homes it was very tempting for a Sherpa to take brand-new equipment away and store it in his house, so as to sell it unused later on. We were concerned that all members should be clothed as well and as warmly as possible and asked Pertemba, the Sherpa Sirdar, to address all the assembled team before we finally left for the climb to impress on them that we expected to see all the clothing on the mountain on their backs, not in their rucksacks.

In addition to the twenty-four tons of equipment and food sent out by trucks from England in the spring, Mike Cheney in Kathmandu had gathered together a fair amount of cooking gear, fuel and tentage as well as a good deal of fresh food for the walk in and for Base Camp. So the final weight we had to handle was almost thirty tons and the approximate breakdown is shown below.

Personal Equipment	4·00 tons
Climbing Equipment	1·00

Tentage Equipment	2·00
Cooking Equipment	0·75
Miscellaneous	1·50
Fuel	2·00
Oxygen and Packing	1·50
Food and Packing	13·00
General Packing and Plastic	3·00

Well over a thousand boxes were packed and weighed and their contents recorded with values in three currencies before loading into the two trucks at Leeds before Customs officials sealed them and released them for the 7000-mile trip to Nepal. Life for me was governed by endless lists and those which follow summarize the work we had put into the design and preparation of our equipment. They also record the suppliers without whose help and support the whole thing would have been impossible.

All the food as it was so vulnerable was packed by professionals and only sent to Leeds for final loading into the trucks but the equipment was packed by a few of the expedition team and a great number of Boy Scouts who gave a lot of their time voluntarily and cheerfully. We owe them a great deal, and I'd like to thank John Jeffrey and his friends in the 19th NW Leeds troop and Andrew Carter, together with all the members of his troop. As volume was as critical as weight, for the overland journey we are also grateful to the RAF, Carlisle, for vacuum packing all our bulky down equipment and foam mattresses.

Personal equipment

The complete equipment issue to climbers and high-altitude Sherpas was intended to cover all requirements on the expedition. This ranged from the waterproof clothing and boots needed for the walk in, which was made in full monsoon conditions, to the five-layer protective system designed to cope with the extremes of wind and cold which we expected on the Face later on in the expedition. The first layer of this system was an excellent two-piece silk undersuit. It was very light and although it was only envisaged as a cold-weather garment, we soon found that it provided first-class protection from the burning sun during the day. Although there were no gloves with the suit, socks and balaclavas in the same material were used. The socks were not very popular and climbers seemed to prefer the more familiar feel of wool but the balaclavas were universally popular either on their own or as an underhood to the brushed wool variety used by climbers the world over.

The second layer was a suit in thermolactyl fibre, better known by the name of the manufacturer, Damart Thermawear. Although the 'double force' material from which our suits were made is normally only available in white, a special batch of navy suits were made for us and balaclavas and gloves from the same material. It was not possible to spend time altering the basic design of the hood which was far from perfect. This was a great pity as I feel sure the relatively windproof material could well have been better than the more open weave of the wool version. Without doubt, however, the gloves made from 'double force' were excellent and all climbers preferred them to the silk gloves normally used as inners to wool or fibrepile overmitts. Especially useful when handling cameras and karabiners, they were also quite adequate when jumaring in all but the coldest conditions. Each climber had three pairs and this proved more than adequate as the material did not wear out as fast as we had feared.

On top of the Damart suit we used a Polyester fibre pile suit made up to our design by Javlin, from material supplied by Glenoit in Leeds. Following a design originally used by an army expedition, improvements were made to the general shaping as well as collar design and the size and placing of four pockets on the front opening jacket. A full-length fly zip reaching to the back waistband was inserted in the trousers to ensure that nature's demands could be adequately met. Sherpa climbers who expected to be issued with a duvet only were initially doubtful about this material which they had not seen before. It soon became something of a uniform when they discovered how warm and comfortable the jackets were and the only complaints were from photographers who despaired of the overwhelming orange colour presented to the cameras.

The fourth and last layer of insulation was the one-piece downsuit developed over several expeditions from the original designed by Don Whillans in the sixties. All the suits were made to measure by Mountain Equipment, who were responsible for all the down gear on the expedition and are arguably the best down equipment manufacturers in the world. Pete Hutchinson worked very hard to meet our requirements and the down suits were filled with twenty-five per cent more down than normal. New pocket flaps were designed and pockets were carefully placed to avoid the climbing harness. The legs of the suit were filled differently to make walking easier and a complicated system of Velcro and zip closures worked out to ensure maximum versatility. The suit shell is two-ounce ripstop nylon which feels very fragile but suffered no damage on the climb. In such a case, however, the material is very easily repaired with the self-adhesive repair strips we took with us.

As the final layer, an outer wind suit is essential; this protects the more vulnerable downsuit from crampons and general abrasion as well as preventing the wind carrying away valuable heat held in the four layers of insulating clothing. In effect a sophisticated boiler suit, our one-piece outer windsuits were made with two-ounce ripstop nylon outer shell and lined with a medium weight ventile. As the climb went so quickly and the weather remained relatively warm, three or four of the climbers removed the ventile lining, prepared to accept the loss of warmth and increase in condensation because of the weight saving and a possible improvement in ease of movement. In the event this proved a good move but had the climb gone on into October, as expected, the double suit would have been invaluable.

All high-altitude Sherpas, although equipped to the same general standard as the climbers, prefer two-piece rather than the one-piece suits issued to the team. This is largely due to the fact that separate jacket and trousers have a better resale value when the expedition is over, but in the better weather we experienced on the trip, they were probably more versatile than the single oversuit. Mountain Equipment Snowline duvet, breeches and down boots were standard issue for them and the ventile oversuits made by Harrison's were front opening, self-lined jackets with single, one-size overtrousers. These commercially available suits made to an American specification have an unusually generous hood with wired visor and could not be faulted for design or performance.

Single Snowline sleeping bags were issued to Base Camp personnel and Ice Fall Sherpas but all expedition members above Camp 2 were given double sleeping bags. The standard Everest bag from Mountain Equipment was lengthened and widened to accommodate an inner mummy bag and a climber in down clothing. The inner was not cut differentially but was made intentionally over size so that the excess material would fill up the air pockets normally left round a sleeping body. In practice nobody needed to sleep in a downsuit as the double bag easily coped with the minimum recorded temperature of $-30°C$. As all oversuits had attached hoods, very little extra protection was needed for the head and the silk or wool balaclavas were quite adequate for the job. For finer weather, or photographic requirements or merely to satisfy nationalistic fervour, all climbers were issued with a Union Jack wool hat.

At the other extremity, feet require far more protection and altogether six items of footwear were needed to meet the varied needs of the expedition climbers.

We used a standard pair of training shoes for camp and some excellent flexible boots from Hawkins, called Astronaut Hikers, for the actual walk-in. These boots have a good leather upper and a very light cellular sole with a standard Vibram pattern. We all found them very comfortable and there was very little blistering. Our feet stayed remarkably dry even though we were walking a lot of the time along paths which were two or three inches deep in monsoon rain.

On the mountain all the expedition members were supplied with sheepskin boots as a general purpose camp boot and a pair of sheepskin socks for use in tents or inside specially developed Neoprene overboots. Ice Fall Sherpas were given a variety of Alpine standard single climbing boots, but climbers and high-altitude Sherpas were all supplied with the Galibier double boot model called Makalu. We had considered three other types, some of which were considerably cheaper, but over the years the French boot had been used successfully by almost all of the team and in the end it was universally accepted to be the only boot we could really risk. The boot is normally supplied with one pair of felt and one pair of fur inners, but the felt alternative is not adequate for Everest conditions, whereas the two pairs of fur inner boots are ideal.

To act as a combined gaiter and outer insulting layer we developed a 5 mm Neoprene overboot which had a smooth nylon outer skin and nylon towelling inner. The boot was like a giant front opening sock and was stretched over the double boot. The sole gave insulation under the boot and despite our fears that the material was not strong enough, no collapses occurred and holes made by crampon spikes could be quickly and easily repaired. We added a non-slip sole to some of these overboots as we thought extra reinforcing would be necessary when walking round camp or to prevent the bars of crampons tearing through the material. This was not necessary, but an added sophistication which would have been worthwhile was the addition of a snowproof closure at the top of the boot and this is now incorporated in the latest development model.

Standard pattern eight-ounce gaiters were issued to Sherpas working in Base Camp and the Ice Fall but a nylon Karrimor overboot, insulated with 3 mm closed cell foam was given to high-altitude Sherpas. These proved too stiff and awkward to wear with crampons and eventually spare Neoprene overboots intended as reserves for the climbing team had to be issued in their place.

Hands also require a number of differing mitts to cope with the very varied conditions experienced throughout the trip. The basic high-altitude provision for climbers and Sherpas alike was split between the classic Dachstein wool mitts and a specially developed fibre pile gauntlet. The Dachsteins were, predictably, very good but some interesting alternatives from Allan Austin in Bradford and Millar in London were equally acceptable and with further development could be even better. The fibre pile gauntlets were lined with the same Glenoit material used in our undersuits and covered with a nylon outer. A four-ounce, bright orange nylon front (for strength) was reinforced with leather and the back was made from two-ounce material. The long gauntlet was elasticated and wide enough to fit snugly over the padded arm of the down suit. The silk or Damart inners already mentioned were used in conjunction with the overmitts.

Finally a number of industrial insulated leather working gloves, normally used by cold storage operators, were given to the Base Camp personnel. They were very much appreciated when handling boxes, yaks or moving stones to build tent platforms.

Jeans were given to all Sherpas and although a lot of them were worn on the expedition the issue is really considered to be part of their wages for use afterwards and as a result the preferred styling owed more to fashion than function.

Except for the highly successful special lettered 'Everest Expedition' T-shirts and matching hats given to the Sherpa team, the remaining clothing was all basically the 'wool wear'.

Almost five hundred pairs of long stockings from different sources were distributed but a particular mention could be made of the all-wool specials made up for the climbers by Star Sportswear in Wakefield, as they were quite luxurious.

A wide variety of sweaters were used, ranging from some hard-wearing, heavyweight Guernseys to the superlightweight Shetlands and Merino sweaters worn mainly as underwear on the mountain but also as smart casuals at the post-expedition receptions.

Some very good Viyella shirts, made by King's of Maidstone proved long enough and warm enough to staisfy our climbing specifications even though they were originally designed for sailors, and as they wore extremely well there seems no doubt that they will survive many more expeditions in the future.

Two final pieces of clothing originally intended for the Ice Fall Sherpas only, complete the softwear provision on the expedition. The first was a really luxurious padded two-piece suit made for us by Tenson in Sweden. Using an already well-proven thigh-length jacket as the starting point, we designed a pair of matching bib and brace overtrousers to complete the suit. Delighted with the result, Tenson generously supplied the climbing team as well as the twenty-six Ice Fall Sherpas and although, as intended, the suits were never really used above Camp 1 by the Sherpas, several climbers took the overtrousers to Camp 2. The second item was breeches and we had three quite different styles and materials on the trip. Breeches for the Ice Fall Sherpas were made from a tweed by Craghoppers in Hebden Bridge and their reputation for warmth and strength was once more demonstrated. Harris Meyer in Leeds had provided some very smart made-to-measure breeches in ski-pant materials for the climbers and they, although professing a reluctance to wear such elegant attire on an actual climb, were impressed with the warmth and snow shedding properties of the material.

For the walk-in, Hoyle's, who are another Hebden Bridge manufacturing concern, supplied special lightweight moleskin breeches for the team. The cut and material made them very popular and they were worn a lot in the early part of the expedition.

Good protection from wind and cold is essential on Everest but complete protection for eyes is vital and we were very lucky to obtain the support of the French firm Bollé through their British organization. The firm had spent a lot of time developing a complete range of glasses and goggles for the recent Chamonix Guides expedition to Everest and we were able to take advantage of their experience when deciding on our requirements. All climbers and high-altitude Sherpas were issued with four pairs of large goggles each fitted with two colours of non-mist lenses as well as two pairs of mirror lens, high-altitude glasses. Hundreds of another smaller goggle were taken for Base Camp personnel, mail-runners and Ice Fall Sherpas but this was false economy. Small goggles restrict vision and, more importantly, suffer greatly from condensation and we should have provided the bigger non-mist goggles to all personnel, even though they were more expensive.

Technically the climbing on Everest is not of a high standard but even using fixed ropes requires a certain amount of hard-wear and each of the Face team were issued with a pair of jumars as well as a Whillans climbing harness from Troll with a slightly narrower crutch strap. This recommendation came from the 1972 expedition as several members on that trip had suffered soreness where the wider strap compressed all the down in the oversuits to a lumpy abrasion.

Each harness was provided with holsters which were used or rejected according to personal prejudices. Sherpas were issued with standard, fairly long ash-shafted Stubai axes and climbers were asked to bring their own particular preferences as the only issue was a terrordactyl hammer which we thought might be an appropriate tool in the Ice Fall. Everyone on the expedition was supplied with a pair of the new Clog adjustable crampons but because they were new, all the climbing team insisted on taking Salewa adjustables as well. Reaction to the Clog crampon varied from initial outspoken criticisms, to an easy acceptance of the new model, felt to be as good as the better known German lightweight. On the mountain most of the trouble in fact came at the fitting stage rather than in use, although in many cases the Neoprene retaining straps cracked after only very short usage.

Everything on an Everest trip, once Kathmandu has been left behind, is carried on backs and consequently we spent a lot of thought trying to design the best but simplest range of rucksacks which would meet all our load-carrying requirements.

Most people, on the walk-in, carried light loads in a Karrimor Lofoten which is a medium-size frameless rucksack for use in the Ice Fall later on. Sherpa load carriers were given a specially strengthened non-welded pack frame, the Euro-trekker, with carrying belt and a sack with no frills, pockets or zips. The high-altitude climbers were supplied with a light-welded orienteer pack frame complete with modified Randon-neur sack to accommodate three oxygen cylinders in locating tubes and a pocket for the demand valve of the oxygen breathing set. Top lid pockets were all deepened so that cameras and accessories could easily be accommodated, and all zips everywhere were fitted with giant tape pullers so that pockets could still be opened even when wearing heavy mitts. We had very little trouble with the hundred and fifty rucksacks which were all provided by Karrimor.

A small addition to our carrying capacity was possible due to the stuff bags provided. These were made in nylon, once again by Karrimor, and were like miniature kit bags, just large enough to hold a sleeping bag or duvet. Small but vital items of equipment like water bottles, lighters, Swiss pocket knives, whistle and plastic insoles were distributed as well as a few housewives. Originally the source of a great deal of ribald expectation, the name housewife is one given to any small collection of useful repair materials such as needle and thread, buttons and string.

For the walk-in, rain or sun, an umbrella is an essential luxury and the same might be said of a plastic pee bottle which can make all the difference to climbers in need in a stormbound face box.

Two other items to comfort the walker during the approach march are a plentiful supply of paper underwear and a sponge mattress. Not everybody agrees about the first, but all would about the second and despite the difficulty in keeping them dry, good thick sponge mattresses are very welcome in the early part of any expedition.

Early morning starts are never ever enjoyable but they are not even possible without good illumination and we were provided with a range of very good torches from Saft. Small disposable torches were probably the most useful and we should have taken more. Six big hand lanterns were issued to the cook and hospital tents, as well as headlamps to each climber. The Saft headlamp gave an excellent light but was rather heavy and the switch mechanism could be turned on accidentally in a rucksack. We used Saft high-power batteries in all these lights, although we were using Mallory batteries in radios and tape recorders.

It was felt politically desirable to issue Sherpas working in the Ice Fall with a crash helmet and we had taken a limited number of Galibier lightweights for that reason. In fact the main danger of the Ice Fall, collapsing séracs, can hardly be

SCALE OF ISSUE

DESCRIPTION	Climbers and four-man BBC TV team	Expedition and BBC high-altitude Sherpas	Camp 2 Cooks	Base Camp staff	Expedition and BBC Ice Fall Sherpas	Mail-runners	Base Camp cookboys	Signallers	Sunday Times Correspondent
	22	39	2	3	29	4	4	2	1
1 Windsuits	1								1
2 Ventile oversuit		1	1	1					
3 Nylon oversuit	1				1	1	1		1
4 Down suit	1			1					1
5 Duvet and down trousers	1	1	1	1				1	
6 Double sleeping bags	1	1	1	1					1
7 Single sleeping bag					1	1	1	1	
8 Down socks	1	1	1	1	1		1		1
9 Nylon pile suits	1	1			1	1	1	1	1
10 Tenson – padded suit	1				1				
11 Overmitts and gloves	4	2	2	2	2	1	1	1	2
12 Inner gloves	3	1	1	2					1

13	Breeches	2				1	1	1
14	Damart undersuits	1	1	1	1	1	1	1
15	Silk undersuits	1						
16	Jeans	1	1	1	1	1		
17	Sweaters – heavyweight	1	1	1	1	1		1
18	Sweaters – lightweight	1	1	1			1	1
19	Wool undersuit	1						
20	Viyella shirt	1	1	1				1
21	Balaclava	3	2	2	1	1	1	2
22	Stockings	4	4	4	3	2	2	2
23	Double boots	1	1	1				1
24	Single boots			1	1	1	1	
25	Walking boots	2	1	1				2
26	Sheepskin boots	1	1	1	1	1	1	
27	Gaiters	1	1	1	1			1
28	Nylon overboots	1	1	1		1	1	1
29	Neoprene overboots	1						
30	Goggles	6	4	3	3	1	1	4
31	Sunglasses	3	2	1	1	1	1	2

SCALE OF ISSUE										
	DESCRIPTION	Climbers and four-man BBC TV team	Expedition and BBC high-altitude Sherpas	Camp 2 Cooks	Base Camp staff	Expedition and BBC Ice Fall Sherpas	Mail-runners	Base Camp cookboys	Signallers	Sunday Times Correspondent
32	Stuff bags	3	2	2	2	2				2
33	Pack frames	1	1	1	1	1	1	1	1	1
34	Pack sacks	1	1	1	1	1	1	1	1	1
35	Ice axes	2	1	1		1				1
36	Crampons	1	1	1		1				1
37	Climbing harness	1	1							1
38	Jumars	1	1	1						
39	Headlamp	1	1							
40	Water bottle	1	1	1		1			1	1
41	Wristwatch	1								
42	Wristwatch		1	1						
43	Wristwatch							1		

44 Gas lighter	2	1	2	2	1	2	1
45 Pocket knife	1	1	1				
46 Housewife	1						
47 Umbrellas	1						
48 Paper underwear	4					4	
49 Pee bottle	1	1	1				
50 Whistle	1	1	1			1	
51 Expedition T-shirt	1	1	1	1	1	1	
52 Climbing helmet	1		1				
53 Hand torches	2	1	2	1		1	1
54 Frameless rucksack	1						1
55 Insoles	1						1
56 Sponge mattress	1	1	1	1		1	1
57 Sheepskin socks	1						

NOTE: In addition, equipment was issued to the five drivers who drove our two lorries overland to Kathmandu.

	PERSONAL ISSUE – DESCRIPTION	QUANTITIES	SUPPLIER
1	1-piece windsuits	22	G. & H. Products
2	2-piece ventile windsuits	45	R. L. Harrison
3	2-piece nylon oversuits	60	G. & H. Products
4	1-piece down suits	22	Mountain Equipment
5	down suits – snowline duvet	45	Mountain Equipment
	snowline trousers	45	Mountain Equipment
6	Sleeping bags – Everest	60	Mountain Equipment
	Lightline	60	Mountain Equipment
7	sleeping bags 1 snowline	35	Mountain Equipment
8	down socks	60	Mountain Equipment
9	2-piece nylon pile suits	120	Javlin
10	Tenson – Jackets	50	Tenson
	Overtrousers	50	Tenson
11	mitts – Millarmitt	40	Millar
	Shoddy	30	Alan Austin
	Pile overmitt	250	Stuart Madeley
	Dachstein	60	Centresport

12	gloves – leather work gloves	30	Hollingworth
	Damart inners	60	Damart
	silk inners	30	Centresport
13	breeches	60	Pickles/Harris Meyer/Hoyle
14	Damart undersuits	130	Damart
15	silk undersuits	20	Zegna
16	jeans	115	Levi/Campari
17	sweaters – heavyweight	100	Channel Island Knitwear
18	sweaters – mediumweight	60	Stuart Madeley
19	sweaters – lightweight	70	Pringle/Bill
20	Viyella shirts	60	David King
21	balaclavas – brushed wool	200	Robert Sim
	silk	20	Zegna
22	stockings	350	Star/Stuart Madeley
23	double boots	65	Richard Pontvert (Galibier)
24	single boots	40	Centresport

PERSONAL ISSUE – DESCRIPTION	QUANTITIES	SUPPLIER
25 walking boots – Astronauts	66	Hawkins
Trainers	22	Stylo
26 sheepskin boots	90	Bama/Moreland
27 zip gaiters	90	Karrimor
28 nylon overboots – KP insulated	55	Karrimor
nylon only	15	Centresport
29 Neoprene overboots	60	Aquairland Sports
30 goggles – Sherpa	100	Bollé/Steiner
HAS and climbers	100	Bollé
31 sunglasses – disposable	100	Bollé
Everest	100	Bollé
32 stuff bags	250	Karrimor
33 pack frames	100	Karrimor
34 pack sacks – Randonneur OXY	60	Karrimor
Orienteer	40	Karrimor
35 ice axes	100	Berghaus/Pascall

36	crampons – Clog	100	Clog
	Salewa	22	Salewa via Karrimor
37	climbing harness and holsters	60	Troll Products
38	lumars	70	Robert Lawrie
39	headlamps	72	Saft
40	water bottles	100	Sigg
41	wristwatches – climbers	20	Certina via ACC
42	HAS	40	Swiss Time
43	others	40	Swiss Time
44	lighters	200	Masters
45	pocket knives	60	Swiss Cutlery
46	housewife	12	Various
47	umbrellas	20	Lawtex
48	underwear – disposable	200	Strentex
49	pee bottles	65	Various

PERSONAL ISSUE—DESCRIPTION	QUANTITIES	SUPPLIER
50 whistles	100	Clog
51 Sherpa T-shirts and hats	100	Danson
52 crash helmets	40	Richard Pontvert (Galibier)
53 torches (hand)	100	Saft
54 day sacks	22	Karrimor
55 insoles	50	Chamberlain
56 mattresses	120	Kay-Metzler
57 sheepskin socks	25	Antartex

countered with a crash helmet no matter how good and a much more appropriate place to use them is on the Face itself. Here small but fast-moving pieces of ice and stone are continually falling, putting climbers in danger and it is always wise to use head protection, preferably lightweight, and the Galibier model was ideal for our needs.

To provide all the expedition members with a watch each may seem something of a perk, but in order to successfully co-ordinate the movements of a hundred men and ten tons of equipment on the mountain, it is essential to use a system of radio calls to relay instructions. Obviously these calls have to be made at pre-arranged times and it is essential, if the programme is to work, that the radio exchanges are on time. The fact that climbers and Sherpas alike all have a synchronized watch is very desirable and in our case was only made possible by ACC Swiss Time, who provided a range of Certina watches to match the relative needs of all the team.

Material suppliers: I should also like to register here our thanks to the great number of suppliers of materials who, when approached, readily gave their support to our manufacturers.

Carrington Performance Fabrics supplied material for the windsuits and other clothing as well as BM Coatings and Ashton Brothers who provided all the ventile for the two-piece Sherpa suits as well as windsuit linings. Selectus supplied all Velcro, and Lightning Fasteners most of the zips, often for the Northern manufacturers, through their distributor J. & P. Coates in Leeds. Javlin were responsible for making the nylon pile suits to our design but the material was supplied by Glenoit UK Ltd, who also provided the material for overmitt lining. These mitts were also reinforced on the palm with leather provided by the Pittard Group Ltd. The Neoprene overboots were made from material supplied by the St Albans Rubber Co. and reinforced with Skiplite, an excellent material supplied by K Shoes in Kendal. The sole was attached by a local cobbler in Leeds, Mr Edwards. Our major equipment sponsor was Karrimor who in turn were given strong support by ICI Harrogate and BM Coatings in Manchester. In addition all their tapes were provided by W. Ribbons and labels by Brough Nicholson & Hall. The details of our packaging and transport methods are covered elsewhere in the book but I would like to add my personal thanks to Mr Turnbull in Leeds who made his warehouse facilities available to us and who also was responsible for making some of the climbers' personal boxes.

Climbing equipment

The first time most of us saw all the expedition equipment assembled in one place was at the Sherpa village of Khumde just before it was issued to all the team members. It looked an enormous amount, but completely lost amongst the boxes of down gear, food and fuel, the actual climbing gear – the hardware that is – looked such a small heap I wondered whether I had made a mistake and forgotten some vital equipment. In fact I had everything we needed, but the fact is on a non-technical climb like the South West Face the only things needed in real quantities are rope, ladders, oxygen and effort.

As weight, in logistical terms, is the key factor controlling the speed of our build-up the attraction of Polypropylene ropes was obvious. Ropes in this material are only two thirds of the weight of nylon ropes, strength for strength, and we spent a lot of time discussing this and other advantages of the rope before we decided that its big drawback – rapid deterioration under ultraviolet radiation – was too big a risk to take. We had to provide rope to cover three areas of activity – the fixed ropes and safety line in the Ice Fall; fixed ropes on the Face; and climbing ropes for teams operating in either situation. All the climbing and fixed ropes on the Face were provided by Bridon Fibres and all fixed rope in the Ice Fall was specially made for us only a couple of days before we left by a Leeds ropeworks – Synthetic Ropes and Cordage.

Climbing rope: 9 mm Dynaflex provided in 90-metre lengths. This was cut in two and issued to all Ice Fall Sherpas who preferred to be roped together, usually three or four to a length, although a few ropes were reserved for climbers operating in the Rock Band. Normal climbing technique was to lead out on Polypropylene or Super Braidline, tying off to deadmen at intervals, leaving the resulting fixed rope for load-carrying Sherpas to follow using jumars.

8 mm Super Braidline: This was a terylene rope with no weight, strength, or abrasion-resistant advantages over nylon, but the one great difference is a comparative lack of stretch and as a fixed rope on the Face it proved ideal. Carried to Camp 2 in 200-metre reels, it was cut into more manageable 50-metre lengths and fixed in that form.

7 mm Dynaflex: In order to protect a possible retreat in bad weather across the exposed traverse above the Rock Band, we had always planned the provision of a fixed rope as far as possible across the Upper Snow Field from Camp 6. Although not as strong as the 8 mm Braidline, this rope was considerably lighter – a point of great advantage at that altitude and very much appreciated by Doug Scott and Dougal Haston when they placed it on the day before their successful summit bid.

We also took limited quantities of 4 mm Kernmantel rope as well as ⅝-inch and 1-inch tape to cut up into slings and tie-offs when required.

10 mm Polypropylene: This was all pink and used only in the Ice Fall. The colour coding was very useful as Sherpas tend to use any rope that is handy but this obvious identification made it easy to make sure that ropes were only used in the appropriate situation. The rope was very light but not easy to knot, and a careful watch was necessary to make sure that anchorages and hand lines remained safe.

4 mm Polypropylene: Made to the same specification as the rope used as handrails, lifelines and braces, the smaller diameter rope was used for tarpaulin ties, guy lines, pack frame lashing and general security everywhere. Needless to say we didn't take nearly enough and double quantities would be nearer the mark.

For anchors in the snow to secure fixed ropes, tents or adder bridges we took deadmen, snow stakes and ice pitons

	CLIMBING EQUIPMENT DESCRIPTION	QUANTITIES	SUPPLIER
1	9 mm climbing rope	200 metres	Bridon Fibres & Plastics
2	8 mm Super Braidline	4000 metres	Bridon Fibres & Plastics
3	7 mm climbing rope	1000 metres	Bridon Fibres & Plastics
4	4 mm tensile rope	500 metres	Bridon Fibres & Plastics
5	1" soft tape	300 metres	Troll Products (Lancs.)
6	$\frac{5}{8}$" soft tape	150 metres	Troll Products (Lancs.)
7	screwgate alloy karabiners	70	Clog (Wales)
8	non-screw alloy karabiners	400	Clog (Wales)
9	tubular snow stakes 30"	200	Aalco (Scotland)
10	deadmen snow anchor	100	Clog (Wales)
11	drive-in ice pitons	20	Salewa
12	tubular ice pitons	75	Salewa
13	standard ice pitons	75	Stubai

14	rock pitons	100	Clog (Wales)
15	bolt kits	2	Troll Products (Lancs.)
16	snow shoes	10	Recreational Equip. (USA)
17	skis	12	Rossignol (France)
18	aluminium ladder	60	Lyte Industries (Wales)
19	marker flags	600	Karrimor Prods. (Lancs.)
20	avalanche probes	10	Tyromont (Austria)
21	snow saws	8	Maeyer & Rec. Equip.
22	ski sticks	60	Europasports
23	Polypropylene rope	3000 metres	Synthetic Ropes & Cordage

but as there was so much new soft snow on the mountain, only the deadmen were really useful and we soon used all our supplies. The snow stakes, which had been invaluable in the harder snow of Bonington's 1972 expedition, were useless in the normal position, so we taped and tied them together before buring them as emergency deadmen and they proved very successful in their modified role.

Although we often seemed short of karabiners, a purge in the camps and a keener look at the often extravagant methods of rope-fixing produced sufficient supplies to meet demands from the lead climbers at the front. A small selection of rock pegs was taken and a few used, but the bolt kits and avalanche probes, thankfully, were not.

We also provided snow shoes and short touring skis in case it was ever necessary to make an emergency trip between Camps 1 and 2. Luckily this too was never necessary, although I had one or two short outings from Camp 1 just to enjoy the experience of skiing at that altitude. The snow saws were not used much, although I think more use could have been made of them. Sherpas cut snow blocks for melting, deepened the floor of the cook tent to give more headroom and a wall was made between store tents as a windbreak, but there was certainly more potential for their use.

Marker flags are essential in good and bad weather on a big route like Everest to ensure that Sherpas follow the selected route safely and we used 18-inch long luminous orange nylon flags tied off to 8-foot long bamboo canes bought in Nepal.

Ladders, heat boxes and the stretcher
by Hamish MacInnes

The 6′ aluminium alloy bolt-together ladder sections, as used on our 1972 expedition, were excellent. The only addition to the design was a suggestion to Dr Mathews, of Lyte Industries – who made them for us – to supply triangular plates which could bolt onto the ladder sections and enable further ladders to be attached at right angles. High-tensile wire could be tensioned from the spanning ladder ends over the end of the ladder placed at right angles. The 'bridge' would then be slung with the 'stuck on' ladder underneath. This enabled us to span larger crevasses and, in practice, it worked well. I had made up also several handrails which were ostensibly ice-fall belay tubes (again $1\frac{1}{4}''$ aluminium alloy) with $\frac{7}{16}''$ holes at the bottom end. Long bolts, fixed through the $\frac{7}{16}''$ holes, and also through the tubular rungs of the ladder, made upright supports of these tubes. A handline could be attached to their tops to safeguard crossing.

Work on heat boxes was done by me and by Leeds Polytechnic to produce a form of container inside which a small butane gas stove could operate with the minimum of heat loss. Various experiments were made with not very favourable results. Eventually, we made up several titanium boxes insulated with Ceramic Fibre, a highly efficient insulating material manufactured by Morgan Refactories Ltd. Although they were taken out to Everest with us it was not necessary to use them, thanks to the success of a propane/butane gas mixture.

A special compact lightweight stretcher was taken out for use on the expedition. It was a tubular, capsule type which I had developed for helicopter rescue work, but which also has mountain rescue application. It weighs 23 lb. and fits in a carrying bag which doubles when extended as a casualty bag, size: $3' 2'' \times 20'' \times 3''$. It has rucksack-type carrying straps with helicopter lift wires attached.

Material suppliers: We should also like to thank Alcan Industries who provided all the ladder alloy; R. Tomlinson for swaging; Tucker's for supplying rivets; and British Ropes for wire rope.

Tentage: MacInnes boxes

by Hamish MacInnes

There is no better incentive for design than to suffer the shortcomings of poor equipment. During our post-monsoon attempt on the South West Face of Everest in 1972, we found that the tentage and boxes were inadequate for the conditions prevailing at that time of year. It was therefore with considerable determination that I tackled the problem of having boxes constructed which would give some degree of comfort in that inhospitable environment.

Initially, I thought of making up only two types: a large 'super box' for use up to Camp 2, to accommodate three climbers in comfort in an inner vestibule, with a similar spacious floor area for equipment and cooking. The other box, now know as the 'MacInnes box', was specifically designed for the Face: extremely strong and utilizing, where necessary, a special built-in platform with legs capable of siting the box on a level plane, even on very steep slopes.

Due to the fact that the MacInnes boxes emerged in their final design as mini-fortresses it was deemed necessary to have a lightweight, easy to erect, 'summit box' and so this last member of the Everest stable was created.

For both the Super and MacInnes boxes, $1\frac{1}{4}''$ o.d. fully heat-treated Alcan aluminium alloy was used for the frames and pressed steel Clinch joints utilized as they are both strong and light. Tube sections were interconnected, using male and female sliding-fit joints, each end individually machined by expanding parallel reamer so that very close tolerances were achieved. Manufacture of the frames was carried out by J. & T. Lawrie of Clydebank. Both the super box and the MacInnes 2-man box use interchangeable 6' tube lengths but, in the case of the MacInnes box, these are in three 2' long interconnecting sections fitted with internal shock cord for rapid assembly. All other parts of the MacInnes boxes are similarly fitted with this elasticated cord to expedite erection in difficult situations and minimize the danger of losing individual tubes.

All internal fixed male tubes for pole connection were riveted with Tucker rivets, as were the Clinch joints. All boxes had high-tensile wires supplied by British Ropes Ltd, crisscross on roof and wall sections for stiffening frames, and stainless steel Bibb turnbuckles were used initially for tensioning them. Later, sections of rope were used for securing the wires; nylon rope proved quite adequate for this, and on

The MacInnes super box

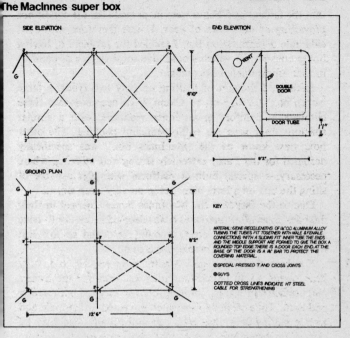

super boxes several coils of solid wire were used also, cut on site for the purpose. The completed super box weighs 124 lb., including the inner vestibule.

To aid fitting the box covers, the frames are angled inwards; this also reduces wind resistance. Not only had the face boxes to be erected in difficult situations, they had also to be proof from falling stones, high winds and, to a limited degree, avalanche proof. On the 1972 expedition we had stones coming right through the walls of the boxes so, to prevent this happening again, I experimented using a Titanium mesh as an outer covering for reef and rear wall. Due to the expense of Titanium mesh, I tried aluminium Expamet instead. Later, after discussing the matter with an ICI representative, a 'bullet-proof' cloth was finally selected; used in three layers, it proved excellent and easy to handle.

On my two previous expeditions to the South West Face,

we had used separate platforms for the face boxes but this seemed unnecessary extra weight. I therefore consulted the British Aircraft Corporation and their Materials Design Section suggested a plastic honeycomb material sandwiched between two layers of thin balsa wood as the optimum platform material for the boxes. We therefore had 'tiles' made up for the floor of the boxes; fitted internally, they rested on the two lower frame longitudinal box members and on two further $1\frac{1}{4}''$ o.d. tubes running parallel to them, close to the centre of the box. As the floor proved to be rather flexible with the eight tiles in place, I had to introduce T-section alloy which fitted between tiles and rested transversely across the floor members. This floor/platform system proved adequate and gave the best possible insulation/rigidity. The outer cover of the box laced underneath the platform.

The legs of the MacInnes box are of square section aluminium alloy, drilled at 2'' intervals on all four faces to give 1''

The MacInnes face box

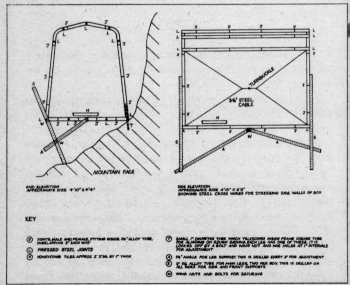

END ELEVATION
APPROXIMATE SIZE 4'10"X 4'4"

MOUNTAIN FACE

SIDE ELEVATION
APPROXIMATE SIZE 4'10" X 6'6"
SHOWING STEEL CROSS WIRES FOR STRESSING SIDE WALLS OF BOX

KEY

(J) JOINTS, MALE AND FEMALE, FITTING INSIDE 1½" ALLOY TUBE, OVERLAPPING 3" EACH WAY

(L) PRESSED STEEL JOINTS

(H) HONEYCOMB TILES, APPROX. 2' X 3'6, BY 1" THICK

(T) SMALL 1" DIAMETER TUBE WHICH TELESCOPES INSIDE FRAME CORNER TUBE FOR ALIGNING ON ROUGH GROUND. EACH LEG HAS ONE OF THESE. IT IS LOCKED OFF BY A BOLT AND WING NUT AND HAS HOLES AT 1" INTERVALS FOR ADJUSTMENT

(A) 1½" ANGLE FOR LEG SUPPORT. THIS IS DRILLED EVERY 2" FOR ADJUSTMENT

(S) 2" SQ. ALLOY TUBE FOR MAIN LEGS, TWO PER BOX. THIS IS DRILLED ON ALL SIDES FOR SIDE AND FRONT SUPPORTS

(W) WING NUTS AND BOLTS FOR SECURING

intervals of adjustment. They had drilled adjustable angle braces from the outer, lower longitudinal frame member, and from each of the two lower end frame members; the legs are held in position by the four angle alloy braces which can be fixed either below or above the horizontal, depending on terrain. The leg braces also help to support the box platform. The square section platform legs attach to the corner of the box with H T bolts and wing nuts. A short 1″ diameter tube is located inside each of the four upright frame corner tubes of the box at the bottom. On the mountain-side of the box they are telescopic and can be locked off to give variable lengths on uneven ground. On the outer aspect of the box, the square platform legs bolt to these short extension tubes.

The box outer cover has small sleeve extensions for making spindrift seals over the attachments to the box frame. The 'bullet-proof' protective cover is fitted over the roof and rear of the box and tied off to the platform legs to the rear with nylon cord. The boxes can be anchored to the face at any convenient point of the platform, or by the legs, or from tape loops fitted to the outer cover. Pre-cut, closed cell foam was used for insulation of floor, walls, and roof, and a 1 oz inner cotton liner can be clipped to the frame once the box is erected. This liner, in all three boxes, is fitted with storage pockets. The final weight of the MacInnes box, less platform, is 66 lb. It can, of course, be used with or without the platform.

The summit box is formed basically from two rectangular aluminium alloy sections, crossed at each end to form an X. All the 1″ o.d. tubing is fitted with internal shock cord for rapid assembly and the two rectangles are permanently bolted together. The theory is that the bundle of short sections of tubing, when shaken out, springs together to form the frame. It is then inserted into the cover which has a fully zipped floor (i.e. zipped round three sides). The frame is then forced out to form the X construction which tensions the cover. Finally, the floor is zipped up. This box proved very rigid, light (weight approximately $16\frac{1}{2}$ lb., plus inner), and easy to erect. Its design is such that, if required, it can actually hang from piton belays (a clip is located at the centre of each

K

The MacInnes summit box

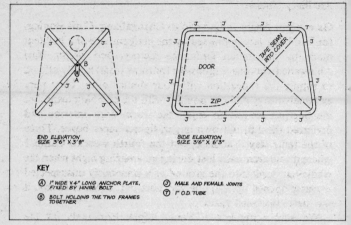

END ELEVATION
SIZE 3'6" X 3'8"

SIDE ELEVATION
SIZE 3'6" X 6'3"

KEY

(A) 1" WIDE X 4" LONG ANCHOR PLATE, FIXED BY HINGE BOLT

(B) BOLT HOLDING THE TWO FRAMES TOGETHER

(J) MALE AND FEMALE JOINTS

(T) 1" O.D. TUBE

X for this purpose) and special wide banding strips are attached to reinforce the floor. Criss-cross thin, stainless-steel wire is used for bracing walls and floor where necessary. For Everest, the box was supplied only with side stainless-steel bracing wires.

I chose BM Coatings, Belflex 40, 1·7 oz, for the outer cover of the summit box, as this offered the necessary strength/weight ratio; the inner was made from artificial silk. Only two summit boxes were manufactured and, as with the other box frames, the prototype was made in Glencoe. One box cover and inner was sewn by the Greenock Sail and Tent Company; the other by Karrimor Ltd. As only green Belflex was obtainable initially, fluorescent crosses were stitched on to the outer cover for locating the box in poor visibility. The summit box cover was painstakingly constructed, using tape reinforcing and zigzag stitching. At each corner a doubled tape was used to attach a nylon line guy. Each of the four guys led from the top corner to the bottom corner of the box and the ends were tied off with a Tarbuck knot for quick adjustment. A single-sleeve ventilator was located at the door end of the box.

Auxiliary tentage

On a recent Anglo-Indian trip to Changabang, Chris Boning-ton had been very impressed by the performance of a bell tent made by the Indian Ordnance factory, and Major Hari Ahluwalia (who was responsible for these tents) kindly offered to supply the expedition with four similar ones. They were extremely heavy and not popular with the climbing team, but the Sherpas seemed to enjoy the warm dark interior and preferred them to our own larger, lighter super boxes. Three of the tents stayed at Base, but the fourth went to Camp 1 where it was eventually lost during an amazing night when the whole tent sank into the ground as a previously unsuspected crevasse opened up. No one was hurt but, needless to say, it was never occupied again.

We used a number of Vango Mark Five tents for the walk-in and at Base as two-man general purpose living tents. But later, as it became obvious that we could develop Camp 2 as an advance base, several of the tents were moved to the Western Cwm where they performed very well until an avalanche swept through the camp and destroyed five of them completely, along with two of the big super boxes. The tents were virtually unaltered commercially available models and I only added a third set of A poles to strengthen the ridge and also took the precaution of fitting a nylon snow valance and protective panel at the foot of the fly sheet.

We had, in addition, four Scott tunnel tents, taken as emergency lightweights, and two simple nylon bivouac sacs which were taken by both summit teams. In fact, when Doug Scott and Dougal Haston were forced into the highest ever recorded bivouac they were able to dig a snow hole and use the bivouac sac as a ground-sheet to sleep on rather than in!

Sleeping on snow means floor insulation is essential and the 9 mm sheets of Karrimat already well known to most climbers performed excellently. At Camp 2 those Sherpas and climbers who had also brought up the open cell foam mattresses used originally for the walk-in slept in real com-fort. On the Face Karrimats were also used as a roof insulation

	TENTAGE—DESCRIPTION	QUANTITIES	SUPPLIER
1	Base Camp bell tents	4	Indian Ordnance
2	Super boxes	7	(Cover) Bradford Cover & Twine (Frames) J. T. Lawrie
3	Force ten Mk. 5	25	Vango
4	Scott tunnel tents	4	Blacks
5	Face boxes	12	(Covers) Karrimor (Frames) J. T. Lawrie
6	Karrimats	200	Karrimor
7	tent brushes	30	Burrow Davis & Sons
8	cook shelters	3	Made in Kathmandu from
9	store tarpaulins	12	material supplied by BM Coatings
10	hypothermia bags	6	Strentex
11	snow shovels	12	Wolfe
12	Summit boxes	2	(Covers) Karrimor & Greenock Sail (Frames) J. T. Lawrie
13	bivouac sacs	2	Mountain Equipment

in an attempt to cut down the condensation which is un-avoidable when cooking is done inside.

Other essential items for the efficient running or erection of camps on the Face in particular were shovels, brushes and tarpaulins. The aluminium shovels were the size normally seen on roadsweepers' carts but they were very light and one soon appreciated that size is essential if platforms are to be dug quickly – a job that takes an age if the only available tools are ice axes. The brushes are not for tent-proud occupants to keep things looking tidy but are used to brush out snow brought in on boots and clothing or blow-in spindrift. If this isn't done the warmth inside the tent soon melts the snow and dampens clothing and spirits alike.

Although recommended strongly by Graham Tiso, the 1972 expedition equipment organizer, I hadn't realized how valu-able is the provision of a good supply of tarpaulins. Luckily we had a good deal of nylon on the roll given to us by BM Coatings. This was sent out to Nepal and made up in Kath-mandu into a variety of sheet sizes. Simply reinforced at the edges and corners and fitted with eyelets at regular centres, these sheets served in turn as tents, temporary cook shelters, covered store areas between tents, emergency flysheets, groundsheets, and as covers over and under equipment boxes stored outside. It is so easy to lose equipment left accidentally outside when snow falls and covers everything. Underneath a generous cover it is easy to find and clear the snow away, and if my turn comes to advise future organizers I would urge them not to forget these apparently unimportant additions to their tent lists.

A number of tents were actually destroyed during the climb and even more had to be abandoned as camps were evacuated in the aftermath of the storm which finished the expedition. Nevertheless, we were able to bring some back with us and these have now been given to the British Mountaineering Council to form the beginnings of the new expedition equipment pool. The three bell tents were loaned to the British Army Spring '76 attempt on Everest by the South Col route and were returned to the pool in the summer.

Material suppliers: We should also like to thank Lightning Fasteners who provided the zips for the tents. Courtaulds who provided the material for the super boxes and Naylor Jennings who dyed it before manufacture, Alcan Industries who supplied all box tubing. Suspension clips were provided by the Hampton Works and dog clips for outside fastenings by Hiatt & Co. The materials for all cook shelters, store tarpaulins and the Face Boxes was provided by B M Coatings who were particularly helpful in developing new materials and coatings to meet our specific requirements.

Cooking equipment

There seems little doubt that as a general recommendation paraffin stoves are far and away the most reliable and economical heat source where large numbers have to be catered for and we used a variety of large domestic stoves up to Camp 2. The main drawback of these stoves, however, apart from weight, is that locally available kerosene is invariably contaminated. We took the very necessary precaution of taking over 200 gallons of specially filtered fuel from this country and used this exclusively above Base Camp where the effects of breakdowns and blockages are far harder to deal with. Supplementary local fuel was restricted, where possible, to Base and only used after filtering, in theory anyway, by the Sherpa cooks. On the Face during the climb, we used gas stoves with disposable cartridges, as this is easily the most efficient way of carrying fuel on the mountain. The cleanliness of the fuel together with the ease of lighting and absence of noxious fumes, all important in a small tent, make this choice almost inevitable. However, this method also has one serious disadvantage. All small stoves use butane as fuel and this is quite susceptible to temperature changes, not volatile at all at $-5°C$, a condition quite common on Everest. Propane is a much better gas to use at lower temperatures, but unfortunately British Specifications do not allow high pressure fuels to be contained in the lightweight disposable cartridges we required. Luckily we were able to purchase from a French expedition in the Himalayas 500 cylinders of a fifty-fifty propane-butane mix and we used this exclusively and with great success on the Face.

Both Hamish MacInnes and I had spent a great deal of time, along with designers and friends in general research, attempting to develop a cooking unit which would improve performance and efficiency. It is very easy to improve performance by protection from wind, but this is never really a problem on Everest, as all cooking is done inside tents. In the end, despite all our work with insulation and double walls, internal flues and textured surfaces, we were unable to make any appreciable savings and even at 28 000 feet on the mountain, apart from special fuel, we were cooking on the standard picknicker's lightweight stove and billy, used by hundreds of hikers every weekend at altitudes nearer sea level than the summit of Everest. Certainly a great endorsement of their performance.

For a single burner gas stove we used the Standard Bluet S200 with stabilizer, no modifications except the use of special fuel.

We took 100 per cent in 7 oz disposable cartridges. In practice, although performance is badly affected by low temperature, if the containers were kept inside there was little problem in getting the stove to light and the rapid rise in temperature within the tent when they were running soon raised performance to normal levels.

The propane-butane mix ensured maximum performance from the start and would have been essential if the worst weather conditions for which we had prepared had developed. Fortunately we completed the climb so rapidly that in common with most of our equipment they were never subjected to the expected extreme conditions and we always had performance in hand.

The Mammoth Optimus No. 3 Domestic single burner stoves gave us very little trouble and the replacement of a few washers and nipples was a small effort in return for their reliable performance, often burning nonstop from two a.m. to ten p.m., only pausing for fuel refills. We did not take with us the very heavy cast-iron hob provided with the stove and had no trouble balancing even the biggest pans which were almost two feet in diameter.

	COOK HEAT AND LIGHT DESCRIPTION	QUANTITIES	SUPPLIER
1	double burner gas stove	2	Tentequip
2	single burner gas stove	28	Tentequip
3	gas cartridges	300	French/Special mixture
		700	Tentequip/butane
4	paraffin stoves	25	Optimus
5	nesting sets	28	Tentequip
6	KFS sets	100	Cobles
	spare spoons	200	Cobles
7	gas lanterns	20	Tentequip
8	plastic one-pint mugs	200	Laughton
9	pressure cookers	10	Prestige
10	gas heaters	4	Tentequip
11	can openers	200	Morfed

12	meta paste	100	Optimus
13	pan scourers	60	Nyleska
14	Thermos flasks	20	Thermos
15	paper kitchen towels	800	Strentex
16	paraffin lanterns	16	Optimus
16	folding tables	20	Wayfarer Leisure (PTC)
18	folding chairs	30	Wayfarer Leisure (PTC)
19	kitchen knives	6	Swiss Cutlery
20	multi-burner stoves	8	Optimus
21	candles	200	Kathmandu market
22	batteries	800	Saft and Mallory
23	hurricane lamps	4	Kathmandu market
24	kerosene (gals.)	250	Rockoil

We also took a number of smaller paraffin stoves as lightweight emergency stoves if the gas cookers proved unsatisfactory, but those were never used. In addition wo provided some industrial heaters, a formidable stove with four burner heads, intended for snow melting. They performed well, but I had omitted to provide a decent stand rfe the billies which is not provided as standard with this model. Consequently they were never used very much, but were never missed as the No. 3 stoves performed so well.

I had hoped to develp a constant feed system direct from the fuel containers, as this would do away with the tricky job of constant refilling and relighting. In the event, there wasn't enough time, but it will be a worthwhile development for some future expedition and another equipment organizer.

Most of the really big five-gallon snow melting and cooking pans were bought in Kathmandu market where they are well made and cheap, although we took lightweight nesting sets from this country and included them in camp kits for the Face. Standard lightweight knife, fork and spoon sets were also taken, together with an unbelievable number of spare spoons as these seem to disappear after ever meal, along with the one-pint plastic mugs which were also constantly in short supply.

Stoves and lights were preheated with Meta paste which seemed better and certainly more efficient to use than the solid type. It was lit by matches, which were included in every camp kit, or with small butane lighters issued personally to every climber and Sherpa.

Most of the general kitchen supplies were bought in Nepal but we included in equipment sent out from England, nylon and metal pan scrubs, the invaluable can opener made by Morfed and kitchen knives from Swiss Cutlery, as well as candles, washing-up bowls, fuel funnels, axes, plates and a huge supply of very useful paper towels. With a great deal of rice and potatoes to cook, the provision of pressure cookers not only makes sense but is essential as the fuel they save far outweighs the relatively small disadvantage of bulk and weight. They were used in all major camps and at Camp 2 the rice and tsampa were precooked before sending up to Sherpa climbers on the Face, saving time and fuel where it was most needed.

We also took a number of Thermos flasks ranging in size from one-pint drink size to almost three-pint food containers and used with a little forethought these too saved time, effort and valuable fuel at Camp 2 and above.

Finally, it is worth writing a few words about what seems a luxury item, folding tables and chairs. If climbers are to perform well on the mountain, it is essential that they eat and rest as well as possible in camp and the benefits of a well-set-up mess tent in the big camps should not need explanation, only emphasizing. The provision of decent, robust chairs and tables, although nothing like as glamorous as the supply of climbing hardware, nevertheless played a real part in ensuring our success.

Material suppliers: Although all our gas equipment was manufactured by Camping Gaz, we were unable to obtain support directly from them and all the equipment was supplied through Tentequip of Ossett. At the last minute we were still short of a number of small items for this section and were helped greatly by Institution Supplies of Leeds who at very short notice made good our shortfalls and in the same way Countess Gravina was responsible for presenting the expedition with an enormous pressure cooker to supplement the standard size models already provided by Prestige.

Although the specially filtered kerosene was obtained through Rockoil as noted, it was sent to Nepal in special 'Paracans' from Harcostar.

Miscellaneous

Under a heading like this one usually finds all the little unimportant bits forgotten until the last minute. In our case, however, there are several most important items and their inclusion here is only because they cannot really be covered by the other classifications.

Packing materials, for example, includes the indispensable heavy duck kit bags which were issued to each climber and

	MISCELLANEOUS EQUIPMENT DESCRIPTION	QUANTITIES	SUPPLIER
1	repair kits (tools)	2	Various suppliers
2	games collection	2	Waddington/W. H. Smith
3	portable offices	2	Sperry-Remington (typewriter)
4	kit bags	100	Cobles
5	assorted poly bags and sheets	1200	Bishop Plastics Ltd
6	boot polish and dubbin	50	Caswell
7	boot oils (suppletect)	36	Cottage Metal Crafts
8	miraclaces	50	Cottage Metal Crafts
9	Yale locks	100	Eaton Corporation
10	low-temperature thermometer	1	Zeal & Co.
11	boot brushes	20	Institutional Supplies
12	cassette recorders	3	National Panasonic
13	Thommen altimeters	2	Lawrie (London)
14	batteries	1200	Saft (France)

15	Anemometer	2	On loan from RGS
16	binding machine	2	UPI (UK)
17	blank cassettes	100	TDK Tape Distributors
18	pre-recorded cassettes	30	EMI
19	paperbacks	80	Penguin Books, Coronet Books
20	compasses	8	Newbould & Bulford
21	spring balances	8	Salter Industrial
22	metal box containers	100	Metal Box Co.
23	alarm clocks	6	Hirst Bros
24	binoculars	2	Newbould & Bulford/ Charles Frank
25	packing boxes	400	MacMillan Bloedel
26	personal and special boxes	40	WCB Containers
27	adhesive tape	600	Smith & Nephew
28	toothpaste, shampoo and soap	400	Colgate

high-altitude Sherpas for general packaging. Bigger bags were used, with plastic liners, to store rice, sugar and flour in both base camps. Almost 2000 assorted plastic bags in different sizes and gauges were taken although the bigger 500 gauge ones were the most useful. Big 10′ × 4′ lightweight sheets were essential as personal cover for Sherpas, under groundsheets for tents, and to keep snow off equipment stored outside. Each climber had his own issue personal box which was lockable and could be left at Base while he was on the mountain, but we had in addition thirty special fibre boxes to store and protect more vulnerable equipment like medical supplies, batteries, and radio equipment.

All equipment otherwise was sent out from England and stored during the expedition in waxed cardboard boxes made especially for us and overprinted with the expedition title and numbered for easy identification. All joints, edges, and corners were sealed and protected with extremely strong waterproof 2″ tape before banding with nylon strapping. This banding was particularly important when the contents were heavy, like oxygen bottles, and it is essential to stop any possible movement within the box which would easily damage the cylinder or burst the container.

The other equipment needed to handle the boxes was a good range of scales to weigh contents during preparation in England and also to make sure that porter loads are correct. Too little in each load soon adds up to a big reduction in carrying power and too much results, understandably, in complaints and trouble from Sherpas who have contracted to carry fixed weight loads. Generally speaking this was 60 lb. on the walk-in and a 40 lb. maximum above Base Camp.

Lastly, two large, comprehensive tool boxes were prepared covering every need from needle and thread and hand cleaner to riveting tool and wrenches.

For entertainment a compendium of games and books is essential, although on this trip only cards and dice were played with regularity. Dice, chess and Scrabble were also played, but basically anything that needed time or brainwork couldn't be sustained and the short-term excitement of gambling was understandably the most popular.

As a background to our evenings of eating and cards a couple of tape recorders were provided and a very mixed bag of tapes taken in an attempt to satisfy musical tastes ranging from heavy rock to grand opera.

Two smaller recorders were also used to record diaries and other conversations as well as a secondary music source. All four were 'winterized' by National Panasonic and played faultlessly during our time on the mountain. The two smaller machines had already had a battering in the overland lorry trip so had been from extremes of heat and dust to cold and snow, and I cannot think of a more rigorous proof of their reliability

Two other machines specially prepared for the trip were the portable Remington typewriters. They were in constant use during the walk-in, at Base Camp, and later Chris Bonington used one at Camp 2 for report preparation, sharing it with Hamish MacInnes who was busily trying to finish his latest novel in between days on the Face. The two typewriters were carried in special boxes – mini-offices really – complete with paper, envelopes, biros, and all the other equipment needed to control and record on paper the progress of the climb.

Material Suppliers: In addition to the games supplied by Waddington and W. H. Smith, we had a small selection from Denys Fisher and also some poker decks from the Continental Casino in Leeds. The compasses supplied by Newbould & Bulford were weight compensated to make them suitable for use on the mountain and finally it is worth noting that the packing boxes provided by MacMillan Bloedel were double-strength waxed cardboard boxes specially overprinted with expedition name and logo.

Conclusion

It took a short six months of very hard work to get our equipment designed, manufactured and despatched before the expedition proper began. The route was climbed in record time and we were back in England almost a month sooner than we expected, but nobody, I suspect, had any idea even then that our post-expedition commitment would be so great. For me it has taken a period of six embarrassing months to complete reports and provide pictures for over one hundred and fifty suppliers to the trip. I had promised all of them material which would make it possible to develop the advertising potential their support deserved, but the mammoth job of looking for appropriate material in the fifteen thousand transparencies we took was bound to take time. In addition, we had to attend an incredible number of receptions and lectures, all of them most enjoyable but all of them time-consuming and this may be the best place to thank them all for their help in the first instance and their understanding and patience in the months since our return. I should also like to add my thanks to my administration team, secretaries, June Slater, Maureen Fernehough, and all the Centresport staff for all their hard work.

On the expedition my time of greatest pleasure was the few days spent at Camp 4 because there at last I was an active part of the climbing effort, in a fantastic camp, but most important of all I was free of the equipment organizer's title. In that unglamorous role one is inevitably preoccupied with impersonal lists of equipment and loading schedules, with little time to relax and enjoy people rather than packing. One eventually resents the situation but it seems to go with the job and one has to look for satisfaction to the successful maintenance of equipment flowing up and down the mountain and feel that it all does help to put the team on top.

So my lasting memory of the expedition will not be of data under control and successfully co-ordinated but it will be of golden sunsets seen from Camp 4 and the warm sound of Sherpa laughter from the tent next door.

Appendix 6

Oxygen Equipment

by Hamish MacInnes

The oxygen apparatus is probably the most important single item of equipment for high-altitude climbing. George Finch and Geoffrey Bruce were the first climbers to use oxygen cylinders on Everest. Sherpas carried them to their camp at 25 000 feet on the North West Ridge in 1922. The climbers reached 27 300 feet before admitting defeat. During the intervening years, several other systems were tried out. On the first successful ascent of Everest in 1953, both open and closed-circuit sets were used. Though the closed-circuit set gives the best possible utilization of a given supply of oxygen, the equipment is bulky and complex. A soda lime canister is used to absorb the expired carbon dioxide and allows the exhaled oxygen to return to a breathing bag. Direction of flow is ensured by two non-return valves. Oxygen which is used by the climber is replaced from an oxygen cylinder. An improved version of the 1953 Everest closed-circuit equipment was used on Kangchenjunga. There is a further disadvantage in that, should the oxygen supply fail for some reason whilst the equipment is in use, the percentage of oxygen in the circulating gas can fall below that in the ambient air without the user being aware of the fact. The set, with one soda lime canister, weighs approximately 19 lb. The canister lasts as long as an 800-litre oxygen cylinder, which is an extra 11·6 lb. Though this system has proved to be reliable, it is heavy and seldom considered for high-altitude mountaineering, though it is used by astronauts.

We considered the various types of equipment available for the 1975 Expedition with particular care. During the 1972 South West Face expedition we had experienced considerable trouble with the diluter-demand system developed by Dr F. Duane Blume and the Robertshaw Company of the USA.

A post-mortem on the sets, which we returned to the Company after the expedition, revealed that a valve had been left in place in error at the end of the corrugated mask hose. This stopped the oxygen flow when the mask froze up – which happened frequently. It was a dangerous fault, as it was often difficult to remove the face mask quickly, when the blockage occurred, whilst wearing two pairs of gloves. Later, we were told that the valves should have been removed by the suppliers of the masks for the special requirements of high-altitude climbing, as opposed to high-altitude flying for which they were originally designed. We were assured that it would not happen again.

I was still in favour of a simple constant-flow system such as the Hornbein equipment which comprises a face mask with a manually controlled variable oxygen supply to the oro-nasal region of the mask. The flow rate can be varied from between 1–4 litres per minute. The system tends to be wasteful of oxygen at the lower respiratory rates and deficient at the high rates but, on the other hand, there is not much that can go wrong with it.

Chris Bonington wrote to Tom Hornbein for his advice in the matter and was informed that, in Hornbein's opinion, the Blume/Robertshaw system was superior. So we decided in favour of the latter, despite our previous ill-luck with the system. Dr Duane Blume had been appointed the Oxygen Officer for the International Everest Expedition in 1971 and he was largely responsible for the development of the diluter-demand system. Similar equipment is used widely in aviation; it works on the principle that, when one inspires, ambient air is also drawn into the mask via a port in the regulator together with pure oxygen from the cylinder in a rucksack on the climber's back. The regulator is a modified aviation type, altered to give four ambient-air orifices in place of the original aneroid valve. This aneroid valve was not sensitive enough for high altitude climbing purposes. Each setting is equal to increments of 2000 feet from 22000 to 30000 feet.

Earlier, I had gone into the possibility of using cartridges of solid oxygen but, although this system is excellent for emergency oxygen supplies in aircraft, it proved to be too expensive and the replenishment cartridge of too short a life for high-altitude climbing.

The question of cylinders for the oxygen was my next problem, and Captain Henry Day who had been working on a similar problem for the British Army Everest Expedition recommended Reynolds Tubes. When I contacted Stan Gould, Manager of Research and Development, I found that he had designed a cylinder which was, at $7\frac{1}{2}$ lb., one of the lightest ever produced. The cylinders which we had used in 1972 had a capacity of 1000 litres which was just too much for the average day's climbing. 800 litres, we felt, would be just about right and, in restrospect, this estimate still holds good. The cylinders were manufactured from HE 15TF aluminium alloy; overall length: 25″, and width: 4″. The working pressure was 3300 lb./in.^{2}; the burst pressure 9500 lb./in.^{2}.

The cylinders were filled with oxygen of a dew point of 6 v.p.m. The cylinder valves were made by Sherwood Selpac, type TV-5441, and these proved excellent; no leakage was observed from any of the cylinders. Burst discs on several cylinders blew whilst they were being transported in one of the two expedition trucks. This was due to excessive heat and in fact the burst discs fulfilled their function in blowing at approximately 5000 lb./in.^{2}.

I studied the possibility of overwrapping cylinders with glass fibre and also with a different material Kevlar 49. Overwrapping steel cylinders with wire had been practised for a number of years and such cylinders were used by the successful Kangchenjunga Expedition, manufactured by the Chesterfield Tube Company, an associate of Reynolds. Glass fibre overwrapping is a more recent innovation and, to date, Kevlar 49 has not yet been used for this purpose. Mr M. E. Humphries, of IMI Engineering looked into the possibility of using Kevlar 49 but unfortunately, due to the lack of time, the testing programme could not be carried out. Perhaps on some future expedition the spherical container with Kevlar overwrapping will provide the ideal oxygen container?

The diluter-demand system which we eventually used is made up from the following components: the oxygen cylinder, with a pressure reducer and pressure gauge attached which fits onto the cylinder valve; a length of high-pressure tubing leading from it to the diluter-demand regulator; and a shorter section of flexible corrugated tubing which links it to the face mask. A further orifice on the pressure reducer is fitted to a plastic medical-type mask for use whilst sleeping. Oxygen for sleeping purposes is supplied to two people via a small T manifold at a flow rate of one litre per minute which, by experience, we have found to be quite adequate. The weight of the complete system with one filled cylinder is 30·1 lb.

In conjunction with Karrimor and Graham Tiso, Karrimor's pack-frame was adapted to carry the oxygen cylinders and other equipment within the sack. Two small pockets inside the bottom of the sack allowed the base of cylinders to be located and strap ties at the top ensured that they were held in position. An aperture was made from the main compartment of the sack to the inside of a side pocket on the left-hand side of the pack-frame to take the high pressure hose. The demand valve was located within this pocket, the side wall of which was made from a breathing material. In fact the

Diluter-demand oxygen system, as used on the expedition

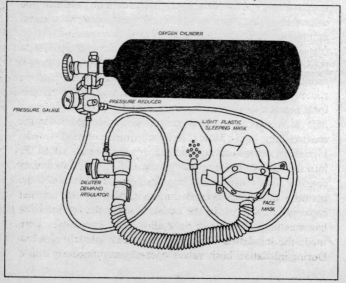

pocket was a spindrift filter. A short sleeve allowed the end of the corrugated mask hose to connect with the demand valve. When the pack-frame was worn, the corrugated mask hose led from under the left armpit to the climber's face. I had the hose lengthened specifically for this purpose.

The face mask was a standard military one: the A-14. It weighs 14 oz and is made by the Sierra Engineering Company. Manufactured from silicone rubber, it gives a reliable performance in cold environments. It is readily crushable in place with a gloved hand – to free ice from the ports and exhaust valve. However, one of the summit parties found that more drastic treatment had to be used for clearing an ice blockage.

Two types of helmet were used for holding the face masks in place. One was the white flying helmet loaned to us by the Swiss Foundation for Alpine Research which we had also used in 1972. The other was an ex-RAF flying helmet supplied to us by Victor Lawrence Supplies, London. Both proved excellent.

Our experiences with the Blume/Robertshaw system on the 1975 expedition were unsatisfactory. Of the eighteen sets supplied to the expedition, only five eventually worked, and several of these were not 100 per cent. Almost without exception, the faults were due to defective demand valves. Even under normal conditions, with no abuse whatsoever to the equipment, failure would occur. The equipment was, moreover, subjected to much less arduous conditions than on the 1972 post-monsoon attempt; the temperatures on this most recent expedition were considerably higher.

It is worth noting that the Japanese did considerable research on high-altitude oxygen equipment and several interesting design aspects emerged. An economizer which fits into the climber's helmet proved successful. This economizer consists of a polyethylene bag designed to accumulate the quantity of oxygen needed during inhalation; the internal capacity is 2·8 litres. In the earlier systems the economizing bag was housed within a light alloy box. Two valves were used: the inhalation valve, and the outer inhalation valve. During inhalation both valves opened simultaneously and a mixture of oxygen and outer air passed through the hose into the mask. During exhalation both valves closed. Oxygen was supplied from the cylinder via a reducing valve to the economizer bag. The reason for not adopting a helmet type economizer for our expedition was that the economizer box was always awkward – located either on the pack-frame, or 'fixed' somewhere more convenient to the climber. There are several other advantages in the helmet-mounted economizer, one being that the inhaled oxygen is slightly warmed before inhalation; another is that the economizer is out of the way and very close to the face mask. This equipment was tested in temperatures of − 50°C. The face mask developed for the helmet-economizer system was the H mask and a great deal of work was put into this design, but it was moulded for the Japanese face and not suitable for our physiognomy.

For the purpose of attempting the South West Face of Everest, the Japanese perfected a system of piping oxygen from the second man to the leader, thereby obviating the need for the leader to carry the cylinder whilst lead climbing. They experimented with 40-metre-long hoses of an internal diameter of 6 mm. When the oxygen was put out from the cylinder pressure reducer at 3 litres per minute, there was only a reduction of 7 per cent at the other end; therefore, by slightly boosting the input flow, a normal supply could be obtained by the lead climber. Another interesting fact emerging from this experiment was that the hose was found to be strong enough to support a climber weighing 70 kg. Perhaps when the South West Face 'Super Direct' is finally made, this will be the oxygen system to be used.

Appendix 7

Food

by Mike Thompson

The letter in the unmistakable Bonington scrawl, once deciphered, read:

> How about coming on the coldest holiday of your life?
> P.S. Will you do the food?

In fact, as it turned out it wasn't *that* cold: but then it wasn't much of a holiday either. 'Doing the food' is a fairly thankless task and the famous dictum, 'The most important thing about food is that there should be some', whilst undoubtedly true, is not the only requirement for satisfaction and success.

During my military days in Malaya an Australian vet attached to the regiment in lieu of a padre pronounced, with that antipodean knack for bibulous vulgarity combined with deep philosophical intuition: 'There's only two things that matter in your life – your belly and what's on the end of it.' On Everest life is even simpler – there is just your belly; for whatever might have been on the end of it has become, at best, vestigial. In consequence food, far from being simply a fuel, becomes the central mystery of existence; the sole remnant of culture and repository of meaning; the metaphor within which all dissatisfaction is expressed.

Only too aware of this, I took the earliest opportunity of consulting that most fluent expressor of dissatisfaction, Mick Burke. With disarming candour he confessed that for him food presented no problems: 'For breakfast, bacon, eggs, mushrooms and fried bread, tea and toast. For lunch, fish and chips. For supper, meat and potato pie and chips.' And that, in a nutshell, is the whole problem: to get as close as possible, with non-perishable foodstuffs, with severe weight restrictions and with primitive cooking facilities, to this ideal diet. But this is only the start of the problem, for there are likely to be as many ideal diets as there are members of the expedition. Of course, if the entire expedition had been recruited from Wigan they would have shared Mick's tastes, but unfortunately other criteria governed the selection of the team and, as its geographically and socially diverse membership grew towards twenty (not to mention the eighty Sherpas and *their* ideal diets), the chances of my satisfying even a small proportion rapidly faded. Denied the opportunity of selecting the members to suit the food, I decided that I could at least satisfy one person, so I chose the food that *I* liked. I took the precaution of sending each member a list of likely items and the sorts of menus they could provide and asked for their objections and suggestions. Nick Estcourt imposed his usual veto on peanut butter, Doug Scott revealed his cravings for granola and French nougat and Chris Bonington urged 'lots of really hot pickles and chutneys', but otherwise the response was slight, so, interpreting apathy as approval, I set to work on the detailed planning.

People often say to me: 'I suppose you start off with a target number of calories and certain ratios of fat, carbohydrate and protein, and then try to achieve these within the minimum weight.' In fact, I do no such thing. I am an anthropologist not a nutritionist and I start off with the *idea* of a meal, and of a day punctuated and made meaningful by a series of meals, and of a succession of days distinguished one from another by different series of meals. A typical starting point would be an outline of a day's eating such as this:

BREAKFAST: Tea
                   Porridge, brown sugar, milk
                   Biscuits, margarine, honey
                   More tea

DURING DAY: Chocolate (Roast almond)
                   Spangles
                   Nuts and raisins
                   Brew of hot fruit juice on return
                   (Possibility of something more substantial
                   if staying in the camp during the day, e.g.
                   tomato soup and digestive biscuits.)

EVENING MEAL: **Tea**

Irish stew, mashed potatoes, peas

Christmas pudding and cream

Coffee, whisky, chocolate

It is this sort of menu that generates the ration packs for use on the Face itself, but most food is consumed at Base Camp or in the Western Cwm and is prepared by Sherpa cooks catering for as many as twenty people. At Base Camp and during the approach march it is a good idea to have as much fresh food as possible and quite a lot of fresh food can be incorporated even at Camp 2 (for instance, we had fresh meat and spinach and even fresh(ish) salad with olive oil and lemon juice at 22000 feet). The Sherpas, of course, like to include as much fresh and familiar food in their diet as possible.

In view of these differences in camp size, in cooking arrangements and in access to local and fresh food, it seemed a good idea to have three different types of ration: 'Base and Approach', 'Advance Base', and 'Face' – an arrangement that neatly fitted in with the changes in load weight on the mountain (60 lb. to Base Camp, 40 lb. to Camp 2 and 30 lb. on the Face).

In deference to the Sherpa preference for local produce the 'Base and Approach' rations were subdivided into 'Climber' and 'Sherpa', the climbers getting $1\frac{1}{2}$ lb. per man-day (and about $2\frac{1}{2}$ lb. local purchase) and the Sherpas 1 lb. per man-day (and about 3 lb. local purchase). The weight allowance for Advance Base (Camp 1 and Camp 2) was a generous $2\frac{1}{2}$ lb. per man-day (and about $1\frac{1}{2}$ lb. of local purchase). For the Face, the rations were broken down into 4 man-day packs each weighing $8\frac{1}{2}$ lb. which gives just over 2 lb. per man per day (which though probably not enough to support life indefinitely is as much, if not more, than anyone managed to eat).

At this stage the planning of the food became intricately involved with Chris's overall planning: the weights, once decided upon, had to be adhered to scrupulously or else the meticulously planned movements of loads and personnel would be thrown out and the narrow logistic margins exceeded. Also I needed to know how many mouths there would be to feed (always a varying and usually increasing, quantity in the early stages of planning) and where those mouths were likely to be situated on the mountain. Eventually, I obtained three figures: estimated number of man-days above Camp 2, between Base Camp and Camp 2, at Base Camp and below. These I then biased slightly in favour of Face and Advance Base (since one can eat Face Rations at Base but not vice versa), multiplied by the weights of food allowed per man-day at the different altitudes, divided by the load weights at the different altitudes, and, assuming the arithmetic was right, I then knew how many boxes of food we would have to take: 480 boxes totalling approximately 11 tons.

The next straightforward but laborious task was to compile a shopping list (149 items including 110 988 tea bags and ninety-six plastic lemons) and then take it down the road to Liptons the Grocers. Allied Suppliers, of which Liptons are the retail outlets, had kindly agreed to provide those items which they themselves produced (under the Liptons and Sunshine labels) at cost, and to obtain all the other items on the list and to gather them all together in one place. In all, fifty-eight separate suppliers were involved and Gordon Lambert of Allied Suppliers had the appalling job of dealing with them all and of persuading them to provide the items free or at a much reduced cost. It is a measure of his success and hard work that the final cost was some £2000 below budget.

I am very proud of the fact that in organizing the food I wrote only two letters but this statistic obscures a lot of leg-work and endless telephone calls. For instance, the dried egg was only obtained after the personal intervention of Sir Geoffrey de Freitas and the cans of cooking oil were, I believe, stealthily diverted from supplies destined for the Royal Household (thank you, Prince Philip). Green's of Brighton queried our order for ninety-six packets of instant pancake mix. Had we, they wondered, left out a decimal point? If not, we would have enough pancakes to pave a footpath all the way to the summit of Everest. The order *was* right and the pancakes were a great success – quite fluffy and not at all like paving stones. In some cases we were asking quite small firms for large quantities of expensive items. The director of Rowland Smith Limited who had received an order for a vast quantity of Ye Olde Oak Hams and Ye Olde Oak Chickens telephoned to ask just what sort of publicity he could hope for in return for helping us. Would I, he asked, guarantee to mention Ye Olde Oak by name in the book? Gambling everything, I said 'Yes.' 'All right,' he said, 'you've got the lot, free.' (Well, there you are Mr Smith, you've got what I promised you, three times over!)

Pitt and Scott who did the packing specialize in fine art removals. Indeed, it is often said of them that they have made the packing of art an art form in itself. They adopted the same reverential attitude to our humble provisions, treating bottles of soy sauce as if they were from the T'ang dynasty and handling jars of Branston Pickle as if they were Henry Moore bronzes.

Not only was the food going to be transported overland to Kathmandu and then handled and mishandled again and again by both yaks and humans, but it had to survive the heat and humidity of the monsoon while stored in Nima Tsering's house in Khumde. The tins would present no problems but such items as cereals, biscuits, chocolate, Christmas puddings and cheese were just as they came off the supermarket shelf in flimsy cardboard and cellophane wrappings. In the hope of retarding their inevitable decay, each water-proofed fibre-board box had a sealable plastic-coated liner; a precaution that really paid off for, apart from the occasional exploding drum of parmesan cheese and some compost-grown muesli that completed its ecological cycle before it could be eaten, these perishable items were still in remarkably good condition at the end of their ordeal. The boxes were wrapped in a tough bitumen sandwich paper and all the seams and folds covered with plastic tape. With heavy symbolism, the boxes were colour-coded: green tape for the pastoral safety of Base Camp, red tape for the dangers of the Face, and yellow for the bit in between. Once wrapped there was no way of telling the menu of a box and this was quite deliberate. The inconvenience of occasionally having the same menu two days running is

Ration Lists

RATION TYPE	COLOUR CODE	PACKAGING UNITS AND WEIGHTS	NUMBER OF BOXES		
Face rations	Red	4 man-day packs each 8¼ lb. (menus A, B, C)	3 to a box (one of each menu A, B, C). Each box weight 30 lb. 165 × 4 man-day packs = 54 × 3 pack boxes	20" × 12" × 8" (pack in double poly bags)	Small
Advance Base rations	Yellow	16 man-day packs. Each 40 lb. (6 menus A, B, C, D, E, F)	44 of each menu A, B, C, D, E, F, giving total 266	20" × 12" × 12"	Medium
Base and Approach (Climber)	Green (Marked 'Climber')	40 man-day packs. Each 60 lb. (3 menus A, B, C)	13 of each menu A, B, C giving total 39	25" × 12" × 12"	Large
Base and Approach (Sherpa)	Green (Marked 'Sherpa')	60 man-day packs. Each 60 lb. (3 menus A, B, C)	20 of each menu A, B, C giving total 60	25" × 12" × 12"	Large

Advance Base (Kitchen)	Yellow (Marked 'Kitchen')	Each box approx. 40 lb.	12	20″ × 12″ × 12″	Medium
Base and Approach (Kitchen)	Green (Marked 'Kitchen')	Each box approx. 60 lb.	12	25″ × 12″ × 12″	Large
Overs (Base and Approach)	Green (Marked 'Overs')	Each box approx. 60 lb.	13	25″ × 12″ × 12″	Large
Overs (Advance Base)	Yellow (Marked 'Overs')	Each box approx. 40 lb.	5	20″ × 12″ × 12″	Medium
Walk-in rations	Pitt & Scott Tape (Marked 'Keep in Kathmandu')	30 man-day packs. Each 60 lb.	19	25″ × 12″ × 12″	Large

FACE RATIONS

Typical 4 man-day pack menu

Sugar (cube)	1 box	
Coffee Mate	6 sachets	
Nescafé	6 sachets	
Tea	12 tea bags	
Rise 'n Shine fruit drink (lemon)		1 packet
Stock cubes	4 cubes	
Soup (Mushroom)	2 packets	
Mint cake	4 × 3 oz bars	
Chocolate (Roast almond)		4 × 2 oz bars
Nougat	4 × 2 oz packets	
Candle	1	
Matches	2 boxes	
Tissues	½ box	

Vitamin tablets	1 strip (4 tablets)	
Salt	2 drums	
Margarine	2 tube × 1 oz	
Tin opener	1	
Readibrek (instant porridge)		8 oz bag
Irish Stew	2 × 16 oz tins	
Smash (dehydrated potato)		2 × 6 oz packets
Surprise peas	1 × 2 oz packets	
High fat biscuits	2 × 3 oz packets	
Xmas pudding	2 × 8 oz packets	
Cream	1 × 4 oz tin	
Choc. digestive biscuits		1 × 8 oz packet
Honey	2 × 1 oz pots	

ADVANCE BASE RATIONS

Typical 16 man-day pack menu

Porridge	1 × 12 oz packet
Marvel milk	2 × 7 oz tins
Sugar (cube)	4 × 16 oz boxes
Sugar (soft brown)	2 × 16 oz packets
Baconburgers	4 × 10 oz tins
High fat biscuits	10 × 3 oz packets

Stock cubes	3 packets of 6
Ovaltine	1 × 8 oz tin
Irish stew	6 × 16 oz tins
Mango chutney	1 × 10 oz jar
Shortbread	3 × 7 oz packets
Honey	2 × 12 oz tubes

Milk chocolate 16 × 1¾ oz bars
Nuts and raisins 16 × 2 oz packets
Pilchards in tomato sauce 3 × 14 oz tins
Tea bags 1 × box of 72
Nescafé 1 × 4 oz tin

Kitchen roll 1 packet
Toilet roll 1 doublet
Safety matches 4 boxes
Salt 1 × 1 lb. 8 oz packet
Ham 1 × 16 oz tin

BASE AND APPROACH (CLIMBER) RATIONS

Typical 40 man-day pack menu

Porridge or muesli 5 lb.
Marvel milk 4 × 7 oz tins
Condensed milk 3 × 16 oz tins
Dehydrated egg 1 × 32 oz tin
Plain chocolate 40 × 1¾ oz bars
Spangles 40 × 1 oz packets
Tea 2 × 8 oz packets
Real coffee 1 × 16 oz packet
Packet soups (2 kinds) 2 × 1 gal.

Irish stew 7 × 16 oz tins
Marmalade 2 × 16 oz jars
Fruit cake (Dundee) 3 × 2 lb. tins
Chocolate Garibaldi biscuits 2 × 4½ oz packets
Kitchen roll 2 packets
Toilet paper 2 doublets
Safety matches 8 boxes
Margarine 1 × 16 oz tin
Salt 1 × 1 lb. 8 oz

BASE AND APPROACH (SHERPA) RATIONS

Typical 60 man-day pack menu

Marvel milk 6 × 7 oz tins
Condensed milk 4 × 16 oz tins
Crunchie bars 60 × 1¾ oz packets
Tea 3 × 4 oz tins
Choc. digestive biscuits 12 × 16 oz packets
Jam (strawberry) 5 × 1 lb. jars

Tuna fish 12 × 8 oz tins
Salmon 6 × 16 oz tins
Margarine 3 × 16 oz tins
Kitchen roll 3 packets
Safety matches 12 boxes
Salt 1 × 1 lb. 8 oz

KITCHEN BOXES: ADVANCE BASE

Olive oil   1 × 1 litre bottle
Cooking oil (Mazola)   1 × 1 gal. can
Jellies   6 assorted
Dehydrated onion flakes   1 packet
Dehydrated garlic   ¼ packet
Curry powder   1 × 16 oz tin
Chilli powder   ¼ packet
Mixed spice   3 tins
Instant batter mix   8 × 7 packets
Golden syrup   1 × 12 lb. tin

Plastic lemons   4
Mango pickle   1 jar
Lime pickle   1 jar
Branston pickle   1 jar
Marmite   2 jars
Baking power   1 tin
Soy sauce   1 bottle
Marmite   2 oz jar
Hunzana cake   2 × 2 lb. tins

KITCHEN BOXES: BASE AND APPROACH

Olive oil   } 2 × 1 gal. oil or 1 × 1 gal. oil +
Cooking oil   } 2 × 1 lit. bottle
Jellies   9 assorted
Dehydrated onion flakes   2 packets
Dehydrated garlic   ¼ tub
Curry powder   2 × 1 lb. tins
Chilli powder   ¼ tub
Mixed spice   3 tins
Instant pancake mix   8 × 7 oz packets
Golden syrup   1 × 2 lb. tin
Plastic lemons   4
Mango pickle   1 jar

Bamboo pickle   1 jar
Branston pickle   1 jar
Marmite   1 jar
Baking powder   1 tin
Dried yeast   3 packets
Chilli sauce   1 bottle
Soy sauce   3 bottles
Marmite   8 oz jar
Marmite   2 oz jar
Margarine   2 × 16 oz tins
Salt   1 × 1½ lb. packet
Apple dice   2 × 1 lb. packet

WALK-IN RATIONS: 30 MAN-DAY PACKS

Lime pickle   1 jar
Cereal (muesli or porridge)   5 lb.
Milk (Marvel and condensed)   4 tins
Dehydrated egg   1 × 2 lb. tin
Tea   1 × 72 box tea bags
Sugar   6 × 16 oz boxes
Rise 'n Shine   6 packets
Stock cubes   6 boxes of 6
Peanuts/nuts and raisins/cashews   48 × 2 oz
    packets
Spangles/Starburst   6 × 5 packets
Jam   2 × 1 lb. jar
Toilet paper   1 doublet
Scotties (tissues)   1 box
Matches   2 boxes: 1 box lifeboat

Hunzana cake   2 × 2 lb. tins
Soup   3 × 1 gal. packets
Pancake mix   1 × 7 oz packet
Apple dice   1 × 16 oz packet
Salt   1 × 1½ lb. packet
Margarine   1 × 1 lb. tin
Cream   2 × 4 oz tins
Fish, various
Ham
Sausages
Chilli con carne
Irish stew
Butter beans
Beans and sausage
Spam

Total of 15 lb.

L

nothing compared with the ill-feeling generated by those in the lower camps consuming the more favoured boxes and passing on the unpopular ones, which is what inevitably happens if the boxes are labelled.

As it happened, there were enough left-overs to keep the Thompson family in steak and kidney puddings for several months *and* to make up nineteen extra boxes for the approach march. Finally, a few boxes of overs were made up for 'Base and Approach' and for 'Advance Base', and some 'Kitchen boxes' containing items for stocking the kitchens, such as cooking oil, curry powder, baking powder and dried garlic which were provided for Base Camp and Camp 2.

ACKNOWLEDGEMENTS

Aerota Packing Co., Allied Services, Allied Suppliers, Associated Biscuits, Atkinsons of Windermere, Barratt & Co., Batchelors Foods, Beatrice Foods (UK), Bovril, Bowater Scott Corporation, Brooke Bond Oxo, Bryant & May, Cadbury Confectionery, Cadbury Schweppes Foods, Carnation Foods, Chiltonian Biscuits, Calthwaite Fudge, Colman Foods, G. Costa & Co., CPC (UK), Crowson & Sons, Ch. Goldrei Fouchard & Son, H. J. Green, John Haig & Co., C. & T. Harris of Colne, H. J. Heinz, J. & H. Packaging, W. A. Jordan & Sons (Biggleswade), Kellogg Co. of Great Britain, Kraft Foods, Lipton Ltd Tea Sales (UK), Lovell & Christmas, Andrew Lusk, Lyons Tetley, Manley Pure Foods, Mars, A. McCormick Foods (UK), Nabisco Foods, Nestlé Co., L. Noel & Sons, Ormo Cake Co., Parrish & Fenn, Pattersons of Livingston, Pitt & Scott, Plumrose, Princes Foods, Daniel Quiggin of Kendal, Rowland Smith, Spillers Foods, Tate & Lyle, UB Snacks Division, United Biscuits, Van der Berghs, H. & T. Walker, Walls Meat Co., Wander, Weetabix, John West Foods, Whitworth Holdings, Wilsons of Scotland.

Appendix 8

Communications

by Ronnie Richards

On a large expedition good communications are essential, since many unforeseeable circumstances occur which require concerted action over a distance in a short time. In contrast to a small expedition, the team is more widely scattered and the problems of co-ordinating and implementing best courses of action are much more complex. In addition, there needs to be provision for getting messages and materials from and to the outside world.

No one on the team was a radio expert but we were able to draw on the experience of the 1972 expedition when Kelvin Kent had organized communications. This alleviated the main problem of identifying a system of radio equipment which was both technically suitable for the different types of link required and would also stand up to the usage and cold. Since the equipment used in 1972 had performed so well there seemed no reason to change and the suppliers generously made sets available.

There were three functions requiring different types of radio: 1. The Rear Link, connecting the main Sherpa village of Namche Bazar with Base Camp and Camp 2, demanded short-wave transceivers having adequate power and range to transmit over terrain including 23 000-feet mountains. For security reasons, the set in Namche had to be housed in the Police Post and any radio messages for Kathmandu relayed on the Nepalese Police net and not our own (our import licence required separate clearance and a permit for the use of radio transmitters).

The Police Radio was out of action much of the time, however, but we were able to pass messages via Syangboche airstrip, just above Namche, whom we also supplied with meteorological data in return for special weather forecasts relayed from Kathmandu. The British Army had kindly loaned us two Gurkha Signallers who operated the short-wave sets at Base and Namche. This was a great help.

2. The Ice Fall net connected Base Camp, Camp 1 and Camp 2 which were non 'line of sight' and so needed higher power VHF sets than those used in the Face. These sets were also for use in case of accident in the Ice Fall etc. where lightness and power might be necessary.

3. The Face net connected Camp 2 with camps on the Face which were all nearly line of sight, allowing a lighter walkie-talkie VHF set to be used. One frequency common to nets 2 and 3 permitted interchangeability.

Details of radio sets

1. *Rear Link* (Base to Namche Bazar)
   Racal Squadcal-HF. Mode: SSB/AM. Frequency: 4.2–4.5 MHz (2 channels). Antenna: Half Wave Dipole or Rod. Output: 5 watts. Power supply: 14 'D' cells or 18v. supply. Weight: 18 lb. complete with case, ancillaries and batteries. No. of sets: 3.

2. *Ice Fall Net* (Base to Camp 1 to Advance Base)
   Racal Telecal-VHF. Mode: Narrow Band FM. Frequency: 40–50 MHz—(2 channels). Antenna: Telescopic Rod. Output: 1 watt. Power supply: 8 'C' cells or 12v. supply. Weight: 3.7 lb. with batteries. No. of sets: 3.

3. *Upper Camp Net* (Advance Base to Camp 6)
   Philips Handy Talkie (Type MC203)—VHF. Mode: Phase Modulation. Frequency: 47–57 MHz—(6 channels). Antenna: Folding springblade. Output: 400 MW. Power supply: 6 Penlight batteries or 9v. supply. Weight, 2.2 lb. including batteries. No. of sets: 8.

4. *Radio Receivers:* Hacker Super Sovereign. Bush VTR 178.

5. *Batteries:* all radios were powered by MN 1300, 1400 and 1500 cells from Mallory Batteries Limited.

The short-wave sets used for the rear link performed well, but for communications on the mountain with Base Camp it was found more convenient to use the light walkie-talkies and relay any messages, if necessary, through Camp 1. Direct communications, particularly from high camps, were often surprisingly good. All types of set developed some faults, mainly in transmission, but we fortunately had sufficient overlap or spare capacity.

Since the airstrips at Syangboche and Luglha (one or two days by mail-runner from Base Camp) did not operate during the monsoon period, mail, press and film despatches had to be sent back by mail-runner all the way to Kathmandu, where they were as ever efficiently dealt with by Elizabeth Hawley, our press agent. Six mail-runners, operating in pairs, were used for the 300-mile round trip and achieved a quickest return within 18 days. Requirements of firewood and fresh food were contracted out to Sherpas and supplies were regularly brought up to Base Camp by yak.

Communications network

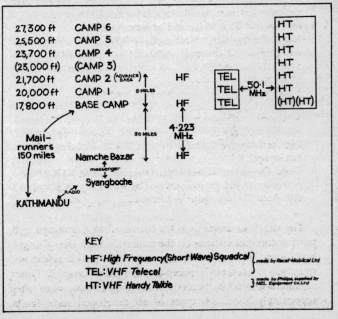

27,300 ft	CAMP 6			HT
25,500 ft	CAMP 5			HT
23,700 ft	CAMP 4			HT
(23,000 ft)	(CAMP 3)			HT
21,700 ft	CAMP 2 (ADVANCE BASE) ↑	HF	TEL	HT
20,000 ft	CAMP 1	5 MILES	TEL	HT
17,800 ft	BASE CAMP	↓ HF	TEL	(HT)(HT)

50·1 MHz

Mail-runners 150 miles

30 MILES

4·223 MHz

Namche Bazar ↓ HF

↑ messenger
↓ Syangboche

RADIO

KATHMANDU

KEY

HF: High Frequency (Short Wave) Squadcal } made by Racal-Mobilcal Ltd
TEL: VHF Telecal
HT: VHF Handy Talkie   } made by Philips, supplied by MEL Equipment Co. Ltd

Appendix 9

Photography

Still photography
by Doug Scott

On Everest in autumn 1975 there was no excuse for not having complete photographic coverage of our expedition. The weather was mainly favourable and every member of the team was well equipped to take photographs.

We were all issued with the Olympus O M 1 body and 75–150 mm zoom lens. We also had the choice of any other lens. Most of us chose either the 28 mm or the 35 mm wide-angle lens. There were also two spare bodies for the real enthusiast plus a plethora of lenses from two macro 50 mm lenses up to a 600 mm telephoto. The camera bodies were ninety-five per cent reliable. The only faults were two broken light meters, one stuck shutter and three A S A rating discs fell off. Considering there were twenty bodies altogether in use, and used pretty well continuously for two and a half months, this was a good performance. The 28 mm lens seemed particularly sharp and the team had no complaints about other lenses either.

We were obliged not to use our own cameras as Olympus had generously supplied all the equipment at a hundred per cent discount. However for the approach march I was able to use a Pentax 6×7 camera with a wide-angle f 3·5/55 lens, standard f 2·4/105 lens and a telephoto f 4/400 lens. Whilst the quality of definition was excellent, I found that the combination of never having handled a large-format camera before, plus its weight, rather counted against the interest of my results. I shot far more 35 mm film but, even accounting for the law of averages, these results tended to be of most value. No other cameras were used for colour photography.

Some of us carried battered Rollei 35 cameras for black and white. I took one, made in West Germany, to the summit and was well satisfied with the sharp results. I kept a 2×2 red filter over the lens at all times mainly because I was too lazy to change it.

Film was also generously supplied free of charge. Kodak gave us the following film.

600 rolls (36 exposure)	Kodachrome 25
100 rolls (20 exposure)	High Speed Ektachrome
100 rolls	Tri X
200 rolls	Panatomic X
100 rolls	Ektachrome X
A small quantity	$2\frac{1}{4}''$ square format film

Bob Stoodley was given the loan of an XL330 movie camera plus 20 cartridges of Kodachrome II Super 8 movie film for the journey with the lorries.

I also had a similar range of film for my 6×7 camera.

The Kodachrome 25 film was by far and away the most popular. The results achieved were superb. One feature that was extremely useful in the often contrasting condition of light and shade was this film's ability to pick out detail in the shadow, whilst allowing full exposure to be given to the lighter areas. In this respect it does seem to be an improvement upon the old Kodachrome II.

The High Speed Ektachrome was either a poor film or we could not handle it properly, for the results it gave were very disappointing.

The Panatomic X black-and-white film proved once again very successful, especially in the bright light condition often prevailing.

Personal considerations

Despite the unstinted help given by Kodak and Olympus the higher we climbed the less we photographed. Masses of good photographs were taken on the walk-in through the Himalayan foothills and there were some superb results from the Ice Fall and the Western Cwm, but there was much less from the Face itself where photography became very much a subordinate activity among the lead climbers. Apart from this, it was not unusual to experience $-35°$ of frost above

Camp 6 (27300 feet) which made it difficult to handle cameras.

Speaking now for myself, there comes also the saddening realization that the view from the top of Everest which I now have in my mind's eye is very possibly no longer the magnificent pure naked wholly coloured vision of the moment, but consequently wholly coloured by the slides I then took and have seen so many times since.

The photographs we took are owned by the expedition, and copyright does not revert to the photographers for two years. Apart from that, the demand for the photographic material is such from sponsors, for lectures, for producing this book, etc., that it is a long time before the actual photographer receives a full set of his own original photographs back again – by which time he may well be embroiled in another expedition.

We were particularly fortunate that Wendy Bonington was able to devote a great deal of time to sorting through the slides and returning all those not required. Those she kept for lecture sets and the book were duplicated and copies sent back to each photographer for his records.

We were also grateful for the care with which Wendy Bonington treated our colour slides and Down Town Darkroom our black-and-white negatives. Would that all others who handled our material so roughly had paused to consider it took a lot of getting.

Cinematography
by Ian Stuart

The BBC film unit consisted of the two producers, Ned Kelly and Chris Ralling; Mick Burke and myself as cameramen; and Arthur Chesterman as sound recordist.

Our brief was to film and record a 75-minute documentary programme and to send back TV news reports and sequences for the 'Blue Peter' programme. A total of 39000 feet of film was used.

Equipment

1. *Sound equipment by Arthur Chesterman* Lightweight, realiability, and convenience of use were the prime factors

that influenced my decision to use the Nagra S N as the main recorder on the expedition, although I did have a Nagra 4·2 and Nagra IS as alternatives. By running the machine at $3\frac{3}{4}''$ per second and using double-play tape I achieved a recording time of 54 minutes per reel without sacrificing quality. I had a lightweight mixer built which provided two microphone inputs and full monitoring facilities which gave the same versatility and capability to the S N as a full-size Nagra. The total weight of the equipment was four pounds and it was small enough to leave in my sleeping bag overnight, to keep it warm. Mallory alkaline cells were used throughout and, although they gave reduced performance under very cold conditions, their performance was superior to ordinary batteries under the same conditions.

The S N gave no trouble at all, in spite of rough treatment and, although it would sometimes take up to three seconds to reach speed, this was almost certainly a battery problem and only happened when it was extremely cold. I used Sennheiser 415 microphones – the 415 is a short gun mike – for most work and Audio Engineering Radio Microphones. These gave no problems and are probably the best microphones for this kind of work.

2. *Camera equipment included the following:*

Cameras
    2 Eclair N P R, 10–1 Angenieux zoom and 10–1 Zeiss zoom
    1 Eclair A C L with spare body and 10–1 Angenieux zoom
    2 Arriflex S T with 10–1 Angenieux zooms
    1 Bell Howell 70 D R
    5 Bell Howell 200T autoloads with either single-lens or two-lens turrets
    1 Bell Howell 200T with electric drive and crystal sync. facility (adapted by the B B C)

Tripods
    2 Ronford fluid 2
    2 Miller
    1 Satchler and Wolfe heavy duty

Additional lenses included
   20–1 Angenieux zoom
   Novaflex outfit 140 mm–600 mm
   Telestigma telephoto
also 2 Ferranti solar battery chargers (developed specially
   by Ferranti Ltd and the BBC Research and Develop-
   ment department)
Film stock
   Kodak Eastmancolor 7247
Filters
   A range of 85 and 85B with neutral density was taken.

Problems

1. *Logistics*   Having our own team of BBC porters meant
that we had no serious logistical problems below Camp 2.
Above this camp manpower is at a premium and climbing
the mountain obviously takes precedence. The BBC front line
was kept supplied, but, due to the speed at which this expedition moved, by a very narrow margin. Some means of making
camera loads immediately recognizable (brightly coloured
bags?) would have been a help at high camps.

2. *Temperature*   The effect of cold on film equipment is
cumulative. At night all gear with moving parts and batteries
was kept inside tents and as warm as possible. At altitude the
sun's radiant heat is tremendous and equipment was exposed
to this for as long as possible each day. The great range of
temperatures experienced can give rise to condensation if care
is not taken. Cameras, magazines and lenses were always
brushed clean of snow and stored at night in closed plastic
bags.

3. *Batteries*   Maintaining a stock of fully charged batteries
is a big worry when working in remote areas. We left a petrol-
driven battery charger at Khumde Hospital (a six-day round
trip by runner) and had sufficient batteries to depend on that
source if necessary. Blessed as we were with good weather,
however, our two Ferranti solar chargers made good use of
the intense sunlight at Camp 2 and kept us fully charged. This

was probably the first time that solar chargers had been used to support a film unit.

4. *Rushes*   Approximately every six days exposed film was taken by runner to Kathmandu (12 days) and air freighted to London by Liz Hawley, our press agent, where they were processed by Denham Laboratories. Naturally this results in a long delay before reports are received.

5. *Photographic Exposure*   Throughout the expedition I relied heavily on a Pentax spot meter, generally relating exposure to flesh tones, especially above the snow line. A Weston Master and a Spectra ware also taken. None of these meters were winterized and all jammed if allowed to get cold.

6. *Oxygen*   The lack of oxygen at altitude makes camera operating difficult, and a tripod is essential for prolonged shooting. Hand holding above 17 000 feet might well be made easier if the operator used an oxygen system. One's ability to sustain creative effort is also drastically reduced. For me six hours' filming at 17 000 feet was more than enough for one day.

7. *Personalities*   Personal relationships can make an expedition an enjoyable or a harrowing experience. Compatibility is extremely important within an expedition film unit. On this expedition relations between the unit members and between them and the climbers were excellent. In particular the friendly, co-operative and frank attitude of the climbers played no small part in making the film a success.

The 3 Eclair Cameras were provided by Soromec of Paris and not winterized; they were guaranteed to function at −30°C. The 10–1 Zeiss zoom was not winterized either but also worked sharply and smoothly throughout the expedition. The bulk of the rest of the equipment was provided by the BBC who winterized it (degreased and regreased with low-freezing-point grease) and carried out modifications where necessary. The Bell Howell 200T with crystal sync. made sync. shooting with the Nagra SN, at high camps or even the summit, a possibility. All the 200T cameras had film identification codes consisting of holes drilled through their gates on the sound track side.

The 600 mm Novaflex took effective shots of climbers above Camp 6 from a position near Camp 2. For camera movement to be successful with this lens a geared head or equivalent is necessary.

Eastmancolor 7247, with its good latitude characteristics, coped well with the extreme contrasts above the snowline. On exteriors it was usually used in conjunction with a Wratten 85N6 filter at f 11 or f 16.

Filming

The camera equipment used on the expedition can be divided into four main categories.

1. Equipment used on the walk in.
2. Equipment used at Base and advance base camps.
3. Equipment used for professional coverage of climbing.
4. Summit and amateur use.

1. Two camera teams filmed the approach march, generally working independently of one another, one team using an Eclair ACL, the other using an Eclair NPR and Arriflex ST. Filming a walk in is difficult. Mountaineers tend to walk rapidly and are usually impatient of delay, some can be downright camera shy. Film units therefore need to start ahead of the main body and have the energy to overtake them once they have passed. The problems are obviously compounded by ill health, as few people complete the walk in without experiencing one or two days below par. The ACL proved to be an ideal sync. camera for this work, being much lighter, more compact and faster to bring into operation than the NPR.

On the approach our cameras were carried by porters. This was not as satisfactory as using Sherpas for this job. Although Sherpas consider it below their dignity to work as porters on the walk in, they can be persuaded by argument and bonuses if these are organized at the time of their engagement. The BBC employed 48 porters and 6 Sherpas on the march in and

6 camera Sherpas at Base Camp and above. In addition to his many better known abilities, the Sherpa can quickly grasp some of the technicalities of filming and can become an indispensable camera assistant. Pasang Temba of Khumjung is such a man.

Our in-service equipment was carrried in rucksacks, padded with foam plastic. A more convenient arrangement would have been zip-around canvas cases, fitted with cut-out Ethafoam and mounted on pack frames.

2. The NPR and ST Arriflex were chosen for use at Base and Advance Base Camps, as they had proved their reliability on Everest in 1971. The NPR generally worked well, but at very low temperatures (−15°C) the mechanism itself functioned normally, but the centre drive sprocket in the magazines seized. It is absolutely essential that cold room tests should simulate actual working conditions as nearly as possible. Magazines need to be loaded with film and all equipment left to freeze for twelve hours before testing for such tests to be meaningful. That old war horse the ST behaved impeccably. The shock wave from an avalanche that hit Camp 2 destroyed the camera tent and spread gear far and wide, where it lay unprotected from the cold for some time. At dawn it was the ST Arriflex that recorded the scene.

3. Mick Burke used an ACL for sync. filming on the mountain. This camera with its push-on 200 feet magazines, although untried, was considered to be the best available for the job. The ACL appears to have functioned well, but detailed information is unavailable due to Mick's tragic death.

4. Amateur coverage on the mountain was photographed with Bell Howell 200T 10 ft autoload cameras. These are clockwork, cassette loading, pocket sized, robust and easy to operate. Their reliability was proved on Everest in 1971. Martin Boysen used an autoload to shoot effective material at Camp 6, the highest cine film used in the documentary. The same type of camera was used by Mick Burke to film Pete Boardman and Pertemba on the summit ridge.

Appendix 10

Medicine

by Dr Charles Clarke

The benefit which every 'Everest doctor' derives from his predecessors is considerable and both Dr Barney Rosedale and Dr Peter Steele gave much useful advice, thus saving a considerable amount of time. At early expedition meetings it became clear that a team of our size, which could be spread over a vast distance and altitude, would need two medical officers. We felt this particularly because of the logistic problem of having the expedition divided between the Face and Base Camp by bad weather. Dr Jim Duff from Kendal, a graduate of Liverpool University, was soon recruited and it was most helpful to have as a partner someone who had worked in Nepal – he had spent the previous year working on the British section of the East–West highway through the Terai and foothills of Nepal.

No two doctors would plan for Everest in the same way; for example, in the United States, I feel sure, the preparations would have been more elaborate. The team members had no formal medical examination but a careful medical history was taken with particular reference to illnesses on previous expeditions. A dental check was strongly advised and all had a chest X-ray, a full blood picture and urinalysis. Blood grouping with antibody screening was also carried out so that we could, in an emergency, consider transfusion. The usual inoculations for smallpox, cholera, typhoid, tetanus and polio were carried out, largely by local general practitioners. BCG (against tuberculosis, which is common in Nepal) would have been given had not all the members reacted to the appropriate skin test. Gamma globulin – excellent short-term protection against infectious hepatitis – was also given and although there is relatively little malaria in Nepal, pyrimethamine (Daraprim) tablets were issued weekly before and during the monsoon approach march.

From this somewhat sketchy prelude there emerged no current illness, although some chest pain and an unusual electrocardiogram, in the case of one member, did in the end lead him to investigation with a coronary arteriogram which was normal. Later he went well to Camp 5. Previous severe occult gastro-intestinal blood loss had occurred in one member.

The accumulation of the ten porter-loads of medical supplies took place almost entirely through the generosity of the pharmaceutical industry. The only point which revolutionized the packing was the large variety of polythene boxes we were given; this made it easy to pack delicate equipment for the varied terrain of the journey overland and the approach march.

Insurance is becoming costly as the numbers of Himalayan casualties rise. We had a Life and Medical Insurance for £6000 per head at a premium of under £50 each.

Although rescue attempts by air are possible in the Western Cwm, the case would have to be exceptional to justify an attempt. It would, anyway, require elaborate liaison in Kathmandu before the expedition. We chose to rely on evacuating patients on foot (their own, if possible) or by stretcher to Base Camp, thence to Khumde (by yak, if necessary) where there is the small, but very well organized, hospital founded by Sir Edmund Hillary. There Dr Paul Sylvester and his wife, Glen, kindly agreed to help us if the need arose. Only exceptionally would we use the home-made ice and rubble helipad at Base Camp to fly a patient direct to Kathmandu – although at the end of the expedition we did use this route to fly out Chris Ralling with some of the film. It is worth remembering that the payload of most of the helicopters operating in Nepal is small, and it may be that no more than two passengers could be airlifted at this altitude. For expeditions elsewhere in Nepal, it would be well worth while contacting the helicopter pilots before leaving Kathmandu and specifying a potential rescue site near one's Base Camp.

Illness on the approach march

The usual discomforts of the monsoon came our way: diarrhoea, a few blisters, infected wounds. Apart from being aggressive about sterilizing drinking water, we took no special precautions and ate anything and drank tea and chang locally. Oddly, the most severe case of sunburn on the whole trip occurred early in the approach march – the 'cloudy-bright' conditions being deceptive.

Illness on the mountain

1. *Acclimatization* The leisure of our stay in Khumde (about 13000 feet) and the march to Base Camp – about eight days for most of us – undoubtedly contributed to the scarcity of serious symptoms of altitude sickness up to 18000 feet. On our return it was alarming to see trekkers planning to do the journey in less than half the time, and easy to understand why pulmonary and cerebral oedema are so common in the Khumbu Valley.

2. *Pulmonary Oedema* We had one case of serious altitude sickness at Base Camp. Keith Richardson, in spite of leisurely acclimatization, developed pulmonary oedema five days after arrival. I chose to evacuate him on foot to Khumde and with oxygen as far as Pheriche, where he made a rapid recovery. Thus, sadly for Keith, there was no possibility of his returning to join the expedition and take part in reporting for the *Sunday Times* from the Western Cwm, as he had planned.

3. *Cerebral Oedema* Two Sherpas became drowsy and listless after several carries from Camp 2 to Camp 4. Both had early papilloedema (swelling of the head of the optic nerve) and retinal haemorrhages. One was disproportionately breathless. Recovery was rapid with oxygen and descent to Base Camp; both were treated with the potent steroid, Dexamethasone.

4. *Frostbite and Hypothermia* The combination of the team's experience of cold and high altitudes, together with superb equipment, contributed to making frostbite a relatively

trivial problem. Dougal Haston, Doug Scott and Martin Boysen had minor frostbite of fingertips at the end of the trip but they recovered rapidly as we came home with no specific treatment. Doug and Dougal's bivouac on the South Summit deserves special mention here as the model of 'how to avoid cold injury'.

We also had an ingenious device for warming oxygen, designed by Dr E. Lelwellyn Lloyd from Edinburgh. This would have been invaluable in the treatment of hypothermia.

5. *Sunburn and snowblindness*   We carried a variety of anti-sunburn creams (Piz Buin and Roche Eversun 7 were the most popular) and several members also wore silk masks. No one was incapacitated by severe sunburn but several noses became very painful. A simple nose-guard – easily made from tape – gives an adequate shadow.

Many of the Sherpas complained of minor snowblindness, largely because they disliked wearing goggles in the morning heat in the Ice Fall. With steroid eye drops they recovered rapidly.

6. *Other illnesses*   Two members developed severe chest pain at Camp 2, which was later shown to be due to rib fracture; one man passed a renal stone at Camp 2. One Sherpa had a severe attack of migraine, also at Camp 2: he had had similar attacks at altitude in previous years.

Mike Cheney, our Base Camp Manager, suffered much severe pain caused by a form of arthritis in the thoracic spine. It later turned out that he had an infection in a vertebra at the site of a previous operation. He bore his symptoms with great courage and only at the end of the expedition did he accept being carried by yak to Khumde.

Hamish MacInnes inhaled part of a soft snow avalanche above Camp 4 and took several weeks to recover. He returned home before the summit bid.

High altitude cough was almost universal, a difficult symptom to alleviate – particularly at night. A variety of cough lozenges, of which Mac and Fisherman's Friend were the most popular, were used freely by everyone. The old-fashioned Dr Nelson's Inhaler (now banned from hospitals because it is unhygienic!) filled with a mixture of Macs, rum and hot water was particularly helpful.

It is interesting to note how long after the expedition the coughs and sore throats persisted in the European members – some of us were still troubled several weeks after returning to Britain.

Morale was high throughout the trip and this certainly contributed to the lack of serious illness. The doctors hoped to keep a 'low profile' on the expedition and our task was made relatively easy by the excellent relations we maintained amongst ourselves and with our Sherpas.

Research

It is often said that a medical officer contemplating serious altitude research on a pure mountaineering expedition should direct his interests elsewhere. It is frequently unpopular, equipment is hard to maintain and there may be much routine or emergency work to do. Our work was correspondingly modest and determined by personal interests. We carried out the following studies which will be briefly mentioned here:

1. A survey, with photographs, of the symptomless haemorrhages in the retina which occur at high altitude.
2. Measurement of the intra-ocular pressure during the early part of the expedition – up to 20000 feet.
3. Some observations on the use of soft contact lenses (Permalenses) at high altitude.

The results of these studies will be published in the medical press. We found a tendency for relative newcomers to high altitude to develop multiple retinal haemorrhages (which were symptomless) whereas in those members who had been over 24000 feet in previous years they were a rarity, as indeed were symptoms of altitude sickness.

There was no change in the intra-ocular pressure during acclimatization – and in particular during the development of the retinal haemorrhages.

Two members of the team were able to use soft contact lenses up to 24000 feet.

Medical Equipment

The choice of supplies was determined largely by our predecessors on Everest and in particular, the 1972 British and 1971 International Expeditions. Where possible, drugs were chosen which would serve two or even more purposes. The surgical and anaesthetic equipment must depend on the experience of the medical officers rather than on their enthusiasm; our equipment was certainly less than others have carried.

We took particular care to distribute supplies widely in small quantities, clearly labelled – almost all the packing was done before leaving Britain – and the details which follow, though long, do give information which may be useful in the future.

DIAGNOSTIC KITS *Packing: polythene boxes. Numbers: two*
1 Littman stethoscope; 1 aneroid sphygmomanometer; 1 auroscope/opthalmascope (Keeler pocket set); 2 low-temperature thermometers; 6 pen torches; 1 bottle Multistix diagnostic strips; 20 spatulas.

RESUSCITATION KITS *Packing: Vickers Laerdal boxes. Numbers: two*
1 Vickers Laerdal resuscitation kit; 2 mucus extractors; 6 needles and syringes; 4 Medicuts; 2 scalpels + blades; 1 crêpe bandage; 10 skin swabs; 1 wound dressing; 1 Steristrip.

Drugs: packed in empty Fortral boxes
8 Diazepam 10 mgm inj; 6 Omnopon 20 mgm inj; 4 Pentazocine 60 mgm inj; 4 Scoline 50 mgm inj; 4 Atropine 1 mgm inj; 8 Frusemide 20 mgm inj; 2 Digoxin 0·25 mgm inj; 4 Nalorphine 10 mgm inj; 2 Chlorpheniramine 10 mgm inj; 4 Dexamethasone 4 mgm inj; 4 Haloperidol 5 mgm inj.

INTRAVENOUS AND ANAESTHETIC EQUIPMENT *Packing: polythene boxes. Number: one*
41 IV giving sets without needles; 2 6-pack Fenwal bags (blood taking), 6 Rheomacrodex 500 ml in saline; 2 1 litre Intravenous Dextrose 5%; 2 500 ml intravenous normal saline; 8 Butterfly needles; 8 Medicuts; 2 crêpe bandages; 2 Micropore tape 2·5 cm; 2 LP needles; 20 Marcaine 0·5% 10 ml inj;

10 Ketamine 100 mgm inj; 100 small gauze squares; 20 anti-septic wipes.

DOCTORS' READY KITS *Packing: polythene boxes. Numbers: two*

50 Codeine Phosphate 15 mgm tablets (sachet); 100 Lomotil tablets (bottle); 24 Panadol tablets (box); 30 Superplenamins (multivitamins) (tin); 500 water sterilizing tablets (bottle); 30 Fortral 50 mgm capsules (sachet); 10 Frusemide 40 mgm tablets (sachet); 20 cough lozenges (foil strip); 2 Omnopon 20 mgm inj + syringes + needles; 30 Ampicillin 250 mgm tablets (sachet); 1 pair of scissors; 1 Elastoplast doctor's set; 6 safety pins; 1 lint dressing no. 6; 1 eye dressing; 2 Elasto-crêpe 7·5 cm bandages; 1 elastic adhesive bandage; 1 theatre and ward dressing; 1 Steristrip sutures $\frac{1}{4}$″; 10 assorted Melolin dressings; 1 pack of moleskin; 1 suncream; 1 lipsalve; 1 anti-septic cream (M&B); 1 Otrivine 0·1% nasal spray; 10 Welldorm capsules (foil strip); 10 insect repellent wipes; 1 insect repellent gel; 1 Tineafax powder 25G; 1 Iodex with Wintergreen; 4 Benoxylate minims; 4 Sulphacetamide minims; 4 Anusol suppositories.

CLIMBERS' PERSONAL KITS *Packing: polythene boxes. Numbers: twenty-eight*

30 Codeine Phosphate 15 mgm tablets (sachet); 20 Lomotil tablets (foil strip); 12 Panadol tablets (box); 100 water-steriliz-ing tablets (Puritabs bottle); 20 cough lozenges (foil strip); 1 tin assorted Elastoplast, code 7291; 3 safety pins; 1 crêpe bandage 7·5 cm; 4 Melolin dressings; 3 Elasoplast wound dressings; 1 suncream; 1 lipsalve; 1 antiseptic cream (M&B); 1 Otrovine 0·1% nasal spray; 10 Welldorm capsules (foil strip); 10 insect repellent wipes; 1 insect repellent gel; 1 Iodex with Wintergreen; 1 Tineafax powder 25 g; 2 Benoxylate minims; 2 Sulphacetamide minims; 4 Anusol suppositories.

CAMP FIRST–AID KITS *Packing: polythene boxes. Numbers: ten*

50 Codeine phosphate 15 mgm tablets (sachets); 100 Lomotil tablets (bottles); 48 Panadol tablets (boxes); 30 Superplena-mins (multivitamins – tin); 30 Fortral 50 mgm capsules (sachet);

10 Frusemide 40 mgm tablets (sachet); 40 cough lozenges
(foil strip, polythene bags); 2 Omnopon 20 mgm inj+
syringes+needles; 30 Ampicillin 250 mgm capsules; 1 pair
scissors; 20 Mogadon 5 mgm tablets; 20 Dalmane 30 mgm
capsules; 1 tin assorted Elastoplast, code 7291; 1 triangular
bandage; 3 safety pins; 1 lint dressing no. 9; 1 eye dressing;
2 crêpe bandages; 1 Sleek 2·5 cm; 1 Elastoplast strip 7·5 cm;
8 assorted Melolin; 10 antiseptic wipes; 2 suncream; 2
lipsalve; 1 Otrovine 0·1% nasal spray; 1 antiseptic cream
(M&B); 1 Anusol cream; 1 Otosporin drops; 4 Benoxylate
minims; 4 Sulphacetamide minims; 1 Chloramphenicol
eye ointment; 1 zinc and castor oil cream 112 g.

DRESSING PACKS *Packing: fibre medical boxes. Numbers: two*
6 Elastoplast theatre and ward dressings; 10 assorted crêpe
bandages; 7 Elastoweb bandages; 80 Melonin dressings
4″×4″ and 2″×2″; 18 Elastoplast dressing strip 3″×1 yard;
10 Elastoplast adhesive bandage 3″; 120 Carbonet dressing
4″×4″ (in foil packs) pieces; 200 Airstrip dressings 3″×⅞″ and
3″×2″; 5 Airstrip assorted dressings (tins code 7291); 3 Sleek
7·5 cm strapping; 6 Duropore 2·5 cm strapping; 12 Micropore
1·25 cm strapping; 6 Micropore 2·5 cm strapping; 5 packs
digit-sized Tubinette bandages+applicator; 12 plaster of
Paris emergency packs 3″×3 yards; 24 safety pins; 500 G
sterile gauze; 1 kg cottonwool; 100 4″×4″ gauze swabs; 10
assorted sterilized lint dressings; 12 eye pads; 240 antiseptic
wipes; 4 dressing packs.

SURGICAL KITS *Packing: large polythene boxes. Numbers: two*
1 scissors 7″ sharp; 1 scissors 7″ blunt; 2 artery forceps 6″;
1 forceps 5″ toothed; 1 forceps 5″ non-toothed; 1 needle
holder; 1 scalpel handle no. 3; 12 assorted catgut and silk
sutures with needles; 12 no. 11 blades; 3 catheter bags; 2
urinary catheters (Foley 16 and 20 FG); 2 spigots; 1 tourni-
quet; 1 disposable proctoscope; 1 dental upper forceps;
1 dental lower forceps; 1 excavator, large; 1 dental spatula;
1 dental mirror; 1 dental forceps; 1 PhisoMed 150 ml; 3
surgical gloves size 7½; 20 Disposagloves; 1 Rikospray
antibiotic; 1 nasogastric tube; zinc oxide, clove oil, Cavit
quickset; 1 neurosurgical Burr Hole kit; 2 collars (padded

polythene, adjustable); 8 scrubbing brushes; 3 dressing packs;
11 pairs scissors.

Packing: Zimmer splint box. Numbers: two
8 assorted ¾" and 1" Zimmer splints; 2 Argyll trochar cannula
sets (thoracic).

Packing: small polythene boxes. Numbers: two
1 Heimlich chest valve; assorted rubber tubing and connectors.

STOCK DRUG PACKS *Packing: polythene boxes. Numbers: two*
400 Ampicillin capsules 250 mgm; 400 Oxytetracycline tablets
250 mgm; 200 Septrin (dispersible) tablets; 400 Phthalylsul-
phathiazole tablets 500 mgm; 30 Triplopen vials; 10 Ampicillin
inj 500 mgm; 100 Flagyl tablets 200 mgm; 300 Daraprim
tablets 25 mgm; 50 Chloroquine tablets; 100 Griseofulvin
tablets 500 mgm; 25 Alcopar sachets 5 G; 4 Mycota cream;
50 Digoxin tablets 0·25 mgm; 10 Digoxin 2 ml inj; 100
Frusemide tablets 40 mgm; 20 Frusemide inj 20 mgm; 100
Opilon tablets; 12 Opilon ampoules; 100 Ronicol tablets;
100 Ventolin tablets 4 mgm; 1 Ventolin inhaler; 100 Praxilene
tablets; 20 Praxilene ampoules; 300 Veganin tablets; 300
Panadol tablets; 1000 Codeine Phosphate tablets 15 mgm;
100 Fortral capsules 50 mgm; 20 Fortral inj 60 mgm; 100
Pethidene tablets 50 mgm; 10 Omnopon inj 20 mgm; 500
Lomotil tablets; 100 Senna tablets; 100 Dulcolax tablets;
36 Anusol suppositories; 4 Anusol cream; 500 Mag Trisil
tablets; 50 Stemetil tablets 5 mgm; 10 Stemetil inj 12·5 mgm;
1500 G Kaolin powder; 200 Diazepam tablets 5 mgm; 10
Diazepam inj 10 mgm; 250 Mogadon tablets; 250 Dalmane
capsules 30 mgm; 200 Soneryl tablets; 50 Largactil tablets
50 mgm; 25 Haloperidol tablets 5 mgm; 5 Haloperidol inj
5 mgm; 25 Kemadrin tablets 5 mgm; 100 Phenobarbitone
tablets 30 mgm; 5 Phenobarbitone inj 200 mgm; 8 Chloro-
mycetin eye ointment 1% 4 g tubes; 20 Pilocarpine minims
2%; 20 Mydrilate minims 1%; 20 Phenylephrine minims;
40 Chloramphenicol minims 0·5%; 20 Sulphacetamide
minims; 40 Benoxylate minims (local anaesthetic); 4 Beta-
methasone eye/ear/nose drops 5 ml; 2 standard eye dressings;
2 eye patches; 20 fluorets; 180 Fersaday tablets; 360 Super-

plenamins tablets; 200 Redoxon tablets 500 mgm; 1 Clinitest set; 15 Dexamethasone/Betamethasone inj 4 mgm; 200 Dexamethasone/Betamethasone tablets 0·5 mgm; 5 Piriton inj 10 mgm; 50 Piriton tablets 4 mgm; 40 water for inj 2 ml; 15 Lignocaine plain 1% 5 ml; 30 assorted syringes and needles; 1 set Vickers inflatable splints; 2400 water-sterilizing tablets (Puritabs); 100 dispensing labels; 100 polythene dispensing bags; 1 Mercurochrome crystals 25 g; 1 Crystal Violet crystals 25 g; 1 Brilliant Green crystals 25 g; 12 Swarm insect repellent tubes; 60 Mijex insect repellent sticks; 48 insect repellent gel (tubes); 600 insect repellent wipes (sachets); 6 Caladryl cream; 36 Tineafax powder 25 g; 6 olive oil cream shampoo; 12 Lenium shampoo; 13 bars of soap; 5 E 45 cream (tubes); 3 Ascabiol 200 ml; 4 M & B antiseptic cream; 8 zinc and castor oil cream (112 G pots); 6 Lorexane powder; 12 Vapona insect repellers; 30 Iodex with Wintergreen (tubes).

SUNCREAM, LIPSALVE, COUGH SWEETS *Packing: fibre boxes. Number: one*
200 tubes suncream (Vanda, Uvistav, Piz Buin, Eversun 7); 250 lipsalves (Little Princess, Piz Buin, Uvistav, Pickles); 3000 cough lozenges (Mac, Dequadin, Bradasol, Fisherman's Friend); 2 Dr Nelson's Inhaler.

HYPOTHERMIA KITS *Packing: loose. Numbers: two*
1 hypothermia treatment kit (Dr Lloyd); 1 mummy survival bag.

Further reading

Mountain Medicine by Michael Ward (Crosby Lockwood Staples, 1975).

Mountain Medicine and Physiology edited by Charles Clarke, Michael Ward and Edward Williams (Alpine Club, 1975).

'Emergencies in Medical Practice Edition', edited by C. Allen Birch, (Churchill Livingstone, Edinburgh, 1975).

Everest South West Face by Chris Bonington, Medical Notes by Dr Barney Rosedale (Hodder & Stoughton, 1973, and Penguin, 1975).

'On surviving a bivouac at high altitude' by Charles Clarke (*British Medical Journal* i, 92, 1976).

Clarke, C. R. A., 'Retinal haemorrhages at high altitude' and 'The use of contact lenses at high altitude' (not yet published).

A Traveller's Guide to Health by Col. J. H. Adam (Royal Geographical Society).

Expedition Travel and Your Health by Peter Steele (Bristol University, 1975).

Acknowledgements

Allen & Hanbury's, BCB, BDH Pharmaceuticals, Beecham Proprietaries, Beecham Research Laboratories, Becton Dickinson (UK), Boots Co., John De Carle, Churchill Livingstone, Ciba, Clement Clarke, Cyanamid of Great Britain, Dr John Dickinson, DRG Wye Plastics, Duncan Flockhart & Co, Dr C. J. Earl, Evans Medical, Prof Irvine Fatt, French & Scott, Glaxo Laboratories, Global Vision (UK), Miss Janet Hearn, Hoechst Pharmaceuticals, ICI Pharmaceuticals, Keeler Instruments, Key Med, Kirby Pharmaceuticals, Lederle Laboratories, Leo Laboratories, Lipha, Dr E. Ll. Lloyd and Peter Bell, Lofthouse Chemical Products, May & Baker, Menley and James, Merck Sharp and Dohme, The Middlesex Hospital, Parke-Davis, Pfizer, Pharmacia, J. Pickles & Sons, Riker Laboratories, Roche Products, Dr J. O. B. Rosedale, Searle Laboratories, Seton Dressing, Seward, Smith & Nephew, Dr W. Sommerville, Jean Sorelle, Dr P. R. C. Steele, Dr and Mrs P. Sylvester, Chas F. Thackray, 3M (UK), Travenol Laboratories, Tupperware, Vanda Beauty Counsellor, Vickers Medical, The Wellcome Foundation, Wm R. Warner, Winthrop Laboratories.

Appendix 11

Glossary of terms

ABSEILING Method of descending steep terrain by sliding down a rope.

ACCLIMATIZATION Process of physiological adaptation to living and climbing at high altitude in thin air and less oxygen.

AID Direct use of inserted piton (q.v.) or other artificial means for further progress on a climb.

ANCHOR The point to which a fixed or belay rope (q.v.) is anchored. Either a natural feature such as a rock spike, a piton (q.v.) in a rock crack or ice, or a deadman (q.v.) in snow.

APPROACH MARCH The walk in at the beginning of a climbing expedition to the point where roped climbing begins. On Everest to Base Camp (q.v.).

ARÊTE A sharp rock or snow ridge.

BASE CAMP On Everest the camp at 18000 ft before the bottom of the Ice Fall (q.v.).

BELAYING Tying oneself to a firm anchor (q.v.) in order to safeguard all other climbers in a roped group.

BERGSCHRUND The gap, or crevasse (q.v.), between the glacier proper and the upper snows of a face (q.v.).

BIVOUAC (BIVVY) Temporary overnight stop on a mountain without a proper tent. Haston and Scott's bivouac on the South Summit of Everest is probably the highest bivouac ever survived.

CHANG Sherpa beer brewed from rice or occasionally millet or corn.

CHEYNE-STOKES RESPIRATION A disordered and irregular breathing pattern experienced at altitude before one is acclimatized.

CHIMNEY A very narrow gully.

CHIYA (CHAI) Tea.

CHORTEN Small wayside shrine.

CLIMBING ROPED If there is no fixed rope (q.v.), climbers rope together on difficult or dangerous ground for safety, and can either all move together or move one at a time, so that one member of the team is constantly belayed (q.v.).

CLIMBING SOLO Climbing completely alone.

CLIMBING UNROPED Climbers on easy ground (or on difficult ground, if they are sufficiently confident) who climb without using a rope.

COL A dip in a ridge (q.v.), usually between two peaks. See South Col.

CORNICE An overhanging mass of snow projecting over the edge of a ridge, formed by prevailing winds.

COULOIR An open gully.

CRAMPONS Steel spiked frames which can be fitted to boots to give a grip on ice and firm snow slopes.

CREVASSE A crack in a glacier surface, which can be both wide and very deep, made by the movement of the glacier over the irregular shapes in its beds, or by bends in its course.

CWM A deep rounded hollow at the head or side of a valley.

DEADMAN Small alloy plate which is dug into the snow to act like a fluke anchor, digging deeper the harder it is pulled.

FACE A steep aspect of a mountain between two ridges.

FIXED ROPE On prolonged climbs up steep ground the lead climber, having run out the full length of rope, ties it to an appropriate anchor (q.v.), and subsequently all climbers move independently up and down the fixed rope, clipped to it, using it either as a safety line or, on very steep ground, for direct progress. The rope is left in place for the duration of the climb.

FRONT POINTING Climbing straight up steep snow or ice by means of digging in the front points of crampons (q.v.) and supporting balance with an ice axe.

GOMPA Buddhist monastery.

ICE FALL Where a glacier falls steeply and creates a series

of crevasses (q.v.) and pinnacles of ice. On Everest the 2000 ft of broken ice falling from the Western Cwm (q.v.) to Base Camp on the Khumbu Glacier (q.v.). Because it is constantly moving, the Ice Fall is one of the most dangerous areas of the mountain, but it is also the essential highroad through which supplies for the upper camps must pass daily.

JUMARING   A method of climbing a fixed rope with a jumar clamp, which can be slid up the rope, but locks on the rope to support weight when subjected to downward force.

KARABINERS   Oval metal snap-links used for, amongst other things, attaching rope to an anchor.

KHUMBU GLACIER   The glacier which descends from the Everest Ice Fall (q.v.), on the head of which Base Camp is situated, and part of the main route in the ascent of Everest from the Nepalese side of the border.

MANI STONE or WALL   Stones inscribed with Buddhist prayers in Tibetan script and built into walls or cairns on paths in the Sherpa country.

MORAINE   Accumulation of stones and debris carried down by a glacier.

NAMASTE   Salutation or greeting in Nepali.

NÉVÉ SNOW   Permanent snow at the head of a glacier.

PITCH   Section of climbing between two stances or belay points.

PITON   A metal peg hammered into a rock crack to support a belay (q.v.).

PORTERS (local)   On Everest those who are employed at a daily rate to carry loads from Kathmandu to Sola Khumbu. See Sherpas.

POWDER-SNOW AVALANCHE   Caused by freshly fallen snow on steep surfaces before it has had time either to thaw or freeze; one of the most spectacular and dangerous avalanche conditions. See also Spindrift, Windslab Avalanche.

PROTECTION   The number and quality of running belays (q.v) used to make a pitch safer and psychologically easier to lead.

PRUSSIKING   A method of directly ascending a rope with

the aid of prussik knots, or friction hitches, with foot loops.

RAKSHI Spirit usually distilled from rice.

RIDGE The line along which two faces (q.v.) of a mountain meet.

ROCK BAND On Everest the 1000 ft wall of sheer rock that stretches across the South West Face (q.v.) around 27 000 ft, at the foot of which five earlier expeditions turned back.

RUNNER (RUNNING BELAY) An intermediate anchor point between the lead climber and the main belay, when the climbing rope runs through a karabiner (q.v.) attached to this anchor (q.v.) The distance a leader would fall is thus reduced and security increased.

SÉRAC A pinnacle or tower of ice, invariably unstable and dangerous.

SHERPAS An ethnic group of Tibetan stock, living below Everest in the Namche Bazar, Khumde and Sola Khumbu area, who have obtained an effective monopoly of high-altitude portering in Nepal. On Everest high-altitude Sherpas are the élite porters who carry loads above Camp 2, and Ice Fall Sherpas are the mountain porters who carry loads from Base Camp to Camp 2.

SHERPANIS Sherpa women.

SIRDAR The head Sherpa.

SNOW BRIDGE A bridge of snow spanning a crevasse (q.v.) or Bergschrund (q.v.), formed by the collapse of the surrounding snow.

SOUTH COL The col by which Everest was first climbed in 1953 by Hillary and Tenzing, and the most frequently climbed route since.

SOUTH SUMMIT The subsidiary summit of Everest at 28 700 ft.

SOUTH WEST FACE Of Everest, 7000 ft high from its base in the Western Cwm (q.v.) to the summit; the first 5000 ft is not technically difficult, being an open gully system, but above this the Rock Band (q.v.) had blocked the way to five previous expeditions.

SPINDRIFT Loose powder snow carried by wind or small avalanche.

SPUR   Rock or snow rib on side of mountain.

STANCE   Place where climber makes his belay, ideally somewhere comfortable to stand or sit.

STEP   Vertical or short steep rise in a gully or ridge.

STUPA   Buddhist shrine.

TERRORDACTYL   Special type of ice-climbing implement.

TOP ROPE   Rope secured from above.

TRAVERSE   To move horizontally or diagonally across a rock or snow slope. Also the ascent and descent of a mountain by different routes.

TSAMPA   Flour ground from barley and sometimes roasted, an important part of the Sherpas' diet.

UPPER SNOW FIELD   On Everest the area of deep snow above the Rock Band (q.v.), across which the climbers traversed to the South Summit (q.v.).

WESTERN CWM   On Everest the cwm (q.v.) above the Ice Fall, leading up to the start of the Face, and extremely dangerous from avalanches.

WHITE-OUT   Conditions of driving snow and mist with a snow background, which make it near impossible to judge distance or distinguish between solid ground and space.

WINDSLAB AVALANCHE   Can occur when a snow layer formed by wind-compacted snow settles insecurely on top of old snow and descends in enormous blocks or slabs.

Index